VOICES OF THE BORDER

VOICES
OF THE
BORDER

TESTIMONIOS OF MIGRATION, DEPORTATION, AND ASYLUM

EDITED BY TOBIN HANSEN AND MARÍA ENGRACIA ROBLES ROBLES, ME

TRANSLATED BY DAVID HILL AND SATHYA HONEY VICTORIA
FOREWORD BY SEAN CARROLL, SJ

GEORGETOWN UNIVERSITY PRESS / WASHINGTON, DC

Library of Congress Cataloging-in-Publication Data

Names: Hansen, Tobin, editor. | Robles Robles, María Engracia, editor. | Hill, David (Translator), translator. | Honey, Sathya, translator.
Title: Voices of the border : Testimonios of migration, deportation, and asylum / Tobin Hansen and Engracia Robles Robles, editors ; translated by David Hill and Sathya Honey.
Description: Washington, DC : Georgetown University Press, [2021] | Includes bibliographical references and index.
Identifiers: LCCN 2020033493 | ISBN 9781647120849 (hardcover) | ISBN 9781647120856 (ebook)
Subjects: LCSH: Immigrants—Mexican-American Border Region. | Refugees—Mexican-American Border Region. | Deportees—Mexican-American Border Region. | Mexicans—Mexican-American Border Region. | Central Americans—Mexican-American Border Region. | Mexican-American Border Region—Social conditions—21st century.
Classification: LCC F790.M5 V65 2021 | DDC 972/.1—dc23
LC record available at https://lccn.loc.gov/2020033493

♾ This paper meets the requirements of ANSI/NISO Z39.48-1992 (Permanence of Paper).

22 21   9 8 7 6 5 4 3 2   First printing

Printed in the United States of America

Cover design by Erin Kirk
Interior design by BookComp, Inc.

For the people who have shared *testimonios* of
life on the move or stuck in place. May we all be
discerning enough to learn from their experiences.

*A todas las personas, en movilidad o varadas, que
han compartido sus testimonios de vida. Que quienes
recibimos sus palabras tengamos una actitud de
discernimiento, para aprender de sus experiencias.*

CONTENTS

FOREWORD

Over thirteen years ago, I made my first trip to the border region of Nogales, Arizona, and Nogales, Sonora, Mexico. I remember participating in the interviews of various people on the Arizona-Sonora border and seeing and hearing firsthand the need for humanitarian support, especially for women and children; I also became aware of the importance of raising awareness among faith-based communities about the reality of migration while promoting just and humane immigration policies. The fruit of these dialogues resulted in the founding of the Kino Border Initiative (KBI), a binational ministry working on the issue of migration through humanitarian assistance, education, and research/advocacy.

In that process, I met Sister María Engracia Robles Robles, a Missionary of the Eucharist, who was already working with migrants in Nogales, Sonora, at the time, and I have worked with her at KBI over the years. I appreciate deeply her energy, her passion for justice, and her innovative and creative spirit—all gifts that she has shared generously and that have helped to make KBI the ministry it is today. She has brought to bear these same talents in editing this powerful and moving volume of migrant testimonies, in which these men and women teach and challenge us in their own words and through their lived experience.

In my work at KBI, I have also come to know Dr. Tobin Hansen, and I am so grateful for his warm and gentle spirit, as well as for the generous service he has provided us over the years. In this project, he has contributed his great research and writing ability toward making this important book a reality. His experience as an anthropologist and as a person who has developed close relationships with migrants in Nogales, Sonora, enriches this text deeply.

All the contributors to this volume have some connection to KBI either as staff, volunteers, or collaborators. Their written introductions contextualize powerfully the testimonies you will read here and enable us to enter more fully into the migrants' testimonies. In an overall sense, this text truly humanizes the critical issue of migration and invites us into deeper solidarity with these men and women along with migrants in our midst. It puts into practice Pope Francis's words in February 2016 during a homily in Ciudad Juárez, Chihuahua, Mexico, when he spoke about the immigration phenomenon with these words: "This crisis which can be measured in numbers and statistics, we want instead to measure with names, stories, families."[1]

In the end, this book reminds me of the privilege and honor it has been to accompany migrants at the Kino Border Initiative. I think especially of Julia (not her real name), who is currently stranded in Nogales, Sonora, with her young son as they wait to access the US asylum process. As she comes for food every day, she unfailingly greets me and our staff with a wide smile and then places her hand over her heart in a beautiful gesture of blessing. Through her dignity and strength, she invites me to receive the same spirit of hope that she has embraced, even in the face of deep adversity. May this text open us all to the lessons these migrant men and women teach us through their moving words and the powerful testimony of their very lives.

—*Sean Carroll, SJ*

PREFACE

N ogales, a city of 234,000 people on Mexico's northern border, one hour south of Tucson, Arizona, is a place of connection. Over the years, it has been a place to stay or pass through for millions of people who wish to migrate or seek refuge in the United States or are deported by the US government, as well as humanitarian and religious workers, activist academics, and community members who stand in solidarity. Nogales brought together the people whose *testimonios* are compiled in this book, as well as the individuals—migrant advocates—who collaborated to write it. Many who have once visited Nogales now find themselves in distant corners of the earth. Taking Nogales as a central hub, as we do in this book, and tracing the routes traveled to and far from it, permits understanding of linkages between histories, regions, local geographies, economies, cultures, and people. This book captures the ways in which the lives of so many become entwined. As you read it, you become connected too.

The first strand in the web of those who collaborated on this book leads to María Engracia Robles Robles, ME, who, with vision and vigor, conceived of this project and guided it to completion. A Missionary of the Eucharist born in the state of Jalisco, Mexico, she began her humanitarian work in Nogales in 2007 with groups of people trying to cross north and with the numerous people who suddenly found themselves deported to Nogales from the United States. Decades after becoming deeply inspired by the Second Vatican Council in the 1960s, Engracia remained focused on the values espoused therein: following Christ by living in solidarity with dispossessed people. It was in this spirit, after decades working as an educator and a community advocate, that Engracia started documenting migrants' *testimonios*—personal narratives of lived experiences—in 2009 at the Kino Border Initiative (KBI).

Engracia learned about people's lives on the move, sacrifices, and perceptions and aspirations. People told her about the obstacles on the road: abuse, mistreatment, hunger, sadness, bitterness, and disappointment. She also heard about the inner strength, solidarity, and surprising joy and relief that people experienced. The importance of migration experiences, and of educating others about them, became clear. Engracia wanted these *testimonios* to be heard, as had the people who gave them, and she started to disseminate them in articles and reports. The overwhelming positive response encouraged her to continue collecting *testimonios* to share with students and volunteers who came to visit Nogales. Upon reflection, Engracia envisioned this book as a larger educational project and set it in motion.

On a searing July day in 2013, I passed through Nogales for the first time, taking a brief detour during a trip from Oregon to Texas. A few hours after crossing the border into Mexico, happenstance led me to meet Oscar and Carlos, who would become close friends, and hear their stories of the weight of deportation and its loneliness, uncertainty, and pain. Oscar, Carlos, and friends of theirs I met on a return trip to Nogales later that summer, other Mexican nationals deported after having lived most of their lives in the United States, encouraged me to write, as an anthropologist, about their experiences. They were, in their words (in English), "the forgotten people" and "the trash that they [the US government] take out." Oscar and Carlos had lived for more than four decades in Phoenix and Los Angeles, been incarcerated for years in US prisons, and struggled to understand what it meant to be permanently banished from home. They invited me to join their struggle. I designed an ethnographic research project and in 2014 started doctoral dissertation research based on community living, participating in everyday life, and conducting interviews. The research highlighted the contradictions and disorientation of legal exclusion from the United States after decades of full participation in US social and cultural life. I also started volunteer work at KBI in 2014, doing kitchen labor in the *comedor* (kitchen and dining area for migrants, asylum-seekers, and deportees) one day a week. Over time, Engracia, who had become a collaborator and dear friend, shared her vision for this book. We began working together.

Many people contributed energy and uniquely cultivated knowledge to produce this work. Engracia imagined the potential reach of this project and, since 2009, has collected hundreds of *testimonios*, including most of those reproduced here. In 2017, Engracia invited me to participate. With her discernment at the fore, we worked together to define the objectives; identify central themes that run through the lives of migrants, asylum-seekers, and deportees; and create a structure for the book. The advocacy, educational, and scholarly work on the ground in Nogales that Engracia and I, as well as the other collaborators, had conducted helped clarify the book's vision and scope. The chapters are centered on the themes that emerged and were finalized over lengthy deliberations in large group meetings with collaborators and during the countless hours of conversations Engracia and I had in Nogales and remotely, when our work and COVID-19 took each of us elsewhere, including Florence, Arizona; Agua Prieta and Puerto Peñasco, Sonora; and Eugene, Oregon. Engracia and I selected relevant *testimonios* for each chapter. We sought to identify *testimonios* that provided a window into the book's salient themes and that reflected the dignity of the lives of people we had worked with and sometimes become close to. We purposely avoided sensationalistic representations of people's lives, instead choosing *testimonios* that felt somewhat familiar to us based on our experience listening to people's stories. Although aspects of *testimonios* become familiar and even "ordinary," we remained cognizant of and driven by the extraordinariness of this historical moment within the grim social, economic, and political contexts of life on the move or stuck in place. Engracia and I worked as co-intellectuals and conscientiously ceded authority and deferred to one another in the process of together laying a substructure for the book and, eventually, constructing a carefully crafted edifice. We discussed details, down to the negligible, regarding the book's purpose, focus, and tone, as well as how to represent people, places, and institutions. Moreover, we recognized in ourselves and spoke often of the virtues and limitations of our respective identities: national, gender, ethnic, linguistic, racial, religious, and vocational. We sought to facilitate a collaboration that brought together the best aspects of approaches cultivated within the realms of religious humanitarianism and publicly engaged scholarship, and that began as and has continued to be a partnership between friends.

For the writing of chapter introductions, Engracia recruited other collaborators, migrant advocates—some motivated by religious faith and others not—who have dedicated their lives to supporting migrants. These individuals brought their unique knowledge, experience, and points of view to the project. They represented a breadth of educational formation, grassroots advocacy, and personal dedication to justice for marginalized peoples. David Hill translated *testimonios* with meticulousness and care.[1] Sathya Honey rendered precise and thoughtful translations of the introductions to chapters 1–5, 7–10, and 12, which were originally written in Spanish. And of course migrants, asylum-seekers, and deported people are counted among the collaborators, speaking up, raising their voices. Their words form the backbone of this document and imbue its spirit. From the founding of KBI, these remarkable individuals have stepped forward to share their *testimonios*, so they could be known beyond Nogales.

Since 2009, Engracia has conducted interviews, taking notes by hand and then making digital interview transcriptions. Using the approach of fast but careful note taking allowed her to be faithful to the *testimonios* and gave her the flexibility of not relying on recording equipment. She could, for example, conduct interviews in the noisy, controlled chaos of the KBI *comedor*. Beginning in 2016, improved portable microphone technology allowed her to make recordings of the interviews and then transcribe them. Engracia made public offers to take *testimonios* at mealtimes in the *comedor*, and people who opted in usually did so after eating. Engracia would discuss with people their wishes to have their *testimonio* published. Likewise, I conducted participant observation and interviews for my research in the community. I worked in people's homes, at their places of work, and on Nogales streets with a notebook in hand; in the evenings, I would digitize interview transcriptions and write fieldnotes. Among my interviews with people who consented to sharing their stories are the *testimonios* included in chapter 9. Jorge A. Andrade Galindo, a collaborator and anthropologist working in Mexico City, gathered in the course of his work the *testimonios* included in chapter 8.

Those of us who collaborated on this book are connected by the conviction that the possibility of living with dignity should be available to everyone. We are joined by the view that freedom of movement should not be a privilege reserved for those born in wealthy countries or who have access to financial means. We believe that circumstances of birth—family wealth, nationality, and access to quality education—should not dictate life options. Regardless of who we are or where we were born, our humanity connects us.

—*Tobin Hansen*

ACKNOWLEDGMENTS

We want to thank the many people who have helped this book materialize. Our parents helped us take our first steps along this path. Our siblings have reminded us, through their lives and love, where we've come from. Thank you to the Missionaries of the Eucharist congregation and the University of Oregon, institutions that have supported our work with those who migrate, are deported, or seek asylum.

We are grateful to our communities in Nogales, from whom we've received unwavering support, friendship, and solidarity. The Kino Border Initiative (KBI) has not only provided the infrastructure which has facilitated the connection between our lives and others, and supported this project financially, but it has drawn to Nogales the collaborators of this volume. Moreover, we thank the volunteers who make KBI's outreach possible. From both sides of the US-Mexico border, people come to give of themselves and their faithfulness, service, warmth, and friendship. They have often been an inspiration during difficult times.

So many people on the move, stuck, or living the aftermath of deportation have opened their hearts and entrusted to us the most intimate aspects of their lives. Many stories are documented in this book, but the vast majority will never be published. This window on their lives, through which we've been able to peek, has brought us closer to these individuals' strength, courage, hardship, and love of family. Moreover, their narratives affirm time and again the injustices of our interconnected and globalized social, political, and economic systems.

Engracia's religious congregation of sisters in Nogales has, since 2006, provided a physical and spiritual home. Their collaboration has facilitated Engracia's service of the most vulnerable. Tobin's wife, Kristine, has supported him in every way possible. He has also received immeasurable support from vibrant relationships with scholars who, over the years, have helped advance his academic and community engagements in Nogales. He especially thanks Dr. Lynn Stephen; since 2013, she has helped bring clarity to his research in Nogales and provided invaluable mentorship. His stays in Nogales have been made possible, in part, by financial support from the Social Science Research Council, with funds provided by the Andrew W. Mellon Foundation; the Wenner-Gren Foundation for Anthropological Research; the University of Oregon's Center on Diversity and Community, Center for Latina/o and Latin American Studies, Center for the Study of Women in Society, College of Arts and Sciences, Department of Anthropology, Global Oregon Initiative, and Wayne Morse Center for Law and Politics; and the University of California, San Diego's Center for US-Mexican Studies.

We thank our acquisitions editor at Georgetown University Press, Al Bertrand, for his timely insights and wisdom, as well as the belief he had in this volume, an unorthodox collection of written and orally recorded texts produced through scholarly and community collaboration. Katie Sharar at KBI looked diligently for a home for the book and, thankfully, put us in touch with Georgetown. Our production editor, Elizabeth Crowley Webber, has left us marveling at the improvements in substance and design that were made at each step. We are appreciative of the comments from two anonymous reviewers. Our gratitude to Alejandra Díaz de León and Iván Sandoval Cervantes, who read parts of the manuscript and bolstered it with their deep expertise of migration in the Americas. We thank the talented photographers April Wong and Avery Ellfeldt and the artistic creations, inspired by personal experience, of Alain Ojeda, José Luis Cabrera Sotero, and Wenceslao Hernández Hernández. Their provocative visuals provide color, texture, and a mental map of Nogales and the surrounding region. We appreciate Sathya Honey for rendering the book's Spanish-language chapter introductions into lucid English. Our team of collaborators has made fundamental and decisive contributions. We express our sincerest thanks, with our whole hearts, to Fr. Sean Carroll, the director of the Kino Border Initiative and to Cecilia, Joanna, Jorge, and Fr. Samuel. David Hill's nimble mental dictionary, cross-cultural sensitivity, and sharp eye have produced faithful and sturdy renditions of *testimonios* in English. Marla Conrad has provided valued friendship and, in 2014, introduced us to one another, thus initiating a professional collaboration that bloomed into a bright friendship and, eventually, this book. Our hearts are filled with gratitude for one another and for the tenacity, faithfulness, consistency, discipline, and professionalism we see in each other. We accomplished together what could not have been done alone.

—*María Engracia Robles Robles, ME, and Tobin Hansen*

NOTE ON NAMES

The names of people who gave their *testimonios* have been changed to protect their privacy. Place-names, dates, and some other identifying details have likewise been altered. The texture of the narratives was maintained to the extent possible, however, by making minimal changes. A focus on the original regions has been conserved, but specific villages or neighborhoods often take alternative names. While all people actively opted in when consenting to participate, some people chose not to give a name. This choice reflects both the level of vulnerability that people perceived, as well as the understanding that they were one more of countless people on the move. In cases where people did not give a name, the *testimonios* are simply identified with *Nombre Reservado / Name Not Provided*. Although in reproducing the *testimonios* some details were changed, no details, including names, were added.

TRANSLATOR'S NOTE ON *TESTIMONIOS*

Some of the things that make the *testimonios* in this book so valuable also make them challenging to translate: their personal nature and the amount of local knowledge embedded in them.

I am profoundly grateful to Sister Engracia for the hours of her time that she gave me, helping me understand particular passages by drawing on her intimate familiarity with each story, her decades of experience working with people from similar backgrounds, and her general cultural and linguistic knowledge. Any translation errors that I did not succeed in eliminating through consultation with Engracia I take full responsibility for.

In addition to translating the text and, in a few notes, explaining or justifying particular translations, I have also, in many other notes, found myself taking on the role of *interpreter*, supplying bits of context without which the text and the story would not be fully, maximally intelligible. For this role I have drawn on general reference information (maps, encyclopedias, and so on) as well as my own acquired knowledge as a resident of Nogales who has been providing services to migrants for ten years. My goal was to bridge the gap between the background knowledge that the individual presupposed when telling their story (especially small, miscellaneous details, which were unlikely to be explained in the thematic introductions) and the knowledge that a reader of this book could be reasonably expected to have.

In translating the text, beyond adjusting for linguistic differences between English and Spanish, I have tried not to monkey with the speaker's point of view. Language around geography is a case in point. For example, if a person in Mexico on the border with the United States says they *have come to the United States* to work, this might cause a reader some puzzlement, since they know the person is in Mexico and has not come *into* the United States.

But that understandable puzzlement is due to a difference in point of view, not a difference between the source language and the target language. For me, a white US citizen with birthright citizenship, *coming to the United States* equates to coming to US territory; because it's not my experience, I'm not used to thinking of the United States as a place with a hard exterior surface and conditional admission, like a bank or a prison. When one goes to a place like that, one of course says that one has arrived before one has gone inside and even if one doesn't go inside. The nature of such a place automatically creates a space, however vaguely delimited, in which one is "there" without being inside. It would not do to overtranslate *vengo a Estados Unidos* as *I've come to the US border* and thus erase a difference in point of view.

For physical quantities, I have used the units that are familiar to US readers: feet, pounds, and degrees Fahrenheit instead of meters, kilograms, and degrees Celsius. I saw no value in being faithful to the original units. Length is length, weight is weight, and temperature is temperature, so whatever unit enables the reader to efficiently grasp the quantity in question is the right choice. Kilograms do not mean something different to someone from El Salvador than pounds mean to someone from the United States.

Similarly, with a few exceptions, I have rendered currency amounts in US dollars, so that these quantities would be meaningful to US readers. I have used 2015 conversion rates given on xe.com as a baseline.

For the format of the dollar amounts, I have chosen not to use the standard abbreviated (numerical) format. The main problems with an abbreviation such as *$1,500* are (1) it may be overly precise numerically, and (2) it is not precise enough linguistically. Informal economies don't necessarily deal in precise amounts, and to capture the flavor of a person's speech one needs to be able to distinguish between *one thousand five hundred dollars* and *fifteen hundred dollars* and *fifteen hundred*. I've opted for a similarly "oral" approach to dates like *November (the) seventeenth* and *May (the) second*. (The Spanish text has been styled in a corresponding way in this book.)

As explained in the "Note on Names," the editors of this book had to change people's names and certain other concrete details to protect their anonymity. The editors made these changes before translation began. I have translated the Spanish text at face value, approaching the *testimonios* on an equal footing with any other reader.

—*David Hill*

ABBREVIATIONS

AEDPA	Antiterrorism and Effective Death Penalty Act
CBP	US Customs and Border Protection
CCA	Corrections Corporation of America (rebranded as Core-Civic in 2016)
CURP	*Clave Única de Registro de Población* (Population Registry Code)
DHS	US Department of Homeland Security
DOJ	US Department of Justice
ENDIREH	*Encuesta Nacional sobre la Dinámica de las Relaciones en los Hogares* (National Inquiry into Dynamics and Relationships at Home)
GDP	Gross Domestic Product
IADB	Inter-American Development Bank
ICE	US Immigration and Customs Enforcement
IIRIRA	Illegal Immigration Reform and Immigrant Responsibility Act
INE	*Instituto Nacional Electoral* (National Electoral Institute)
INFONAVIT	*Instituto del Fondo Nacional de la Vivienda para los Trabajadores* (Institute for the National Housing Fund for Workers)
INM	*Instituto Nacional de Migración* (National Migration Department)
IRCA	Immigration Reform and Control Act
ISSSTE	*Instituto de Seguridad y Servicios Sociales de los Trabajadores del Estado* (Government Workers' Social Security and Social Services Agency)
KBI	Kino Border Initiative

OECD	Organization for Economic Co-operation and Development
PFS	*Programa Frontera Sur* (Southern Border Program)
PGR	*Procuraduría General de la República* (Attorney General's Office)
PTD	Prevention through Deterrence
UNHCR	United Nations High Commissioner for Refugees
UNICEF	United Nations International Children's Fund
USBP	US Border Patrol
WB	World Bank
WHO	World Health Organization

1

Testimonios from Nogales

Tobin Hansen

Miguel recounts years of agricultural work.[1] His brown eyes become glassy and his shoulders slump. Over decades Miguel has moved between Oaxaca, in southern Mexico, and the Pacific Northwest, following crops through fertile valleys, hills, and lowlands. After several years in Oregon and Washington, he returned to Oaxaca some years back to work his own small farm there. He hoped to provide a decent living for his family, be closer to them, and live a fuller life.

But in November 2017, he says while telling me his *testimonio*, he found himself traveling north again. The prospect did not sit well with him. But he was heading back to Oregon *por necesidad*, out of necessity, because in Oaxaca *ya no hay trabajo*, there's no more work. The trip to Nogales—a Mexican border town an hour south of Tucson, Arizona, where he and I were talking—took three days on a cramped bus. Once here, he connected with a guide, called a *guía* or *pollero*, to lead him through an arid ecoregion of the Sonoran Desert called Altar, whose extreme temperatures make it simultaneously the hottest desert in Mexico as well as one with subzero temperatures certain times of year. Under a blackened night sky, walking on scrabble-clay earth outside the city, the cold bit his hands. His mind flashed to his kids and elderly parents. "I couldn't keep up. I was just going up and down these rocky hills. And I fell down, like, several times. I got scared and couldn't keep going. I started crying. The group kept going. I sat down and started crying and crying. And I asked myself, 'What am I doing here? What am I doing so far from home?'"

Miguel felt a poignance and unease. Seemingly the last option he had—that of long hours of work in western Oregon's lush but unforgiving vegetable and fruit farms—had disappeared. Miguel wandered under the night sky and, because he had only begun the several days' walk northward through the desert, made his way south across an area of the US-Mexico border not even marked by a fence and east back to Nogales. Days later, talking with me, Miguel reflected on his life and speculated about his options. Was there a less arduous way to get where his labor would be valued? And if people were so eager to hire him in the United States, why is getting there to work made so difficult for people like him? How long would he be stuck in Nogales? What would come next?

This book offers historical context and draws attention to the voices of people, like Miguel, who have experienced life on the move. It illuminates the terrain that Miguel and countless others have traveled as they have migrated, sought refuge, or been deported from the United States over Mexico's northern border. Miguel's questions form the book's starting point: What are people doing around the US-Mexico borderlands, in motion and in stillness? Why has the border, and places they have come from or where they are going, become a site of suffering, whether they are there for a long or short time? How has the arc of history from colonialism to the present—the evolution of nation-state power, shifting immigration laws and policies, the squeeze of global capitalism, diverse familial and financial situations, persistent faith—shaped the options available to people? These questions are vital for understanding human movement and learning more about aspects of life in the US-Mexico borderlands. And the book takes a particular structure in order to answer them. The following chapters each have a thematic focus and begin with short introductions written by migrant advocates, humanitarian aid workers, religious leaders, and scholars to explain the broad, historical contours of these themes. Each chapter then presents two or more *testimonios*—first-person narratives that bear witness to historical events through lived experiences—to amplify the voices of people like Miguel and document the circumstances surrounding human movement to, from, and across the US-Mexico border today.

The people at the center of this book seek positive change, and yet local and global dynamics guide their journeys along unpredictable and arduous paths. The uncertainty of their course propels sudden motion and then, just as suddenly, immobility. At one moment not another second can go by, and then, in an instant, there is no choice but to stay put and wait for days, weeks, months, or years. These abrupt changes in hopes, plans, and possibilities are not born of capriciousness. The brute facts of global markets, harsh immigration controls, and social and political conflicts deeply affect peoples' lives and constrain their options. Despite these obstacles, people in these situations navigate their circumstances with determination and ingenuity. They want to do. To endeavor. To live.

This book focuses on those who migrate, seek asylum, or have been deported and have passed through or ended up in Nogales, Mexico. The labels "migrant," "asylum-seeker," and "deportee," occasionally used in this book, are a practical shorthand and reflect processes of physical and social mobility and stasis. But the labels encapsulate only a narrow slice of the full humanity of the people featured in this book. They do little to capture the rich, infinitely complex personhood of each individual, and these categories themselves are not fixed but fluid and imprecise. Migrants find themselves on the move to reunite with family, search for work, or escape vulnerable situations. Asylum-seekers are migrants who request recognition—by the US government, in this case—of a fear of persecution in their place of nationality. Deportees have been coercively removed by the US government over the US-Mexico border. But all have unique experiences, personalities, and personal identities.

People who migrate, seek asylum, or are deported end up in Nogales, for a few hours or a few years or more, in myriad ways. Some might trek for several weeks by bus, truck, on top of a train, and on foot: from northern Honduras, over the Guatemalan border, across the Suchiate River into Mexico, and over the expanse of countryside, railroad tracks, highways, and urban centers that is Mexico.[2] Others may have come as children to the United States from rural Mexico in the 1960s, '70s, or '80s, to live decades in Arizona or California only to later be identified by immigration enforcement officials, detained, jailed, processed, and eventually driven to the US-Mexico border in a US government–chartered bus in handcuffs and shackles, to be let out and walked over the international boundary.

People arrive in Nogales with diverse plans. Some are eager to leave. Nogales is another stop on the migrant journey to Chicago or Seattle. From Nogales, it's a bumpy ride in a cramped van just minutes or hours westward, to stage with a group of people migrating and be guided north through deadly desert. Or Nogales is the first taste of a type of freedom for people being deported after the coercive restraint of immigration prison in the United States; the first step on Mexican soil when led over the border from southern Arizona, a place from which to catch a bus back to Piedras Negras, Veracruz, or Apango, Guerrero. People may spend an afternoon in Nogales, if that. Other people may have no bus to catch and spend a few days or a week, waiting for the right time to move on. People wait because traveling south is unsafe or people say crossing north is especially dangerous at the moment. Maybe there's no guide available. Perhaps a body is exhausted by the journey and needs time to recover. The money could have run out. A relative might

Migrants trek northward through the desert. Wenceslao Hernández Hernández.

be on the way. For a minority of people who come, the weeks in Nogales stretch, becoming months and years. For deported people who have lived many years in the United States, there is no home anywhere else. Or upon arriving at the doorstep of the United States, fleeing violence elsewhere in the world, people seek the chance merely to plead with a US official for an asylum hearing. If an asylum claimant is not deemed to express a "credible fear," then it's back to Mexico or Honduras or Brazil or Haiti. And what then? Back home, in the communities from which people fled, life is too perilous. But if people make it back to northern Mexico, having already been denied asylum in the United States, a clandestine desert crossing into southern Arizona in search of safety is too potentially fatal. Nogales is a place full of people who have burst into motion and then stood still, whose plans may change or remain constant. They are people looking for a way forward.

Miguel's perspectives, and those of others on the move, matter. They give insight into the lives they lead, choices they make, options available, and day-to-day experiences. Although some politicians, media commentators, and others in the United States fixate on immigration, the strength of their beliefs and opinions is outsized given that their knowledge of mobile people's lives and the structures that shape them is frequently scarce. Some vocal pundits, public officials, and everyday people herald border "crises," mischaracterize and demonize immigration, and speculate about who people are and how they live with little grasp of the situation on the ground or historical context. Others have firsthand knowledge, as community members who live near or visit the border, or have become involved as migrant advocates. Still others have become informed by the growing historical record compiled by the solid reporting of dedicated journalists and the insightful research of social scientists. For those who wish to learn more, this book permits insight of a particular kind: it takes the midsized city of Nogales, Mexico, as a hub of diverse forms of movement and stasis about which less is known than the metropolitan areas of Ciudad Juárez, Matamoros, Nuevo Laredo, Reynosa, and Tijuana. Moreover, we reproduce *testimonios* to elevate voices of those who have come to Nogales, usually passing through, to shed light on the emotional, psychological, embodied, and experiential aspects of life stuck in place or on the move. The act of testifying and of documenting *testimonios* also enriches historical narratives surrounding contested aspects of life.[3] According to anthropologist Lynn Stephen, writing about the importance of testimony in the context of truth commissions, "oral testimony has become a vehicle for broadening historical truth by opening up the range of who can legitimately speak and be heard and, ultimately, who participates in the construction of shared social memory."[4] Giving, recording, reproducing, and listening to or reading *testimonios*, then, are acts of legitimation, of history-making and of broadening spaces wherein marginalized people become seen as authentic, proper, and warranted participants *in* history as well as makers *of* history. The voices of people on the move in and around Nogales matter not only for the unique point of view that they provide, but because people on the move matter as full participants in communities, nations, and in an interconnected world.

The book emerged as a collaboration between people seeking to draw attention to *testimonios*. Those of us who have collaborated are all deeply and personally attached—via professional, vocational, religious, or humanitarian commitments—to the Kino Border Initiative (KBI), a migration advocacy organization. Kino is based in Nogales, Mexico, in the Mexican state of Sonora, and its sister city, also called Nogales, that adjoins the US-Mexico border on the north, in Arizona. Kino runs several programs in Mexico and the United States. It provides direct services to migrants, deportees, and refugees; advocates on behalf of humane migration policy; collaborates with

People stand outside the Kino Border Initiative *comedor*. April Wong.

scholars to advance research; and educates youth and adult populations alike on migration-related issues. Our collaboration grew from the vision to create an educational resource for those who seek to understand stories like Miguel's, as well as the cycles of migration, deportation, and political asylum; the public policies and social and economic circumstances that invigorate or disrupt these cycles; and the consequences of these dynamics. It also emerged through the connection to Nogales that each of us, writers of introductions or sharers of *testimonios*, has come to establish as we also have come into contact with the city.

NOGALES IN HISTORICAL CONTEXT

Nogales, Sonora, Mexico, grew historically through human movement and settlement and abuts what today is one of the longest and most regulated international borders in the world. Nogales has a population of about

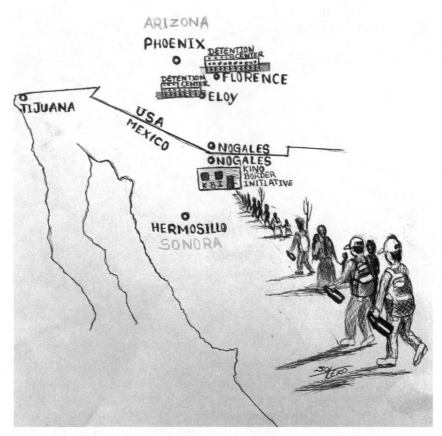

Map of Arizona-Sonora borderlands region. José Luis Cabrera Sotero.

234,000 located in a basin-and-range area of the Sonoran Desert, where the Santa Cruz River snakes northward. The landscape is a crumpled napkin. Hills, ravines, and desert washes cut from volcanic rock over millions of years reach an altitude of 3,480 feet above sea level and, atop sheer ridges, some 5,610 feet.[5] Average high temperatures in July, despite the mitigating altitude, reach ninety-two degrees Fahrenheit while in January lows average thirty-six degrees and frequently dip below freezing. Enormous factories line the southern edge, residential neighborhoods dot the expanse of the city, and, where the border fence juts horizontally across its northern edge, souvenir shops sell Mexican handicraft kitsch and no-frills eateries cater to tourists strolling into Mexico from Arizona.

Mountains in the Sonoran Desert. Avery Ellfeldt.

A few centuries ago, this sparsely populated, twisting series of ridges and gullies comprised Spanish territory. A trail traversing the area provided a critical connection between New Spain's northernmost settlement, Tucson, some sixty miles north, and points south.[6] Apaches, Opatas, Pimas, Tohono O'odam, and Yaquis lived and moved in this area where *mestizos*—people of combined European and Indigenous descent—and so-called Anglos also occasionally passed on horseback through the hard clay terrain of prickly pear cactus, mesquite trees, ocotillo, cottonwood, and cedar or juniper, usually making their way between Tucson and towns or villages further south. By 1821, the region became subsumed into the newly independent Mexican Republic. In 1854, the Gadsden Purchase (or Treaty of Mesilla) converted the area into US territory; life on the ground, however, changed little at the time. The binational Boundary Commission, a team of Mexican and US engineers and surveyors, worked its way along the 1,954-mile border between Tijuana/San Ysidro on the Pacific Ocean and Matamoros/Brownsville on the Gulf of Mexico. They left a pile of stones in 1854 to mark the US-Mexico boundary at the Nogales Pass.[7]

Since emerging as a far-flung outpost in the 1880s, the twin townships of Nogales, Sonora, and Nogales, Arizona, have grown together. Citizens of both countries, particularly those racialized as white or "Mexican," moved unimpeded throughout the Sonora-Arizona borderlands region—working, living, and assumed to belong. In general, the physical and social mobility of Indigenous and Afro-descendant peoples as well as of Chinese immigrants and their descendants, was more circumscribed by discriminatory laws and social marginalization, though the governmental control of movements across the international boundary that did exist focused not on people, but on regulatory duties on goods.[8] People of diverse racial, ethnic, and national heritages contributed to a vibrant and growing local community. Moreover, they proved crucial for filling various labor needs throughout the broader region including, in the local area, construction of the north-south linkage of the Atchison–Topeka–Santa Fe railroad system through Nogales, which solidified the town's ongoing importance.[9] By 1900, the population on the US side reached two thousand inhabitants and on the Mexican side three thousand.[10] In the latter nineteenth century and at the turn of the twentieth, Mexican citizens continued to be actively recruited to provide much-needed labor for mineral extraction, cotton production, and other work that reflected the global economy's increasing industrialization.[11] Moreover, just decades from the annexation of almost half of Mexico's territory, those who lived and moved between northern Mexico and the Arizona Territory (which would achieve statehood in 1912) were recognized as family people and workers with full membership in the region.[12] At the turn of the twentieth century, it would be difficult to distinguish between the Mexican and US sides. Famously, John Brickwood's saloon straddled the border in Nogales and, in a move simultaneously cheeky and practical, sold cigars on the Mexican side of the establishment and American liquor on the US side in order to evade the collection of import duties.[13] People moved across the US-Mexico border regularly to work, shop, and spend time with family. Although a fifty-foot easement, or reserve strip, was created on either side of the border to more clearly demarcate it and reduce the illegal transportation of cattle and produce and the smuggling of Chinese people, it took until 1918 for the first binational barrier, a barbed-wire fence, to be installed.[14]

The racialized anti-immigrant sentiment of the early twentieth century prevalent in the United States, coupled with the impulse to consolidate and securitize national territory during and after World War I, led to a gradual hardening of the southwest US border.[15] For the first time in 1917, the movement of Mexican citizens was regulated by the need to pay an eight-dollar head tax to enter the United States.[16] Payment, however, was easily avoided by evading the few customs posts in the city and, after the formation of the

US Border Patrol in 1924, the several dozen agents working on horseback who were charged with patrolling vast expanses of desert. Capital interests desiring pliable labor and local residents and officials in US border towns such as Nogales, Arizona, sought to keep the Border Patrol at a distance, so that northern movement, and the economic activity it brought, would not be impeded.

The assumed belonging of Mexican and Mexican American people in and around Tucson and Nogales, whose ancestral ties to the region dated back centuries, coexisted and contrasted with the broader US national ethos of racially motivated xenophobia. Anti-immigrant and anti-Mexican sentiment continued to animate border enforcement policies and removals of millions of Mexicans, including some Mexican American US citizens, in the 1930s and spiked again in the 1950s.[17] Repatriations coincided with the active recruitment of Mexicans to work in the United States, especially on farms and in the service sector. The US and Mexican governments even negotiated a temporary-worker agreement, known as the Bracero Program, in 1942 to counteract US labor shortages that resulted from World War II. The program extended well beyond the end of the war, continuing until 1964.[18] The apparent paradox between anti-immigrant feeling and harsh enforcement and, at the same time, active recruitment in Mexico of workers to come north reflects the complexity of immigration as a national policy debate and its usefulness to politicians who stridently perform anti-immigration demagoguery, while tacitly condoning, through a lack of employer sanctions, the hiring of people whose work has been made unlawful.[19]

Today, Nogales shares characteristics with other Mexican border cities. Lining the southernmost edge roughly twelve miles from the US-Mexico border, *maquiladoras*, or assembly plants, manufacture all manner of goods for importation to and consumption in the United States and elsewhere. *Maquiladoras* employ about 70 percent of the city's active workforce. Areas far from the historic downtown are the most recently developed and comprise lower-middle-class tract housing built in recent decades with the support of INFONAVIT (*Instituto del Fondo Nacional de la Vivienda para los Trabajadores*, Institute for the National Fund for Workers' Housing). Closer in, a small upper-middle-class district houses boutiques, eateries, professional offices, and a mall. Surrounding the downtown area, irregularly developed working-class neighborhoods twist and cling to the steep grades of the east, west, and south hills. In the several dozen square blocks around downtown, on the south side of the border fence, is the flat, low-lying urban grid-platted core of restaurants and inexpensive food stalls and carts, souvenir shops, money exchange houses, pharmacies, and government buildings. Tourism—cultural, food, medical, dental, and sex—in this area accounts for a portion of the

View of a portion of downtown Nogales and the Buenos Aires neighborhood, nestled in the east hills and abutting the border fence that demarcates southern Arizona. Avery Ellfeldt.

local economy. Although Nogales today appears similar to other midsized cities throughout Mexico, it is a hub for northern migration. The surrounding areas manifest ramped-up, militarized border policing and its consequences: sophisticated smuggling networks and the suffering and death of migrants.

Since the 1990s, a focus on the "security" of the US southwest border has led to increased migrant hardship. Fence construction, technology and heavy weaponry deployment, and urban saturation patrols, as discussed in chapter 6, accompanied the Border Patrol strategy of Prevention through Deterrence (PTD) implemented in 1994.[20] The stated goal of the strategy was to dissuade would-be migrants by sealing off crossing points in urban cores such as El Paso, Texas, and San Ysidro, California, and reduce clandestine crossings. Notwithstanding this putative objective, its effect was to funnel people into more difficult, isolated crossing areas and entrenching rural routes through rugged deserts and mountainous terrain, such as that surrounding Nogales.[21] Simultaneously, changes made the enterprise of guiding unauthorized crossings more dangerous. In the twentieth century,

View of the Patagonia Mountains. West of Nogales, looking west. Avery Ellfeldt.

friends or family from a shared hometown somewhere in Mexico knowl-
edgeable of the route or, alternatively, entrepreneurial locals in cities such
as Nogales often led people into the United States.[22] Under the era of forti-
fied border "control," however, a highly lucrative, dangerous, and callously
calculated organized crime business, discussed in chapter 8, costs migrants
much more in terms of the financial cost of crossing as well as the risks of
kidnapping, extortion, or abandonment in the desert.[23]

Since its rollout, the US government's PTD policy has correlated with high
levels of apprehensions, the criminalization of migrants, and increased
deaths. Between 1999 and 2018, the US Border Patrol (USBP) made a staggering 959,802 apprehensions *per year*. In USBP's Tucson Sector, in southern Arizona, between 2009 and 2018, a ten-year period, 112,513 annual
apprehensions were made.[24] And simultaneous efforts to punish border
crossers through a zero-tolerance approach engender more consequences
than ever for those apprehended. For example, Operation Streamline is
a joint Department of Homeland Security and Department of Justice initiative started in 2005 whereby those apprehended are charged with the

A migrant suffers in the sun and heat of the desert and receives help. Wenceslao Hernández Hernández.

misdemeanor crime of illegal entry or the felony crime of illegal reentry. Previously, such apprehensions would have led to quick processing and release at the border, in a process known as a return, or voluntary departure.[25] In Operation Streamline proceedings, dozens of people appear before a judge in one large courtroom at the same time for an impersonal, hasty en masse trial and, almost invariably, end up convicted of a federal crime. Convictions lead to federal prison sentences of thirty days or more for illegal entry, up to twenty years for illegal reentry, harsher sentencing for future arrests, and an order of removal that remains on official records and reduces the possibility of attaining a US visa in the future.[26] Death has been the starkest outcome of PTD. Between 1998 and 2020, more than 7,505 people have lost their lives while attempting to cross the treacherous US-Mexico border and suffering heat stroke, dehydration, hyperthermia, and drowning.[27]

In addition to death and the misery of bodies broken other ways, deportations of astronomical proportions have characterized recent years. The US government classifies expulsions of people, what are called "deportations" in everyday language, in two ways: as a (1) removal, with a formal order from an immigration judge or a deportation officer, or a (2) return, which entails processing someone at the border and expelling them without a formal order. In all of Mexico, Nogales is among the cities that receive the most deported people, along with Ciudad Juárez, Mexicali, and Reynosa. It received thirdmost in 2019, with 30,296 expulsions, behind only Tijuana and Nuevo Laredo.[28] With deportations come family separation, disorientation, vulnerability to violence, unemployability, and unstable housing.[29] Between 2015 and 2019, there were on average 22,444 deportations to Nogales each year. While this seems to be a substantial decrease compared to the peak of 158,471 removals and returns in 2009,[30] it is in part the result of the US government's narrowed focus on formal orders of removal, such as those that emanate from the prosecution of illegal entry crimes through Operation Streamline or from other moments of detection—during arrests, prosecutions, convictions, imprisonment, or postprison supervision—by police, jails, and prisons at local, state, and federal levels. Previously, when the administrative process of return was more frequent, one person could be expelled multiple times in just a few days or even in one day, and since the Mexican government counts repatriation events, not people, this process made it seem like more people were deported to Nogales. While returns from the United States numbered 582,567 in 2009, by 2018 they were only 109,083. Meanwhile, deportations with a formal order of removal numbered about 369,000 per year over that same period.[31] Most of those who are deported to Nogales from the United States do not stay in the city. They may try to travel north covertly to rejoin families in the United States or set off south to return to relatives elsewhere in Mexico. But deported people in Nogales form part of a constant coming and going, and while most leave, many end up staying in Nogales for a period of time or indefinitely.

The history of the US-Mexico border, along with the *testimonios* in this volume and the US government's draconian enforcement regime, invites us to rethink borders and bordering generally. Commonsense notions envision borders as lines that separate one side from the other. On a map, the eastern portion of the US-Mexico border darts and scurries, while the western portion snaps with straight lines and right angles. On the ground, the border traverses the Rio Grande to the east and west. What appears to be a rectilinear boundary is a border that meanders over hills, down into ravines, over crags and nooks, and across flat clay, loam, and other topsoil. Whether looking at the US-Mexico border on a map or on the ground, it may feel

timeless and permanent. At the same time, the story of the line's formation, as in the paragraphs above, makes it feel historically contingent and
produced by humans within a particular set of circumstances. It invites us
to imagine a line somewhere else—or none at all. But the border is not produced only in a historical moment—at the signing of a treaty, the surveying
of land, or the erection of a barrier—but in many ways and in many places.
In fact, the border can be thought of as produced or performed in little acts
all the time. The meaning of the border shapes how people and things move
and act, freely and unencumbered, or hemmed in and blocked.

GLOBAL CONTEXT AND *TESTIMONIOS*

US immigration policies and the making of the US-Mexico border reflect
global trends of exclusion and displacement. As of 2020, there were an esti-
mated 258 million international migrants, 41.3 million internally displaced
people, 25.9 million refugees, and some 3.5 million people seeking political asylum.[32] Expulsions and exclusions of people from the Global North
to the Global South continue as migratory control regimes have intensified
in the United Kingdom, Israel, Australia, some countries of the European
Union and the United States, and even now in countries such as Saudi Ara-
bia, South Africa, and, as explored in chapter 8, Mexico.[33] Global immigration developments hold significance for human well-being in the world. In
the United States, although close attention is paid to domestic immigration
policy, the voices of people on the move or displaced are often neglected,
save for some insightful and richly contextualized journalistic and academic
work or memoirs and other literary modes. Listening to those voices permits
new understandings of global mobilities phenomena, provides context for
discerning US-related immigration matters, and encourages a recognition of
shared humanity with those implicated in transnational migration regimes.

To attend to people's voices and the rich experiences that those voices
echo we turn in this book to *testimonios*, or narratives in which individuals
speak for themselves. The genre of *testimonio* allows people to tell stories
in their own words and present lived experiences from their point of view.
Giving *testimonio*—witnessing, or assuming the role of witness—is an act
of documenting history for posterity.[34] Moreover, it promotes histories of
resistance, sometimes running counter to official narratives set forth by
government actors. *Testimonios* bring in the voices of those who have been
excluded from accepted versions. Therefore, sharing or recording a *testimonio* is also a political act that conveys experiences shaped by unjust social
and political arrangements and unevenly distributed resources. In this

book, the *testimonios* of those directly affected reveal the consequences of such arrangements.

The *testimonios* of poverty, political conflict, and violence in Guatemala, El Salvador, Honduras, and Mexico connect historical processes such as resource extraction by Global North countries and corporations, US military and political interventions, and, in recent years, the deportation of gang members from the United States to Central America. These narratives underscore the influence the United States has had on the social, political, and economic landscape of Latin America; they show that we live in an interconnected and interdependent world and that what is done in one place sends reverberations to others. Moreover, *testimonios* reveal the government neglect and staggering inequality in Mexico and Central America that have led to flagging economies, the radical reconfiguration of traditional indigenous practices, a paucity of education and health services, intensifying poverty, and, often, the violence that neither local nor federal governments can allay and in which they are often complicit.

Testimonio also produces knowledge about diverse experiences, identities, and points of view configured by movement, time, and place. By voicing experiences and perspectives that have been shaped, in part, by the ways people negotiate the world in their physical bodies, *testimonio* "permits people to represent personal histories within fused/inseparable identity categories of gender, race, ethnicity, class, and sexuality."[35] In this sense, *testimonio* is not merely replicative—the dissemination of information, facts, or data—but also provides original ways of considering social life and its meanings for the fullness of individuals' humanity. Knowledge is produced through *testimonios* over time as events are lived, recounted, and retold, and across place, as new considerations of various aspects of life in and between places are revealed and themselves travel. Nogales becomes a site of novel understandings through contact between mobile people tied to multiple locations in the world but whose trajectories have brought them here.

The *testimonios* in this book showcase a broad range of backgrounds and perspectives. The people represented here were mostly born in working-class or working-poor conditions. They hail from different parts of the Americas, but mostly Mexico, El Salvador, Honduras, and Guatemala. They grew up in a ranch or a small village working the land and producing, preparing, and transporting its yield through freezing high mountains, arid low deserts, or lush jungles. Or they came from urban areas teeming with people on bustling sidewalks, at home with glittering skyscrapers; screeching metros; and streets clogged with cars, trucks, buses, and motorcycles. In flux—now standing still, now in motion—each person feels unique motivations for moving and is passing through or has ended up in Nogales. Some are fleeing violence in their home communities in El Salvador, Guatemala, Honduras, or Mexico. Some seek work in the United States as an escape from crushing poverty or simply to earn a better life for their families. Others find themselves deported from the United States. Deportees may have tried to cross the desert and been apprehended by USBP agents. Others lived in the United States for a time, perhaps even decades, and found themselves apprehended and held in custody by Immigration and Customs Enforcement (ICE).

These *testimonios* capture a fundamental tension between the tremendous capacity of people and the limits that are imposed on them. The individuals who walk into KBI's *comedor* have extraordinary skills and potential to weave the strands of social life as part of a family, community, and nation; living out creativity and cultural traditions that date back generations; sharing knowledge of land and its natural and social ecology; producing oil or watercolor paintings, pencil or charcoal drawings, vocal and instrumental music, and various forms of dance; developing and using computing and internet technologies; and contributing labor to local, national, and transnational economies. However, the life options available—that for the moment potently constrain innovative potential—result from international trade, labor, and immigration policies that devalue human flourishing and the products of toil in stores, workshops, and factories. In a moment of postindustrial capitalism, labor surpluses result in low wages and extended work hours of repetitive tasks that do not often lead to social, intellectual, or spiritual satisfaction. Moreover, the desire for tractable labor underpins relentless immigration enforcement regimes that permit enough unauthorized human movement to satisfy employers' needs while confining people to situations of perpetual illegality and deportability.

The book is organized around eleven salient themes that have emerged through the work that collaborators have done in and around Nogales. Each one contextualizes the circumstances surrounding people's movement or immobility. The second chapter looks at wealth inequality within Latin America and between the United States and Latin America. The following chapter explores the intricate threats presented by organized crime, as well as the uncertainty, instability, fear, and helplessness it can cause in individuals. The fourth chapter examines gender inequality and violence against women and perpetrators' near-total impunity. Chapter 5 deals with family separation and the legal, social, and psychological problems it engenders. The following chapter discusses how main crossing routes over the US-Mexico border have been displaced from urban areas to the desert and the dangers associated with this shift. Chapter 7 considers the abuses committed by authorities and the perversity of governments that end up harming human life instead of protecting it. Chapter 8 explores the southward thickening of the US border. Next is the topic of migrant criminalization in the United States. Chapter 10 deals with the deportation of long-term residents. The subsequent chapter explores the difficulties people have accessing the US government's asylum system. The final thematic chapter turns to spiritual life, and, subsequently, the book ends with a brief concluding chapter.

The personhood and experiences of those who migrate, seek asylum, or are deported merit recognition. And the historical forces that encourage and normalize human mobility must be understood and reckoned with in order to develop humane responses to people on the move around the world. The *testimonios* that are included were not selected for being extraordinary; on the contrary, they reflect a range of similar experiences that thousands upon thousands of people have had. As this book reveals, people on the move are not heroes. But they have voices that deserve to be heard.

2

Wealth Inequality and Migration

Introduced by Tobin Hansen

Wealth inequality at local, national, and global scales influences contemporary experiences of transnational migration. Socioeconomic motivations for migrating merit a close look, in addition to motivations of political and social conflict, family reunification, the threat of interpersonal violence, climate change, and historically patterned cultural practices. Some questions worth asking include: Historically, what has led to uneven wealth distribution within Latin America? And how has the economic gap between the United States and Latin America come to be? What economic factors have motivated migration from the Global South to the Global North? The historical context of current migration patterns is partly explained by the precarious economic positioning of some migrants within broader local and global systems of uneven wealth accumulation. Wealth inequality in the Latin American region as well as between the United States and Latin America, in part as a result of US resource extraction and the US government's search for political influence abroad, has shaped economic insecurity for many people who perceive migration as a viable option.

Wealth inequality in Latin America has a long history. From the early stages of Latin American colonialism in the sixteenth and seventeenth centuries, a European and Euro-descendant political and economic elite living in both the Old and New Worlds sought wealth through resource extraction. The Spanish colonial system of *castas* created stratified caste- and race-based categories that recognized rights, privileges, and obligations relating to land ownership, administrative and political positions, participation and leadership within the Catholic Church, tax payments, and manual labor. Spaniards and their descendants were positioned at the top of the hierarchy and below them Indigenous, Afro-descendant, or so-called mixed-blood people. The system of *castas* was difficult to implement uniformly in areas under Spanish control; however, in some regions it influenced the structure of the *encomienda, repartimiento,* and *hacienda* socioeconomic systems, wherein a privileged few owned land and received wealth tributes, personal services, and the benefits of others' work. Elites accumulated wealth and transferred it to family by overseeing the toil of peasants who tapped mineral deposits such as gold, silver, and copper and produced cash crops such as sugar, coffee, pulque, and cacao.[1] Gaps between rich and dispossessed people in Latin American countries persisted after independence from then-European empires in the nineteenth century. Entrenched economic disparities continued to shape opportunities and limit class mobility and reinforce notions of Indigenous and Afro-descendant peoples' inferiority vis-à-vis Euro-descendant people.

The US government and US-based corporations, moreover, exerted increasing political and economic control of Latin America through a combination of military might and extractive economic and trade policies. The US government's Monroe Doctrine of 1823 declared the entirety of the Americas to lie solely within its sphere of influence. It instituted US "protection" of the region, stating that "American continents, by the free and independent condition which they have assumed and maintain, are henceforth not to be considered as subjects for future colonization by any European Power."[2] Conceived in this way, the geopolitical order justified US military and counterintelligence interventions, such as in Mexico during the 1840s, Cuba and Puerto Rico in the 1890s, Panama in the 1900s, Nicaragua and again Mexico in the 1910s, Honduras in the 1920s, Guatemala in the 1950s, Cuba and the Dominican Republic in the 1960s, Argentina and Chile in the 1970s, Nicaragua and El Salvador in the 1980s, Colombia and Peru in the 1990s, and Venezuela in the early 2000s, to name several.[3]

At the same time, Latin American elites with ties to the US government controlled their nations' politics and governments while market oligopolies—with few large sellers and limited competition—permitted US corporate participation, deepening the disparities between the wealthy few and a poor majority. The nineteenth century saw a proliferation of US transnational business activity in railways, fruit production, and mining. A more recent version has endured, through the implementation of various so-called free trade agreements, such as the North American Free Trade Agreement and the Central America–Dominican Republic Free Trade Agreement. These agreements limit tariffs on the importation of US goods that may, as in the case of Iowa corn, be produced with US government subsidies, favor certain sectors of the US economy, and exacerbate existing poverty in Latin America.[4]

Also in the second half of the twentieth century, international development institutions such as the World Bank (WB) and the Inter-American Development Bank (IADB) encouraged the dismantling of social assistance systems of Latin American countries. The market logics of these so-called reforms recast individuals as autonomous actors who must maximize earnings potential through judicious financial decisions.[5] National development programs in the region are based on many WB and IADB philosophical principles: they are founded on "personal responsibility" and the individual's place within a globalized market, ignoring the social and economic structures that perpetuate inequality. Essentially, this view blames the paltry opportunities available to citizens on individuals themselves.[6] Governmental programs nominally designed to help working-poor people—such as in Mexico PROCAMPO (*Programa de Apoyos Directos al Campo*), which subsidizes certain crops, and *Prospera*, which offers education and health assistance, plus small sums of conditional cash transfers—do little to alleviate poverty but regulate individuals' behavior and provide political cover.[7] Per capita gross domestic product (GDP), a yearly measurement of average individual productivity and prosperity, further exposes the economic imbalance between the Global North and Global South. While in Latin American emigrating countries such as Mexico, Guatemala, El Salvador, and Honduras, this figure is US$7,300, the US per capita GDP is almost *eight times higher*, at US$57,700.

Average income and wealth measures reveal macrolevel inequalities but obscure the economic precariousness of women and Indigenous and Afro-descendant people, among the most historically subordinated people in Latin America. Legacies of wealth accumulation, discussed above, have shaped ongoing discrimination and high rates of poverty among Indigenous and Afro-descendant people today. Gender, moreover, is associated with intensified marginalization and abuse, particularly in regions where different forms of gendered privation, dispossession, and violence have been concentrated.[8] In the first *testimonio* in this chapter, Yésica recounts how her experience with sexual violence and extortion by a transnational gang compound the financial hardship she faces. Yésica's narrative reflects what anthropologist Lynn Stephen has observed in Guatemala in situations where "the social remittances [across national borders] of masculine culture can result in new patterns of gender subordination that overlay those previously embedded through war and its aftermath."[9] Critically, women and racially and ethnically subordinated people also experience, beyond mere financial precariousness, barriers to stable housing, safe drinking water, efficient sewage, education, health care, and information.[10]

Financially insecure people from Latin America have migrated northward not only in response to a lack of opportunities in the region, but to active recruitment by US businesses for the production of goods and the delivery of services that depend on low-wage work. There is a long tradition of US businesses recruiting in Latin America through family networks and through direct advertising in newspapers, radio, television, and the internet.[11] Even more explicitly, especially in the early twentieth century, some businesses would send recruiters to Mexico. These *enganchadores* (recruiters) would roam the country promising high wages and favorable conditions in the United States.[12] The US government itself worked out an agreement with the Mexican government to enable the entry of more than two million Mexican citizens to labor in the United States.[13] The Bracero Program, as it was known, was active from 1942 to 1964, and further entrenched a pattern of circular migration to and from or of settlement in the United States. In other instances, when migrants entered the country without explicit authorization from the government, authorities were pressured by influential US landowners and agribusinesses to turn a blind eye, ensuring access to an expendable workforce.[14]

Economic dynamics—in conjunction with political, social, and cultural factors—have promoted the current state of inequality in the hemisphere's development. The US government and US businesses have made sustained efforts to include foreign workers as an economic engine and at the same time blame Latin American migrants for perceived hardships of crime, wage stagnation, and cultural decline within the United States. A clear-eyed understanding of the economic and social contexts of migration—and the direct role that the US government and US capital interests have played historically in encouraging migration—would lead to the realization that responsibility for human movement extends beyond the discrete choices of individuals, that migrants should be considered rightful members of the United States, and that inclusive and humane immigration policies should reflect their belonging.

YÉSICA

Soy Yésica, de Guatemala. En mi familia fuimos siete hermanos: cinco hombres y dos mujeres. Fue muy mala nuestra situación. Mi papá le pegaba a mi mamá. Yo tenía cinco años y veíamos cómo le pegaba a mi mamá. Cuando yo estaba grande, ella me platicaba que donde quiera, él quería tener sexo. A ella le daba mucha vergüenza que la encontrara la suegra en esa situación. Y porque ella se resistía, él le pegaba. De tanto golpe, decidió dejar a mi papá.

Se llevó dos hermanos y a mí y le dejó a mi papá a los otros. Nos fuimos a vivir a otro departamento. Mi mamá empezó a trabajar de lavar ropa. Muchísima ropa tenía que lavar para sostenernos. No tuvimos estudio por este motivo. Cuando fuimos pequeñas, nos quedábamos en la casa encerradas. A veces no teníamos nada que comer. Después, mi mamá se quedó sin trabajo y nos llevó a trabajar al campo, a cortar café. A la una de la mañana nos levantábamos para hacer la comida, torteábamos, hacíamos el lonche, nos íbamos y regresábamos a las siete de la noche. Teníamos que sacar el café cargándolo en la espalda, para llevarlo a donde lo iban a recoger. Lo llevábamos en la espalda. Yo tenía ya doce años. A esa edad, yo empecé a trabajar en cortar pasto y cortar caña. Nos pagaban doscientos pesos a la quincena.

Cuando cumplí catorce, empecé a trabajar con papeles falsos. Adquirí una cédula, para poder trabajar en una fábrica. Trabajé de los catorce a los dieciocho años. Luego ya pude sacar mis papeles verdaderos. Después resulté embarazada de mi hija, a los dieciocho años y con la mala suerte del papá de mi hija, que no quería que la tuviera. Me pidió que la abortara. Me llevó cosas para que tomara, porque él no se sentía capaz de ser padre; yo sí me sentía capaz de ser madre. Y con él o sin él, yo entré a trabajar, oculté mi embarazo para que me pudieran dar trabajo y yo sacaba adelante a mi mamá también, porque mis hermanos ya tienen a sus parejas.

Toda mi vida he trabajado para sacar adelante a mi mamá y a mi hija. Yo renté un cuartito para vivir y hasta hoy en día, puse una tiendita para poder sostenernos. Por ese motivo y porque me amenazaron de que me iban a matar, porque me extorsionó la mara Salvatrucha y me amenazaron si no pagaba. Por ese motivo me vi obligada a salir de mi país. Dejé a mi hija con mi mamá. Mi hija va a cumplir once años.

El viaje lo hice pidiendo un préstamo para pagarle a un coyote que me trajera. Ese préstamo fue de treinta mil quetzales. Esa persona sólo me robó el dinero y me dejó perdida. Le pagué treinta mil quetzales. Yo hasta en el camino me di cuenta, que no es así como se lo dicen a uno. Él me prometió que me iba a llevar hasta a los Estados Unidos del Norte y hasta a conseguir trabajo. Todo fue engaño.

Me dejó en Agua Prieta. De ahí, yo no sabía qué hacer. Durante el camino, él nos guiaba, él nos compraba los boletos. Encontré a unas personas que me preguntaban si tenía quien me ayudara. Ellos me dijeron en qué bus me montara para venir aquí a Nogales. Llegué a la terminal. De ahí me salí y ya no hallaba para dónde agarrar. Me encontré una señora que dijo que me iba a ayudar. Me dijo que me iba a buscar quien me pasara. Me llevó a su casa, pero yo la escuché hablando para venderme con hombres. Antes me había dicho que si me salía, ella me iba a encontrar. En una escapadita me salí y regresé al estacionamiento de buses. Ahí me encontré otra señora y ella me mandó para el comedor. Me dijo que tal vez ahí me podían ayudar con una comida y ropa. Así fue como llegué al comedor de Iniciativa Kino.

Estoy en el albergue. Sigo con el plan de ir a los Estados Unidos, aunque yo no tengo allá a nadie que me pueda ayudar.

IIIIIIIIIIIIIII

Okay, I'm Yésica and I'm from Guatemala. In my family there were seven kids: five boys and two girls. Things were really bad for us. My dad used to hit my mom. I was five, and we saw how he hit my mom. When I was an adult, she would tell me that no matter where they were, he would want to have sex. She would be really embarrassed at the idea of her mother-in-law finding her like that. And since she would resist him, he would hit her. From all the beatings she decided to leave my dad.

She took two of my siblings and me with her and left the others with my dad. We went to live in another department.[15] My mom started doing clothes-washing work. She had to wash a whole lot of clothes to keep us fed. That's why we didn't get an education. When we were little, we would stay home alone by ourselves. Sometimes we didn't have anything to eat. Later, my mom ended up unemployed and took us to work in the fields picking coffee. We'd get up at one o'clock in the morning to make our food. We'd cook tortillas, make our lunch, leave, and come back at seven o'clock at night. We had to get the coffee out of the fields by loading it on our backs, to carry it to where they were going to pick it up. We carried it on our backs. I was twelve years old now. At that age, I started working cutting hay and cutting sugarcane. We got paid twelve dollars every two weeks.

When I turned fourteen, I started working with fake papers. I bought someone else's ID card, to be able to do factory work. I worked from age fourteen to age eighteen. At that point, I was able to get my real papers. After that, I found myself pregnant with my daughter. I was eighteen and my luck was bad in terms of who my daughter's dad was—he didn't want me to have her. He asked me to abort her. He brought me stuff to take because he didn't feel like he could be a father; I did feel like I could be a mother. So, with him or without him, I went back to work, hid my pregnancy so they could hire me, and I was providing for my mom too, since my siblings were in relationships by then.

I've worked all my life to provide for my mom and for my daughter. I rented a little room for us to live in, and just recently I opened a little shop so we can keep ourselves fed. And that's why—and because I got death threats, because the Mara Salvatrucha demanded money from me and the threats were if I didn't pay—that's why I felt I had no choice but to leave my country. I left my mom in charge of my daughter. She's about to turn eleven.

I made the trip by taking out a loan to pay a *coyote* to take me with him. The loan was for four thousand dollars.[16] That person just stole my money and left me stranded. I paid him four thousand dollars. Only on the way did I realize, the reality isn't like they tell you. He promised me he would take me all the way to the US and even get me a job. It was all a lie.

He left me in Agua Prieta. From there I didn't know what to do. Throughout the trip, he was the one that guided us, he was the one that bought the bus tickets. I ran into some people who asked me if I had anyone to help me. They told me which bus to get on to get to Nogales. So, I arrived at the bus terminal here. I walked out and couldn't figure out where to go next. I found a lady who said she'd help me. She said she'd look for someone to get me through.[17] She took me to stay at her house, but I heard her making phone calls to sell me to be with men. Before that, she had told me if I left, she would find me. When there was a little free moment, I left and went back to the bus station. I found another lady there and she pointed me in the direction of the *comedor*. She told me they might be able to help me there with a meal and clothes. That's how I ended up at the *comedor* of the Kino Border Initiative.[18]

I'm staying at the shelter.[19] My plan is still to go to the US, even though I don't have anyone there who can help me.

SANTIAGO

Soy Santiago. Nací el trece de febrero de 1955 en Oaxaca, en el Municipio de San Juan de la Cal. Provengo de una familia de dieciocho hijos, del mismo papá y de la misma mamá. Mi infancia fue muy pobre. Andaba descalzo, con poca o mínima posibilidad de estudiar. Éramos muchos y al final quedamos pocos. Murieron ocho, por mala alimentación, falta de desarrollo. Cuando mi mamá tenía qué darnos de comer, estábamos contentos. Pero muchas veces mi mamá nos dejaba con hambre, porque tenía que salir para ver qué conseguía. Fuimos una familia sin juguetes, sin infancia, casi sin ropa, sin huaraches, sin cuadernos para la escuela. Nos dedicaban al campo, a trabajos de la casa, crianza de puercos, de pollos; ayudábamos a mi mamá cuando sabíamos que el dinero no alcanzaba. Recuerdo que, cuando yo tenía cinco años, el hermano mayor murió de veintitrés años. Tuvo leucemia. Muchos sufrimientos, pero lo que más recuerdo es la pobreza. Yo veía a mis amigos de escuela, con mochila, con tenis, con los útiles escolares que necesitaban. Nosotros descalzos, sin cuadernos, una hoja que nos daba por ahí algún compañero, sin duda por lástima, era donde escribíamos. Los otros niños tenían juguetes, nosotros hacíamos juguetes de lodo, o de maderita para poder jugar.

Cuando falleció mi mamá, ya tuvimos la posibilidad de salir a trabajar fuera, porque mientras ella vivió, no nos dejaba. Salí de la casa a la edad de veintiséis años. Mi mamá tenía un año de haber fallecido. Me vine a Estados Unidos de raite y llegando a Mexicali con unos amigos que me habían recomendado, trabajé. Trabajé con un señor que tenía un restaurante, pero no me pagaba, sólo me daban la comida . . . o cuando bien me fuera, me daba cincuenta pesos mexicanos a la semana. Eso cuando yo se lo pedía, porque tenía a mi papá y le tenía que mandar dinero. Aguanté por año y medio con él y luego, cuando salí, me andaba buscando, diciendo que lo había robado. Yo le dije que me había salido porque yo salí de mi casa para trabajar, pero él no me pagaba lo suficiente. Me fui a la iglesia. Cada ocho días iba a la misa de la catedral y ahí encontré un señor, que es coyote y me llevó a su casa. Lo ayudaba a enseñar el himno nacional a los que son centroamericanos y a los mexicanos les daba de comer. Estuve seis meses con él. Le dije que tenía al otro lado un primo y que me quería brincar. Sólo me cobró 250 dólares, porque ya lo había ayudado mucho también a él. Estando en aquel lado, mi primo pagó los 250 dólares, porque yo no tenía. Al llegar a Estados Unidos, también fui explotado. Me tenían como criado y no me dejaban trabajar. Llegué con unos primos hermanos. Ellos tenían doble trabajo y al llegar yo, ellos querían que yo les hiciera el trabajo de casa: bolearles los zapatos, hacer comida. Decían que mientras nos acomodábamos. Pero nunca llegó ese día, hasta que me escapé. Estuve tres o cuatro meses trabajando ahí con ellos.

Me fui a la playa de Santa Bárbara y ahí encontré un paisano de México. Le dije lo que estaba pasando y me dio veinte dólares. De ahí agarré trabajo de lavar trastes y renté mi cuarto. De lavatrastes duré tres años. Me pasé a preparador de cocina y luego cocinero. Ahora puedo guisar de cinco tipos de comida: china, americana, italiana, japonesa y mexicana. La francesa, un poco. Ahí he pasado treinta y tres años de puro restaurante. Un tiempo trabajaba, cinco años por ejemplo, luego cambiaba de dueño el restaurante, pero el que dejaba, o sea el anterior dueño, nos recomendaba y así pasé. Un tiempo trabajaba, otro no.

Como cuatro veces vine a México y me quedé un mes, dos meses. Antes pasaba uno sin problema. En México me casé, me llevé a mi esposa, tuve tres hijos. Ellos están allá en Estados Unidos. Ahora yo salí porque vine a enterrar a un familiar, luego regresé a los Estados Unidos y me encarcelaron. Presenté mi caso, peleé durante tres meses, me pusieron fianza de tres mil quinientos dólares, mi familia la pagó y salí. Estando en mi casa, me llamaron por teléfono y mandaron citatorio. Me presenté y me sacaron ese mismo día. La causa de citarme fue porque cuando se pagó la fianza, yo di la dirección de una persona con tarjeta verde. Ella nos había prestado su dirección para pagar la fianza. Posiblemente ella me reportó. Ahí iba a llegar la correspondencia. El dinero de la fianza era de nosotros, pero por esa persona estoy acá. Tengo cheques allá que no puedo cambiar. Se me quedaron sin cobrar. Tenía la costumbre de siempre tener uno guardado, por lo que pudiera presentarse. Siempre guardaba uno y cobraba uno. Se me juntaron cuatro cheques. Tengo cuatro mil seiscientos dólares que están tirados a la basura. Ya hablé a la compañía y dicen que están vencidos y me los harían de nuevo si voy yo, en persona, a cobrarlos.

La latina que me deportó me despidió diciéndome que se habían acabado mis encantos. Sentí que me insultaba muy feo con eso. Yo nunca arreglé mi estancia legal, porque nunca se me vino la idea de que esto pudiera pasar. A mí, con el record de dos reentres y una deportación que me dieron, tengo que pedir un perdón. Ahora lo que estoy sufriendo es que Migración no me entregó mis cosas. Y temo el día en que ya no me den de comer aquí. ¿Qué voy a hacer?

|||||||||||||||||||

I'm Santiago. I was born on February thirteenth, 1955, in Oaxaca, in San Juan de la Cal municipality.[20] I come from a family with eighteen children all from the same dad and the same mom. My childhood was really poor. I went around barefoot, had little to no opportunity to get educated. There were a lot of us, and then in the end there were not too many of us. Eight died, due to poor diet, underdevelopment. Whenever our mom had some food for us, we were happy. But a lot of times my mom would leave us at home hungry, because she had to go out and see what she could find. We were a family with no toys, no childhood, almost no clothes, no sandals, no workbooks for school. They had us working in the fields, doing housework, raising pigs, chickens; we helped my mom whenever we knew she was short of money. I remember when I was five years old, my oldest brother died at twenty-three. He got leukemia. Yeah, we went through a lot, but the main thing I remember is the poverty. I would look at my friends from school, with backpacks, with sneakers, with the school supplies they needed. And us barefoot, no workbooks, some friend or other would give us a sheet of paper, out of pity, no question, that was what we would write on. The other children had toys, *we* made toys out of mud, or from a bit of wood, to have something to play with.

When our mom passed away, it became an option for us to go somewhere else to work, because as long as she lived, she wouldn't let us. I left home at twenty-six years of age. My mom had been gone a year. I hitchhiked to the

US, and as soon as I got to Mexicali to stay with some friends someone had recommended to me, I started working. I worked at this one gentleman's restaurant, but he didn't pay me money, he just gave me food . . . or if I was lucky, he would give me three dollars a week.[21] Only when I asked him for it, because I had my dad to take care of and needed to send him money. I held on for a year and a half with him, and then, when I left, he came around looking for me, saying I'd stolen from him. I told him the reason I'd left was because when I left home, it was to work, and he hadn't paid me enough. From there I went to the church. Once a week, I would go to Mass at the cathedral, and that's where I met this gentleman, who was a *coyote*, and he took me to stay at his house. I used to help him teach the national anthem to the Central Americans.[22] The Mexicans, I made food for them. I spent six months with him. Then I told him that I had a cousin on the other side and I wanted to make the jump.[23] He only charged me 250 dollars for helping me because I had helped him a lot too. Once I was on that side of the border, it was my cousin who paid the 250 dollars because I didn't have it.

When I got to the US, I was taken advantage of there too. I was kept like a servant and not allowed to work. I stayed with some first cousins. They were working overtime, and when I arrived, they wanted me to do their housework: shine their shoes, cook meals. They used to say, "just while we're getting situated." But that day never came, till the day I got myself out of there. I spent three or four months working there in their house.

I went to the beach in Santa Barbara. I met a fellow Mexican there. I told him what my situation was and he gave me twenty dollars. From there I picked up some work washing dishes and rented a room for myself. I washed dishes for three years. I moved over to kitchen prep and then to cook. I can cook five types of food now: Chinese, American, Italian, Japanese, and Mexican. French a little, too. I've spent thirty-three years there, all in restaurants. I'd work for a stretch of time, like five years, then the restaurant would change owners. But the one who was stopping, the previous owner, would recommend us. That's how I did it. I'd work for one stretch, then not for another.

About four times I came to Mexico and stayed for a month or two. You used to be able to get through with no trouble. In Mexico I got married, took my wife back with me, had three kids. They're there, in the US. The reason I left this time was because I came for a family member's funeral; then I came back to the US, and they put me in jail. I presented my case, fought it for three months. They set me a thirty-five-hundred-dollar bond, and my family paid it and I left. When I was home, they called me on the phone and sent a summons. I showed up and they threw me out that same day. The reason for the summons was that when my bond got paid, I put the address of somebody who had a green card. She had let us use her address for paying the bond. It may have been her who reported me. That's where the correspondence was supposed to arrive. The bond money was ours, but because of her, I'm here. I have checks there that I can't do anything with. They've ended up going uncashed. What I used to do was always have one check stored, for whatever might come up. I would store one and cash one, store one and cash one. I accumulated four checks. So I've got forty-six hundred dollars that are in the trash at the moment. I called the company, and they told me they're expired and they'd do new ones for me if I went and picked them up in person.

The Latina who deported me, the last thing she said to me was that my charm had run out.[24] I felt like she was saying something really insulting and ugly to me. The reason I never took care of my legal residence was because it never crossed my mind that this whole thing could happen. Now with the record they've given me, two reentries and a deportation, I have to apply for a pardon. Right now, what I'm dealing with is that Immigration didn't return my stuff to me.[25] And I dread the day that they stop letting me eat here.[26] What am I going to do?

NIEVES

Nació el veinticuatro de agosto de 1974 en Atlamajalcingo del Monte, un municipio de Guerrero. Tiene treinta y cinco años. Habla únicamente mixteco. Nunca asistió a la escuela, por falta de recursos. Su vida ha sido de sufrimiento y de carencia. Se juntó con un hombre, padre de sus nueve hijos: ocho mujeres y un hombre. Su padre la entregó a este hombre, que es su marido, por dinero, conforme a la tradición.

El saco de maíz se compra a precio de trescientos pesos. Es suficiente en una familia para comer de dos a tres semanas. La comida es tortilla con chile y, algunas veces, frijoles, si los tienen. El marido trabaja en el campo y le pagan setenta pesos al día, mismos que tienen que alcanzar para alimentar, vestir y demás, a once personas, correspondiendo a 6.37 pesos mexicanos a cada persona por día. Con esta cantidad la familia sólo puede comprar un poco de tortillas.

Decidieron ir a Estados Unidos ella y su marido, para darles comida y estudio a sus hijos. Para venirse, dejaron a los hijos solos y, como único capital para vivir durante su ausencia, un saco de maíz, con la esperanza de que llegarían a los Estados Unidos, trabajarían y enviarían dinero a los hijos.

Los ocho hijos se quedaron bajo la responsabilidad de una adolescente, la mayor, que tiene dieciséis años. Cuando los agarró la Migra, a ella la deportaron luego. A él lo dejaron detenido.

IIIIIIIIIIIIIIIIIIII

She was born on August twenty-fourth, 1974, in Atlamajalcingo del Monte, a municipality in Guerrero.[27] She's thirty-five. Mixteco is the only language she speaks. She never went to school, for lack of resources. Her life has been one of suffering and want. She moved in with a man, the father of her nine children: eight girls and a boy. Her father handed her over to this man, her husband, in exchange for money, as is the tradition.

A sack of corn costs eighteen dollars.[28] It's enough to feed this family for two to three weeks. Food consists of tortillas with chile and, sometimes, beans, if they have them.[29] The husband works in the fields and they pay him four dollars a day, which has to cover food, clothes, and more for eleven people, allotting thirty-eight cents to each person per day. For that amount, all the family can afford is a few tortillas' worth.

They decided to leave for the US, Nieves and her husband, in order to feed and educate their kids. To get here, they left their kids on their own, with a sack of corn as their only resource to live on during their parents' absence.[30] The hope was that they would reach the US, work, and send money to their kids.

Responsibility for their eight kids fell to a teenager, the oldest child: she is sixteen. When Immigration caught them, Nieves was deported immediately. Her husband remained under arrest.

SAMUEL

Soy del Estado de Tabasco. Tengo dos niños gemelos. Soy pescador y quiero darles un mejor futuro a mis niños. Pero fue mucho lo que perdí. La mamá de mis cuatitos murió cuando ellos nacieron. Los dejé con mis suegros. Ahora regreso derrotado y no quiero llegar así con mi familia.

El veintiuno de febrero del 2013, intenté entrar a Estados Unidos por Sonoyta. Llegando a Sonoyta, me llamaron unas personas y preguntaron si quería trabajar. Yo no sabía de qué se trataba, pero la idea de conseguir algún dinero, no me caía mal. Dije que sí. Llegué donde me indicaron y me dijeron que se trataba de llevar la mochila. Yo no quería, pero me obligaban y si no, mi vida corría peligro. La mochila pesa como veinticinco kilos y llevaba, además, ocho galones de agua cargando. Caminé cuatro días y medio. Íbamos diecisiete personas en total. Tres llevaban cargando sólo latas de comida para el grupo. A cada cuarenta y cinco minutos descansábamos diez a quince minutos. Hicimos cuatro días y medio. El trato con la mafia era que, si me quedaba en Estados Unidos, me darían quinientos dólares y me llevarían a un lugar donde me pudiera recoger mi familia. Si regresaba para llevar otra carga, ofrecían pagarme mil ochocientos o dos mil dólares, según decían. Pero tienes que regresar a la línea para que te paguen. Yo llevaba ochocientos dólares de cosas que había vendido para venirme, entre esas cosas mi lancha, que era mi instrumento de trabajo.

Nosotros, el grupo que íbamos, cuando ya vimos a Migración, escondimos las mochilas y corrimos a la sierra, al cerro. Allí llegaron ellos en cuatrimotos. Nos asustamos mucho porque cuando llegó Migración, un hondureño corrió y Migración empezó a disparar. Eso nos causó pánico. Creímos que nos iban a matar. A él lo agarraron. Quién sabe cómo lo tratarían. A nosotros nos dijeron que nos quitáramos todo lo que traíamos, pero ahí me quitaron los ochocientos dólares que traía desde Tabasco, de lo que yo había vendido. Eso sí me dolió y me sigue doliendo. Ahora regreso mucho peor de como venía, perdí mi instrumento de trabajo y no logré nada.

Migración me llevó y me tuvieron quince meses en la cárcel, días que perdí de trabajar, además mi dinero que no me quisieron regresar. Dijeron que era la prueba de que me habían agarrado con droga.

Lo más duro en la detención, es que la autoestima te la ponen hasta el suelo, porque en las revisiones, te desnudan totalmente y eso es duro y humillante. Lo único bueno, que lo hacen parejo con todos. En eso, no discriminan.

Ahora quiero conseguir algún trabajo, porque no quiero regresar así, con las manos vacías y ya sin medios para trabajar.

|||||||||||||||||||

I'm from Tabasco State. I have two children, twins. I'm a fisherman, and I want a better future for my children. But I ended up losing a whole lot. My twins' mom died when they were born; I left them with her parents. Now I'm going back totally beaten. I don't want to show up at my family's door like this.

On February twenty-first, 2013, I tried to enter the US through Sonoyta. Right as I was arriving in Sonoyta, some people called me and asked if I wanted work. I didn't know what it involved, but the idea of making some kind of money didn't sound bad. I said yes. I got to the place they'd given me, and they told me it involved carrying the backpack.[31] I didn't want to, but they were making me, my life was in danger if I didn't. The backpack weighs about fifty-five pounds, and I carried a load of eight gallons of water on top of that. I walked for four and a half days. There were seventeen of us in all. Three were carrying nothing but cans of food for the group. Every forty-five minutes, we'd stop and rest for ten or fifteen minutes. We did four and a half days. The deal with the mafia was that if I stayed in the US, they'd give me five hundred dollars and take me to a place where my family could pick me up. If I went back for another load, they were offering to pay me eighteen hundred or two thousand dollars, so they said, but you have to go back to the border for them to pay you.[32] I had eight hundred dollars on me from stuff I'd sold to get here, including my boat, which was my tool of my trade.

The group I was in, when we saw Immigration coming, we hid the backpacks and ran for the mountains, the hillside. They reached us there on ATVs. We got really scared because when Immigration reached us, one Honduran guy ran and Immigration started shooting. That panicked us. We were sure they were going to kill us. They did catch that guy. God only knows how they treated him later. For us, they told us to take off everything we had on, but that included them taking my eight hundred dollars that I had on me since Tabasco, from what I had sold. Now *that* hurt, and it still hurts. I'm now going back a lot worse than when I came: I lost my tool of my trade and I didn't accomplish anything.

Immigration took me away, and they kept me in jail for fifteen months. I lost that many days of work, on top of my money that they refused to give back to me. They said it was proof that they'd caught me with drugs.

The roughest thing about detention is your self-esteem; they take it down to rock bottom. During inspections, they take all your clothes off, which is rough, humiliating. The only good thing is that they do the same to everyone. On that, they don't discriminate.

Right now, what I want to do is find some kind of work. I don't want to go back like this, empty-handed and now with no way to work.

3

Violence and Maras

Introduced by Jorge A. Andrade Galindo

The violence caused by the gangs that operate in Central America—and which extend their reach into the United States and Mexico—has forced thousands of families from the Northern Triangle (El Salvador, Guatemala, and Honduras) to flee and seek refuge in Mexico or in the United States. These are people who fear the possibility of being murdered, having their children recruited into a gang, or their young daughters being raped because they caught the eye of a gang leader.

In El Salvador over 60 percent of crimes committed are the work of the Maras, a group that is composed of two rival factions: MS-13 (Mara Salvatrucha) and Barrio 18, which in recent years have grown larger and more complex.[1] Many of these crimes involve acts of unbridled violence. Three of the most dangerous places in the world are now found in the Northern Triangle: San Salvador is ranked seven, with 83 homicides per 100,000 people; Distrito Central, Honduras, comes in fourth, with 85 homicides per 100,000; and also in Honduras, San Pedro Sula is ranked third, with 112 per 100,000.[2] Just like El Salvador, Honduras and Guatemala (which is ranked the twenty-third most dangerous city, with 52 homicides per 100,000 people) are suffering a wave of violence generated by Mara criminal gangs.

The data about the Maras' violence is undeniable. It is therefore important to ask questions about where and how these groups came to be and to strive to understand more about the level of danger they actually present. It's worth pointing out that the context they emerged from is tied to the Salvadoran Civil War (1980–92), which occurred within the timeframe of the Cold

War—the most decisive moment in the political, ideological, economic, and military confrontation between the United States and the Soviet Union.

The Salvadoran government, which had been accused of fraudulence, was allied with the US government. This bond was strengthened throughout the military conflict, with the United States training Salvadoran military officers at the US government's School of the Americas in Georgia, helping establish some of the most violent elite squads (especially with regards to their actions against civilians).[3] The United States also provided innumerable heavy weapons. The dire situation in El Salvador led the US government to grant asylum to thousands of Salvadorans. Many were sent to suburbs or urban areas, where poverty and gang violence also had a strong hold. The young were especially vulnerable, and some of them would end up joining gangs. These groups grew strong in the prisons where their members were sent. The solidarity that bound gang members together was crucial to the formation of groups like MS-13 and Barrio 18. The Chapultepec Peace Accords of 1992 put an end to twelve years of civil war in El Salvador. In the following years, the United States deported many *mareros* (members of the Maras), who then consolidated their power by forming relationships with other sectors of organized crime, such as Mexican and Colombian drug cartels.

Theft, extortion, homicide, drug and weapons trafficking, kidnapping, rape, small-scale drug dealing, and *cobro de guerra*—the Maras engage in these and other criminal acts under cover of the collusion and omission of the authorities, which of course complicates terribly the process of bringing these acts to justice.[4] So many of the people just trying to get on with their lives in both urban and rural settings are put under huge pressure from implicit or explicit threats. The pressure may come from *mareros* or even from the authorities, whose supposed mandate is to protect the citizenry. Often, setting off north becomes the only choice.

A challenge for those traveling north is that the Maras' influence is not contained by national borders. In 2012 the US Department of Treasury classified the Maras as Transnational Criminal Organizations (TCOs). Beyond the undertakings previously mentioned, other transnational criminal activities attributed to them include people smuggling, human trafficking, organized crime, and extortion.[5]

We have discussed the complexity of the Maras (especially MS-13) operation, which is based on an intricate network of connections that are organized in a hierarchical structure and which operate through *la clica*.[6] Furthermore, they have established links with other TCOs (like the Zetas) or other organizations that provide access to heavy weapons and to militarized training. These relationships with other groups within organized crime have allowed them to take over the transportation of drugs at the Mexico-Guatemala border.

It's important to point out that the Maras have diversified their criminal activities. One of these is their collaboration with *polleros* or *coyotes*, that is, individuals who take migrants from the Northern Triangle to the border with Mexico or the United States. According to *testimonios* heard throughout the migration route through Mexico, the Maras deliver migrants directly to organized criminal groups. These in turn charge the families of those who have been kidnapped in order to set them free. The amounts demanded can range from three thousand to seven thousand US dollars.

Another activity that has been documented is the *cobro de vía*, which is similar to a toll charged for the use of a road. This charge entails Maras concealing themselves among the migrants who travel to the northern Mexican border via the cargo train known as *La Bestia* (The Beast). Once they are in place and the train is in motion, the hidden Maras start charging fees of a hundred US dollars per person in order to allow migrants to continue the trip. According to *testimonios*, people, including women and children, who refused to pay or who simply did not have money would be thrown off onto the train tracks, decapitated, or attacked with a machete.

The rampant violence in the Northern Triangle countries is disturbing. Central American governments have tried different strategies to try to mitigate the rise of these criminal organizations. However, due to a lack of funds, precarious public policy, corruption, and the existing collusion between sectors of law enforcement and criminal groups, these actions have had a limited impact.

There is no simple solution. It is clear that governments hold the key to preventing and stopping violence, but they must change their approach. The United States, for example, rather than building walls to close its borders, trying to stop migration through mass deportations, or hardening its anti-immigrant stance should instead look beyond its interventionist focus and channel some of the resources into programs that strengthen the institutions and support the governments of emitting countries. On the other hand, El Salvador, for example, should test out some of the many approaches that are available, such as cleaning up its law enforcement agencies, strengthening its institutions, establishing public policy aimed at young citizens, creating reintegration programs for gang members, generating employment, establishing incentives for agriculture, or supporting cultural programs.

ANA CAROLINA

Soy Ana Carolina, de Guatemala. Tengo treinta y nueve años. Sólo estudié primaria. A los quince años me junté con un hombre y tuve siete hijos: tres hombres y cuatro mujeres. Con excepción de los asesinados, son los hijos que traigo. Mi hija mayor tiene veinte años y el menor doce. Tres hijas son menores de edad, entre ellas una que fue secuestrada, así como el niño de doce años. Los otros dos varones, mayores, fueron asesinados.

El padre de mis hijos ha sido una persona muy buena, pero a los cuatro meses de tener a mi hijo menor, él empezó a irse de la casa, porque antes él me mantenía. Desapareció dos meses y me dijo que había intentado cruzar a los Estados Unidos. Yo lo perdoné, pero estuvo quince días y se volvió a desaparecer. Pasé cinco años esperándolo. Me puse a trabajar en una maquila. Ahí conocí personas y me fui desenvolviendo. Lo esperé siete años, pero me cansé y me busqué este hombre con el que vengo. Mi marido regresó, pero ya no lo acepté.

Cuando me junté con el hombre que vivo, pusimos una tienda de mercaduría mexicana. Teníamos un mes trabajando cuando comenzaron las extorsiones. Los mareros querían renta: tres mil quetzales a la semana. Puse la denuncia. Confiaba en Dios y el catorce de septiembre del 2008 me mataron a mi primer hijo. Él venía de trabajar. Tenía dieciocho años. Lo mataron como a un criminal y él era un buen hijo. Lo mataron con arma grande y lo dejaron irreconocible. Yo enloquecí. Pasé dos meses ida. Mi esposo me ayudó llevándome a doctores, porque quedé mal. El día de su muerte, quise ir a la escena del crimen. Cuando vi a mi hijo, no pude caminar. Se me fue la voz, me paralicé. No se hizo justicia.

A otro día de enterrar a mi hijo, tuve que salirme de la casa donde estábamos porque nos amenazaron de acabar con todos. Mi hijo, el que seguía de él, se salió de estudiar porque ya no teníamos dinero. Nos fuimos a Paraíso del Frutal sin nada. Brayan, así se llamaba, quería trabajar en mototaxi y empezó a hacerlo llevando pasajeros a todos lados. Todo marchaba bien. No obstante, yo vivía con el temor. Íbamos a cumplir un año allí y un día dijo mi hijo: "Vi un carro, como que me andaba siguiendo". Yo le decía que no trabajara, pero la situación era difícil. A él me lo secuestraron, el hombre del carro que él me había dicho. Lo bajaron del mototaxi y se lo llevaron. La policía me llamó. Yo guardaba la esperanza de recuperarlo. A otro día mi hijo estaba maniatado y muerto.

Nuevamente quedé mal. Me pasaba encerrada, las fuerzas se me habían ido. Yo dije: "Si me matan, que me maten. No voy a andar huyendo". Pero luego me secuestraron a mi hija Isaura. Fue a comprar pan. Llegó la mujer de la panadería y me dijo que la habían subido a un carro. Fui a la policía, levanté la denuncia. A otro día nos hablan: "Queremos treinta mil quetzales". Mi hija estaba siendo torturada. Dos meses y medio la torturaron. Ella iba a cumplir quince años. La tenían vendada. Y le decían cosas horribles como: "Si no paga la perra de tu madre, te vamos a hacer pedacitos, como matamos a tus hermanos". Vendimos un carro, malbaratado, para dar el rescate por mi hija, y la liberamos.

En el 2013, decidí sacar de ahí a mi hija. Saqué a toda la familia y la llevé hasta la montaña. Ellas se quedaron allá, yo me vine con mi marido rumbo a Estados Unidos. Cruzamos por aquí por Nogales. Nos agarraron en el desierto junto con mi esposo. Me llevaron a Tucson. Me dijeron que iban a tenerme seis meses detenida. Firmé mi deportación. A otro día me llevaron para Eloy. Ahí conocí a una persona de Nogales. Yo lloraba por mis hijas. Le conté todo a ella y me ayudó para pedir asilo. Logré la entrevista. Les conté mi caso. Les dije: "No tengo apoyo, ni dinero". Pedí mi deportación y me aconsejaron que no lo hiciera. Una señora me ayudó y a los tres días salí de la cárcel. Me llevaron a su casa. Ellas me apoyaron, recogieron una ofrenda para mí y mandé dinero a mi familia. Me consiguieron trabajo. Me pagaron mi primera semana y mis hijas estaban contentas. Después, ellas me mandaron decir que habían llegado dos cartas de amenaza. Yo me volví loca y me quería venir. Ya no pude quedarme. Me regalaron dólares y me vine. Me quedé en la frontera México-Guatemala y un pariente fue a traer a mis hijas. Me atropellaron a Alam, mi hijo menor. Me llevaron a mis hijas a la frontera, estuvimos en Hidalgo, Chiapas. De ahí nos deportaron tres veces a Guatemala. En Tapachula estuvimos siete meses. Ahí nos dieron apoyo y arreglamos permiso.

Total, en México llevamos año y medio sufriendo. Unas veces en las cárceles de Tapachula, otras trabajando o viajando, a veces sin un peso en la bolsa. Yo lloraba y decía: "¿Qué van a comer mis muchachitos?" Ahora aquí estamos, nuevamente para pedir asilo en los Estados Unidos.

llllllllllllllll

I'm Ana Carolina, from Guatemala City. I'm thirty-nine. I only finished sixth grade.[7] At age fifteen I moved in with a guy, and I had seven kids: three boys, four girls. Except for the ones who have been murdered, it's the same kids I have with me here. My oldest daughter is twenty and the youngest is twelve. There are three girls who are under eighteen. One of them got kidnapped once.[8] There's also my little boy, the twelve-year-old. The other two boys, when they were grown, they were murdered.

The father of my kids has been really decent, but four months after I had my youngest, he left home for the first time. Because before that, he paid the bills. He disappeared for two months, told me he had tried to get across to the United States. I forgave him, but he stayed for fifteen days and disappeared again. I spent five years waiting for him. I went to work in an assembly plant. I met people there, started to feel comfortable. Seven years I waited for him, but I got tired of waiting and found myself my current man

I came here with. My husband did come back, but this time I didn't take him back.

When I moved in with this man I live with now, we opened a Mexican-goods store. We got through the first month of work, and then the extortion started. The people from the gang wanted us to pay rent: four hundred dollars a week.[9] So I filed a complaint, put my trust in God, and on September the fourteenth, 2008, they killed my oldest boy. He was coming home from work. He was eighteen, and they killed him like a criminal and he was a good boy. They killed him with a high-caliber gun and left him unrecognizable. I went crazy. I spent two months out of it. My husband helped me by taking me to see doctors, because I was a mess. The day it happened, I chose to go to the crime scene. When I saw my boy, I couldn't walk. I lost my voice, I froze. No one was held responsible.

The day after burying my son, we had to get out of the place where we were living because they threatened to get rid of all of us. My son, the second oldest after him, he left school because we couldn't afford it anymore. We headed to Paraíso del Frutal with nothing.[10] Brayan—that was his name—he wanted to be in the motorcycle-taxi business, and he got started, he was taking passengers all over the place. Everything was moving along. But still I was constantly afraid. We had been there just about one year and then one day my son says, "I saw a car. Like it was following me." I started telling him not to go to work, but things weren't easy. This time, what happened to my son was that he was kidnapped.[11] It was the man from the car he had told me about. They pulled him off his motorcycle taxi and took him away. The police called me. I held out hope of getting him back. The next day my boy was dead with his hands tied together.

I was a mess all over again. I stayed home all the time. The strength had gone out of me. I said, "If they kill me, let them kill me, I'm not going to run." But then they kidnapped my daughter Isaura. She went to buy bread. The woman from the bakery showed up and told me they had made her get in a car. I went to the police, filed the report. They next day we get a phone call: "We want four thousand dollars."[12] My girl was being tortured. For two and a half months they tortured her. She was about to turn fifteen. They kept her blindfolded. And they said terrible things to her like, "If that bitch of a mother you have doesn't pay, we're going to cut you into little pieces, just like we killed your brothers." We sold a car, way underpriced in order to pay the ransom for my daughter, and we got her out.

In 2013 I decided to get my daughter out of there. I got the whole family together and took them all the way to the mountains. They stayed there, and I left with my husband for the US. We crossed near here, at Nogales. They caught us in the desert, me and my husband. I was taken to Tucson.

I was told they were going to keep me in custody for six months. I signed my deportation. The next day I was taken to Eloy.[13] I met someone who was from Nogales there. I was crying a lot about my girls. I told her everything and she helped me request asylum. I was able to get the interview. I told them my case. I said, "I don't have any support, or any money." I asked to be deported and they advised me not to do it. A lady helped me, and in three days I was out of jail. They took me to stay at their house, these ladies— they supported me; they took up a collection for me and sent money to my family. They got me a job; they paid my first week, and my girls were happy. But then, my girls sent me a message that two threat letters had arrived. I went nuts, and I wanted to leave. I couldn't stay any longer. Someone gave me some money and I left. I stayed at the Mexico-Guatemala border and a relative went to bring my daughters. My youngest son, Alan, had gotten hit by a car. So they brought my daughters to the border. We were in Hidalgo, Chiapas. We got deported to Guatemala three times from there. In Tapachula we spent seven months. They gave us support there and fixed a permit for us.

In all, we've been in Mexico for a year and a half so far, suffering. Some of that time in the jails in Tapachula, some of it working or on the road. Sometimes without a nickel in our pocket. I used to cry and say, "What are my little guys going to eat?" Right now, we're here, to ask for asylum in the US again.

HÉCTOR ARTURO

[*Narra su historia entre llanto. Al narrar de los golpes de la mara, temblaba y tenía las manos heladas*].

Soy Héctor Arturo, originario de El Salvador. Nací en el '79, en la mera guerra. Soy casado. Tengo dos hijas. He trabajado como pescador de altamar.

Mi padre me abandonó al año de que nací. Viví en el Puerto de Acajutla con mi madre y otros dos hermanos. Mi madre nos mantenía con la venta de tamales de elote. Después se fue a una fábrica de mariscos. Vendíamos cocteles de concha.

El problema para mí empieza porque me peleé con mi primo, que era marero. En mi país existen las maras Salvatrucha y 18. Donde yo vivo está la MS. Yo trabajaba como pescador de altamar. Entraba a pescar rentando una lancha, y a la salida empezaron las maras pidiéndome pescado. Al ver que yo continuaba con el producto, empezaron a aumentar su pedido. Si al principio eran 2 los que iban, fueron aumentando a 3, 5, 10, 12 y a todos debía darles pescado. Eso era a la fuerza. Las maras, si uno se resiste a lo que piden, lo quieren golpear y matar. Ellos son dueños de cinco lanchas y se sienten dueños del muelle.

Pasado el tiempo, yo les dije que no podía seguirles dando. ¿Qué les iba a llevar a mis hijos? Como me negué, un día me dijeron que querían platicar conmigo. Fui con uno de ellos a una casa, donde me citaron. Ahí estaban tres más. Me hicieron pasar a un cuarto, pusieron música a todo volumen y uno de ellos iba con un bate con el que se juega béisbol, era de aluminio y me dijeron que era para que no me les anduviera rebelando. Me dieron como sesenta batazos porque tenía que aprender que, cuando me pidieran algo, yo tenía que acceder. Me empezaron a golpear. Cada batazo era muy fuerte. Como a los diez golpes caí al suelo.

Cada vez que caía al suelo me exigían con insultos y amenazas que me parara y continuaban golpeándome. Además, cada vez que caía, se me engarrotaban las manos como que me iba a dar un shock de nervios. Y sentía en el rostro como que me recorrían miles de hormigas, por la cuestión de los nervios. Así pasé esa amarga experiencia. Gateando salí de ahí, no podía caminar y tenía que subir un montón de gradas para llegar a la casa de mi mamá.

Una tía me llevó al hospital. Yo no podía ni hablar de dolor, solo le pedí un vaso con agua. Ella me preguntaba qué me había pasado. Yo no quería hablar de eso. Pasé tres meses tirado en la cama casi sin comer. No podía dormir sino boca abajo. Fue un momento terrible.

A veces la gente nos juzga a los centroamericanos. No saben el dolor que hemos vivido. Yo sufro muchísimo al recordar a mis hijos.

Una vez recuperado, seguí pescando. Pesqué como tres veces o cuatro veces más y ellos ahí se reunían, en el muelle donde atracan las lanchas. Cada vez que salía, me veían y se burlaban de recordar el dolor que estaba viviendo cuando me golpeaban. Veía sus gestos.

Como a la cuarta o quinta vez que fui a pescar, se me volvieron a acercar a decirme que querían pescado. Yo no llevaba nada. Ahí fue cuando me quisieron llevar a la colonia de mi madre. Yo les dije que me esperaran, que iba a entregar cuentas al dueño. Me dijeron que no me fuera a ir. Mandaron a un niño como de unos doce años a cuidarme. El niño se fue conmigo. Yo les dije que sí iba a regresar. Fue cuando corrí y ya no me alcanzaron.

Me fui a la capital de El Salvador. Me fui a trabajar a la central de abastos. La "Tiendona" le llaman, y ahí predomina la Mara 18. Me investigaron de dónde era y hasta me registraron documentos de donde vivía. Se enteraron que venía de donde estaba la otra mara. Me dijeron que me iban a matar, sólo por haber vivido donde domina la MS. En ese momento, que sólo tenía cinco dólares, compré dos cuartos de agua para vender. Me fui a dormir a la calle a donde llegan personas cristianas a repartir alimentos.

Ya habíamos orado y me había recostado en la acera cuando escuché plática de mareros, y estaba uno de los pandilleros que me había dicho que no quería verme ahí en el Puerto de Acajutla, ni en otro lugar donde mandara la MS, porque me iban a matar. Al escuchar eso, agarré mis zapatos y mi mochila, me fui despacio y me empezaron a perseguir. Cuando me alejé como unas cuatro o cinco cuadras, le pedí ayuda a un agente de seguridad, le dije que me hiciera el favor de llamar a la policía, porque me iban siguiendo unos mareros. Le pedí que llamara a la policía, y al voltear la cabeza me dijo que él era marero de la 18, que me hincara, que no corriera porque me iba a matar. Así me dijo que iba a llamar a los demás "perros" para que me fueran a matar ahí donde me tenía hincado él. Se retiró como dos o tres metros para llamar a los demás mareros y pude correr y escapar. Iba pasando una patrulla del GRP. Les pedí ayuda y me la dieron. Les dije la situación y cómo en el que confié para ayuda resultó ser un pandillero también. Luego él me dijo que me fuera. Le demostré que no tenía números ni letras de maras. Yo quería mi mochila. En ese momento, uno de ellos se bajó de la patrulla y me acompañó.

De ahí me escapé para una estación, donde se mantienen en vigilancia dos soldados. Ellos me cuidaron hasta las dos de la madrugada. Y al siguiente día, con dos dólares que me habían quedado, con esos me vine para México.

Llegando a la frontera, empecé a pedir raite. Un trailero me dio raite hasta Escuintla, Guatemala. Luego empecé a caminar por la carretera cuatro días. Comía mangos y nances, era lo que comía. Fueron doce días caminando. Llegando a Tecún Umán, un señor de un taller de soldadura me ofreció trabajo, me preguntó a dónde iba. Yo le dije que sí necesitaba trabajo. Me dio trabajo y para dos pasajes de combi. Logré llegar hasta Tapachula. Ahí me agarraron los de Migración. Estuve ocho días en el corralón. El trato no es malo si uno se apega a cumplir las reglas. Hay que hacer grandes filas para comer. Estando ahí, pedí a Migración platicar con COMAR. Sí platiqué, pero no me dio ni solución a mi problema ni ningún tipo de ayuda. Me pidió hacer una petición por escrito, explicando mi caso, pero no hubo ayuda. Cuando pasaron lista y me llamaron, sólo fue para deportarme. Volví a llegar a El Salvador, sólo para ver a mi madre, me volví a encontrar a los muchachos y ahí me siguieron y de una pedrada me quebraron el brazo. [*Muestra la cicatriz de la cirugía*]. Como pude me fui al hospital, me pedían un donante de sangre. En el hospital pasé dos meses. Me operaron y pusieron dos tornillos y un pedazo de alambre. A los cinco días me dieron de alta. Salí del hospital. No tenía a donde ir. Con el brazo enyesado y recién operado me vine de nuevo. Tengo dos meses viajando. Ahora estoy aquí. No sé lo que voy a hacer.

|||||||||||||||||||

[*Sobs as he recounts his story. When telling of being beaten by the gang, he trembles and his hands get cold.*]

I'm Héctor Arturo. From El Salvador originally. Born in '79, right during the war. I'm married. I have two daughters. I've got experience working as a deep-sea fisher.

My father left me the year after I was born. I lived at the Port of Acajutla with my mother and two brothers. My mother supported us with what she made selling corn tamales. After that she went to a seafood factory. We sold clam cocktails for a while.

My problems started when I got in a fight with a cousin of mine who belonged to a gang. In my country there are the Mara Salvatrucha and the Calle 18 gang.[14] The place where I live is MS territory. I used to work as a deep-sea fisher. When I would go in to fish, I would rent a boat, and the gangs started asking me for fish on the way out. When they saw that I kept producing, they started increasing what they were asking. First maybe 2 of them would come, then it kept increasing to 3, 5, 10, 12. And all of them I had to give fish to. I didn't have a choice. The way the gangs are is that if someone is resistant to what they ask, they want to beat him and kill him. They own five boats, and the way they see it, they own the dock.

As time went on, I told them I wasn't going to be able to keep giving them fish. What was I going to take home to my kids? I refused, so one day they told me they wanted to talk to me. I went with one of them to a house, a place where they'd asked me to meet them. There were three more of them there. They took me in a room where they put some music on full blast, and one of them came in with a bat, the kind you play baseball with, made of aluminum, and they said it was so I wouldn't be rebelling against them anymore. They hit me with the bat about sixty times, because I had to learn that when they asked me for something, I had to agree to it. They started the beating, and every time they hit me, it was really hard. At about the tenth blow, I fell on the floor.

Every time I fell on the floor they used insults and threats to demand that I get up again, then they would go back to beating me. Also, every time I fell, my hands went numb, like I was going to go into shock. And on my face, it felt like thousands of ants were crawling all over it, for the same reason, the shock. So that's what it was like, a bitter experience. I *crawled* out of there, I couldn't walk, and I had to climb so many stairs to get to my mom's house.

One of my aunts took me to the hospital. I couldn't even talk for the pain—I just asked for a cup of water. She kept asking me what happened to me. I didn't want to talk about it. I spent three months flat on my back in bed without eating almost anything. I couldn't sleep except facedown. It was a horrible period of my life.

Sometimes people judge us Central Americans. They don't know what kind of pain we've had in our lives. I suffer a whole lot when I think about my kids.

Once I'd recovered, I went back to fishing. I fished maybe three more times, four more times, and they hung out right there, on the dock where the boats are. Every time I went out, they would see me and make jokes about remembering the pain I went through when they were beating me. I could see the looks on their faces.

About the fourth or fifth time I went fishing, they came up to me like they had before, saying they wanted fish. I didn't have anything. That was when they decided they were going to take me to my mother's neighborhood. I told them to give me a minute, I was going to settle up with the owner. They told me not to try to leave. They sent a little kid along, like twelve years old or so, to watch me. The kid went with me. I told them I was definitely going to come back. That's when I took off, and they haven't caught up with me yet.

I went to the capital of El Salvador. I went to work at a street market. La Tiendona it's called, and it's a place where Calle 18 is dominant. They looked into where I was from; they even searched my documentation to see where I lived. They figured out that I came from where the other gang was. They told me they were going to kill me, just for having lived where MS is in control. Only having five dollars at that moment, I immediately bought two small bottles of water to sell.[15] I went to sleep in the street, in a place where people from a Christian church come and hand out food.[16]

We had prayed, and I had laid myself down on the pavement, when I heard gang talk. There he was: one of the gang members who had told me that he didn't want to see me there at the Port of Acajutla, or anywhere else MS was in charge, because they were going to kill me. When I heard them, I grabbed my shoes and my bag. I started to walk away slowly, and they started to chase me. When I got about four or five blocks away, I asked a security guard for help. I told him, do me a favor and call the police; some gang members are following me. I asked him to call the police and the next thing I know he says that *he's* a gang member with Calle 18 and to get on my knees, not to run because he's going to kill me. That's what he said, he was going to call all the other "dogs" so they could come and kill me right there where he had me kneeling. He stepped away maybe two or three yards to call the rest of his gang, and I was able to run and escape. A GRP patrol truck happened to be passing.[17] I asked them to help me and they did. I told them what was happening and how the guy I put my trust in for help turned out to be a gang member too. Later, the GRP officer told me I could go. I showed him I didn't have any gang numbers or letters.[18] I wanted my bag. One of the officers immediately got out of the truck and went with me to get it.

From there I escaped to a bus station where there are always two soldiers on duty for security. They guarded me until two in the morning. And the next day, with two dollars I still had, with that I got away to Mexico.

When I got to the border, I started hitchhiking. A truck driver gave me a ride to Escuintla, Guatemala. Then I started walking along the highway. For four days I ate mangos and *nance* fruit; that's what I ate. It was twelve days' walk in all. When I got to Tecún Umán, a gentleman with a welding shop offered me some work, asked me where I was headed. I told him I did need work. He gave me work *and* money for two shuttle rides. I managed to get all the way to Tapachula. They caught me there, the Immigration people. I was in "impound" for eight days. As far as the treatment, it's not bad if you follow the rules to the letter. You have to stand in long lines to eat. While I was there, I asked Immigration if I could speak to COMAR.[19] I did, but they didn't give me any solution to my problem or any kind of help at all. They asked me to make a written request, explaining my case, but there was no assistance. When there was a roll call and my name was on it, it was only to deport me. I got to El Salvador again, only went to see my mother, ran into those guys again and of course they followed me, broke my arm with a rock. [*Shows the scar from the surgery.*] I went from there to the hospital as best I could. They were asking me to get a blood donor. I spent two months there. They operated on me and put in two screws and a piece of wire. Five days after that, they released me. I walked out of the hospital. I didn't have anywhere to go. With my arm in plaster, and the operation still fresh, I came north again. I've been on the road for two months. Now I'm here. What I'm going to do next, I don't know.

4

Gendered Violence

Introduced by Cecilia Guadalupe Espinosa Martínez

The stories of the women in this chapter represent different ways of being a woman. In her book *The Second Sex*, Simone de Beauvoir proposes that women are not born as such, but rather it is through our history, culture, context, and family that one becomes a woman. So how do migrant women come to be women? They give us the clues to the answer themselves. The key to understanding lies in looking back over a whole life story and the community that surrounds it. Furthermore, the foundation of this explanation is the constant decision-making that happens in the here and now—to migrate, to remain, to create spaces here or there—and that continually reconfigures their futures. Other factors come into play in the ongoing process of becoming a woman. For many, these include situations of unfathomable violence starting from childhood and continuing all the way to the moment when they take shelter somewhere along the Mexico-US border.

The process of becoming a woman takes place within structures of gender inequality, and even gender violence. These factors shape women's station within society. How do we define discrimination against women? At the UN Convention on the Elimination of All Forms of Discrimination against Women, "discrimination" was defined as "any distinction, exclusion, or restriction made on the basis of sex which has the effect or purpose of impairing or nullifying the recognition, enjoyment, or exercise by women . . . in the political, economic, social, cultural, civil or any other field."[1]

With that definition as a basis, we can go on to determine—in terms of context, culture, and history—the discrimination that women face. Another definition, this one from 1994, to take into consideration: violence against women is "any act or conduct, based on gender, which causes death or physical, sexual, or psychological harm or suffering to women, whether in the public or the private sphere."[2] Both definitions shed light on the situations within which migrant women become women.

Gender inequality must be considered to understand the *testimonios* below. The lack of access and opportunity that women experience versus that of men configures immigration patterns. Migration is not a voluntary choice but a consequence of social and economic contexts, which result in having to face various forms of violence in transit until deciding on a place to live. Even then, overlapping discrimination, inequality, and violence shape everyday life.

The state of inequality between men and women in Mexico becomes starkly clear when we look at the spheres of employment, nutrition, education, domestic violence, political power, family care, and acceptable recreational activities. Let's look at the wage gap, for example. In 2010 women made up 40 percent of the economically active population. However, they were paid 8 percent less than men for doing equal work.[3] In terms of access to nutrition, in 2012, 24 percent of families with a female head of household had nutritional deficits, compared to only 21 percent of those headed by men.[4] In access to education, especially higher education, only 27 percent of Mexican women ever make it to higher education, according to the Organization for Economic Co-operation and Development (OECD).[5] In terms of violence, according to the 2016 *Encuesta Nacional sobre la Dinámica de las Relaciones en los Hogares* (National Inquiry into Dynamics and Relationships at Home, ENDIREH), 66 percent of Mexican girls and women fifteen and older had experienced at least one incident of emotional, physical, sexual, or economic violence, or discrimination. This was a 3 percent increase over ENDIREH's results from 2011.[6] In terms of access to political power in popularly elected positions, only 2 percent of political parties' budgets are earmarked for generating political leadership by women. Even though legislative measures have been passed to promote access for and political participation by women, there are not yet any visible results in the form of an increased number of women holding political office in Mexico.[7] When it comes to home care, it is still women who perform this work, including the work of caring for children and for the family's elderly members.[8] Finally, there is the sphere of recreation, where, on average, women have thirty fewer minutes of free time than men. Women tend to spend that time watching television or interacting with friends and family members, while men tend to spend that time in public places, such as bars or sports arenas.[9] Together, these data paint a picture of an inequality that women are subjected to simply for being women, beginning in childhood and persisting until old age.

This framework allows us to analyze the narratives of migrant women that make up this chapter. First of all, they elucidate why women migrate north, and second, they allow us to understand the continual violence that accompanies them on their journey.

Migrant women live through countless violent episodes starting from childhood, within both their family and community. (The circumstances discussed so far take place in Mexico but are not different in many other countries.) It is precisely these realities, together with the background of social and economic inequality, that lead them to decide to begin a journey in search of work and better economic situations that will offer greater opportunities for their sons and daughters. However, they are also fleeing the myriad instances of physical, psychological, and sexual violence. This inequality is not exclusive to their place of origin, and it continues to follow them throughout their travels and at their destination. The fact that discrimination and violence materialize in new relationships established in a new place and time suggests that these problems have structural causes. Furthermore, once women are traveling and out of their usual element, their lack of safety becomes more acute, since they are vulnerable to extortion, kidnapping, sexual violence, and human and sex trafficking.

Institutionalized discrimination and personal history make up the context within which one becomes a woman. Through the narratives shared here we can glimpse the realities that migrant women live. They challenge political, social, and economic systems to act to guarantee women's right to a life free of violence in every sphere of life.

The *testimonios* presented below permit crucial social, economic, and political analysis, given their personalization of the consequences of discrimination, social and gender inequality, and violence against women's bodies. I invite you to read these not as the stories of just Rocío, Julieta, and other women who narrate their experiences as migrants but as stories that illustrate the reality of thousands of women who face violent acts, discrimination, and inequality on a daily basis just by virtue of being female. Moreover, they reflect the alternatives sought to improve conditions around them and restore and guarantee their rights. Reading the *testimonios* to better understand those realities pushes us to see our surroundings more critically and skeptically and encourages us to find new ways of focusing on rights, equality, and equity.

ROCÍO

Mi infancia fue muy dura. Viví pobreza extrema. Mis padres me golpeaban. Yo pensaba, ¿Por qué mis papás no me quieren? La vida no tenía sen-
tido para mí. Tres veces intenté suicidarme. Una vez me fui detrás de la
casa con un cuchillo, pero mi hermana llegó y no me dejó. Otra vez tomé
suavitel, cloro y pinol revueltos. Me hizo efecto. De pronto pensaron que
estaba borracha y no me hicieron caso. Después, vieron que estaba echando
espuma por la boca. Se dieron cuenta de lo que pasaba y me llevaron al
hospital. Esa vez duré inconsciente cuatro días.

A los nueve años fui violada por un hombre del pueblo. A los once años,
me fui a trabajar al DF. Cuando tenía quince años, estando allá, una vez
vi que alguien me iba siguiendo. Me alcanzó y con el brazo izquierdo me
agarró por el hombro y con el derecho, me amenazaba con un cuchillo al
cuello. Me llevaron a unos árboles, me rompieron los vestidos con el cuchillo y me violaron. Yo perdí la conciencia. Lo demás, no recuerdo. Pero me
dicen que fui a la casa de mi patrona, llegué estilando sangre y con una risa
muy rara. Había perdido la conciencia y estaba como loca. Me llevaron al
médico, luego al manicomio. Ahí estuve más de un año.

Desde primaria, tenía un amigo. Fue por él que me golpearon mucho
una vez, cuando me quise suicidar. A los diecisiete años me junté con él.
Cuando me junté, ya tenía un hijo de él. Tuve otros dos hijos. Vivíamos en
una casa que era de mi suegra y de nosotros. Ella iba cada mes a estar ahí. Mi
compañero se fue a los Estados Unidos. Poco después de un año, me dijo
que había otra mujer pero que a los hijos no les faltaría nada. No cumplió.

Mi hija se enfermó de un soplo en el corazón. Mi suegra me dijo que,
si salía de la casa, ya no volvería ahí. Y efectivamente, tuve que salir a llevar
a mi hija al doctor. Cuando regresé, mi suegra ya no me dejó entrar ni por
mis cosas. Algunas me las dio por la ventana. Me echó a la calle. Me fui con
mi mamá con mis tres hijos. Ella tenía una casita muy, muy pequeña, pobrí-
sima, construida de maguey y lodo.

Para sostener a mis hijos, decidí ir a los Estados Unidos y dejar a mis
hijos con mi mamá. Me fui con un hermano por Reynosa. Nos robaron.
Pasamos frío intenso. El coyote que traíamos nos entregó a un tipo que nos
llevó al hotel. Ya en la noche, él dijo que íbamos a ir de compras él y yo.
Los hombres que estaban no dijeron nada. Nos fuimos en un carro. Allá me
violó y me amenazó que, si le decía algo a mi hermano, nos mataba a los
dos. Al regresar, mi hermano notó que había llorado. Me preguntó si estaba
bien, pero nada pude decirle.

Había otro hombre, tatuado y que se drogaba. El coyote me llevó con
él y le dijo que si hacían el trato y que sería en lo convenido. El trato

era venderme. Él dijo: "Déjame ver qué tan buena está". Se acercó para tocarme. Yo empecé a gritar. Mi hermano y los otros hombres vinieron. También vino la mujer del tatuado. Ella entró y le dijo que se pusiera en paz. Si no hubiera sido por los hombres y la mujer, no sé lo que hubiera sido de mí.

Al llegar a Carolina del Sur, el pollero que me había sacado para llevarme y que me abandonó, me lo encontré allá. Fue mi desgracia porque mi mamá me había encargado con él. Se sentía dueño. Quería decidir por mí. No me permitía salir, quería dominarme. Y era quien me había causado tantos males. Él era quien me había querido vender.

Yo era muy seca. No salía de mi casa. Quise agarrar el vicio de tomar. A veces golpeaba a mis hijos. Pensaba suicidarme. No tenía ganas de reír.

ıııııııııııııı

My childhood was really rough. I lived in extreme poverty. My parents beat me. I thought, why don't my mom and dad love me? Life just made no sense to me. I tried to kill myself three times. One of the times I went behind the house with a knife, but my sister got there and stopped me. Another time I drank fabric softener, bleach, and disinfectant mixed together. It started to have an effect on me, and they immediately assumed I was drunk and ignored me. But after that, they saw I was foaming at the mouth. They figured out what was going on and took me to the hospital. So that time I stayed unconscious for four days.

At age nine someone raped me, a man who lived in the same town as me. At age eleven I went to Mexico City to work. One time when I was fifteen, living there, I noticed someone was following me. He caught up with me and with his left arm he grabbed me by the shoulder. And with his right he was threatening me with a knife, holding it to my neck. I was taken to some trees, had my clothes torn open with the knife, and was raped. I lost consciousness. I don't remember the rest. But I was told that I went to the house of the lady I worked for, dripping blood and laughing very strangely. I had lost consciousness, and I was like a crazy person. They took me to the doctor, then the insane asylum. I stayed there for more than a year.

There was a guy who had been my boyfriend since elementary school. It was because of him that I got beaten badly one time, one of the times I decided to kill myself. At seventeen I moved in with him. When I moved in with him, I already had one kid with him. Then I had two more kids. We were living in a house that belonged to his mom and to us. She came every month to spend time there. Then he went to the United States. A little more than a year later, he told me there was another woman, but as far as the kids went, he wouldn't neglect them. He didn't come through.

My daughter got sick, a heart murmur. My kids' grandmother told me, if you leave the house, you won't be coming back. And sure enough, I had to leave to take my daughter to the doctor. When I came back, she wouldn't let me come in even to get my stuff. She gave me *some* of it through the window. She had thrown me out on the street. I went with my three kids to stay with my mom. She had a house that was really, really small, a total poor person's house, made of agave and mud.

To keep my kids fed, I decided to go to the US and leave my kids with my mom. I went with my brother, through Reynosa. We got robbed. It was freezing cold. The *coyote* who came with us, he turned us over to a dude and he took us to the hotel. In the evening, he said we were going to go do some shopping, him and me. The men who were there didn't say anything. We left in a car. He raped me there and warned me that if I said anything to my brother, he would kill both of us. When we got back, my brother noticed I'd been crying. He asked me if I was okay, but I couldn't say a word to him.

There was another man, who had tattoos and was taking drugs. The *coyote* took me to see him and asked him if the deal was on. And he said if so, it would be on the agreed terms. The deal was to sell me. The man said, "Let's see how tasty she is." He came up close to me to touch me. I started yelling. My brother and the other men came. So did the wife of the man with the tattoos. She came in and told him to behave. If it hadn't been for those men and that woman, I don't know what would have happened with me.

When I got to South Carolina, I ran into the *coyote* there. The guy who had gotten me away from the others in order to take me away, the guy who also left me behind.[10] It was my bad luck, because my mom had put me in his care. He felt ownership. He wanted to make the decisions for me. He didn't let me go out; he wanted to dominate me. And he was the one who had caused me so much harm. It was him who had tried to sell me.

I was a really cold person for a while. I didn't leave the house. I chose to take up a drinking habit. Sometimes I beat my kids. I thought about killing myself. I never felt like laughing.

NOMBRE RESERVADO / NAME NOT PROVIDED

Voy a contar un poco de mi vida. Soy de Chiapas. Mi niñez fue muy triste. Éramos diez hermanos y yo la única mujer. Mi mamá fue muy estricta conmigo. A los seis años, aprendí a tortear a mano. Mi mamá me quemó las manos porque no podía hacerlo y así aprendí, pero mi mamá me pegaba mucho. Cuando mi papá llegaba del trabajo, me quejaba, pero él no me defendía. Él quería más a mis hermanos porque ellos eran hombres y yo era mujer. Mi papá tal vez no me quería. Esa niñez tan triste que tuve, no la quiero para mis hijos. No quiero hacer con ellos lo que hicieron conmigo. Y aunque mis papás hayan sido duros conmigo, aprendí a hacer muchas cosas, como a trabajar y ser responsable. Comencé a trabajar a los nueve años. Trabajaba e iba a la escuela. Pero me sentía muy sola. Porque yo dormía en la casa donde trabajaba y mi mamá solo llegaba cada mes para cobrar mi sueldo y no me dejaba nada para mí, para llevar a la escuela. La persona con la que trabajaba me regalaba ropa. Yo estaba agradecida, pero a la vez me sentía muy triste porque cuando cumplía años nadie se acordaba de mí. Nunca tuve un abrazo de cumpleaños.

Me casé a los quince años pensando que mi vida iba a cambiar. Con la persona que me junté, me iba muy mal. Me pegaba mucho, y aunque estuviera embarazada, a él no le importaba. Me golpeaba, me pateaba. Yo vivía atemorizada. Ya cuando lo oía llegar, me preparaba. Y después que me pegaba, me pedía perdón y yo lo perdonaba porque yo decía que lo quería. Él tenía el doble de mi edad.

Pasó el tiempo y él seguía pegándome. Nos venimos a Torreón a vivir en casa de su tía. Mi sufrimiento seguía cada vez más. Para que los hombres me vieran fea, con unas tijeras me trasquiló. Yo no me defendía por el miedo que le tenía, pero ese sufrimiento era tan grande que no se lo deseo a nadie.

Conocí a una señora y ella me vio golpeada, con un ojo morado. Esto sucedía con frecuencia. Me golpeaba, me pateaba. Me aconsejó que no debía dejarme golpear por nadie. Ese día yo escapé de la casa donde vivía y me fui a la casa de la señora que conocí, quien me brindó su casa y su amistad. Me dijo que iba a estar bien. El hombre con el que yo vivía, se enfureció y llamó a la policía, pero la mujer que me recibió en su casa me dijo: "Déjalo. Ya verá este hijo de su chingada madre cómo le va a ir". Me llevó a levantar demanda. Fueron testigos de cómo me golpeaba, y estaba la evidencia en mi cara de cómo me encontraba. Él me había amenazado de quitarme a mis hijos, pero en nada ganó. Me preguntaron que qué quería para él. Yo lo único que pedí, que no me volviera a molestar, que me dejara en paz.

Desde entonces mi vida cambió mucho. La mujer que conocí me admitió a quedarme en su casa. Me consiguió trabajo y esa pesadilla dejó de existir. Yo trabajaba mucho para sacar adelante a mis hijos. En mí nunca pensaba. Desde entonces soy padre y madre para ellos.

Pasaron cinco años y conocí al papá de mi hija, la más pequeña. Pero cuando lo conocí, tenía miedo que me pasara lo mismo que con el primer esposo. Me dio tiempo para conocerlo. Entre tanto, yo trabajaba para tener un patio. Ahí hice mi casa de tabla. Yo decía: "Pobre, pero es mi casa".

Yo le dije al papá de mi nena, que yo tenía dos hijos, que si me aceptaba así. Tenía miedo porque pensaba que tal vez podría hacerles daño. Pero yo le dije: "Si les haces algo, te mato". Él me dijo que jamás los iba a tocar. Yo siento que a mis hijos nadie los va a tocar, a humillar ni a pegar. Yo me esfuerzo por ellos, aunque siento que soy muy dura en el aspecto de la educación en la escuela, pero se han educado bien. No bajan de calificaciones. Yo siempre trabajaré para ellos, para sacarlos adelante. Y hasta que Dios me dé vida, yo estaré con ellos, porque son mi prioridad. Me gustaría ser mejor madre. Yo quisiera que ellos fueran unos profesionistas los tres, ya que yo no pude serlo. Mis padres son muy pobres y éramos diez hermanos.

Con mi pareja actual, a veces ya no aguanto la situación. Es muy celoso, me grita y tal vez ya no cambie. Me gustaría que me quisiera más, que no me cele ni me grite. A veces pienso en dejarlo. Lo aguanto porque quiere a mis hijos, los dos que no son de él. Y mientras él sea bueno con mis hijos, yo lo aguantaré. Le pido a Dios que me dé fuerzas.

A mis hijos les hablo y los animo. Aunque esté lejos, los llevo en mi mente y en mi corazón. Sé que ellos me extrañan como yo a ellos. A veces siento que no debí alejarme de ellos, pero mis hijos sacan buenas calificaciones y quiero que sean hombres de bien en la vida. También mi hija, que es muy linda y educada y tiene el primer lugar.

A veces me siento vieja y que nunca me he dado tiempo para mí. Siempre ha sido trabajar pensando en ellos. Pero tal vez en el futuro voy a tener demasiado tiempo.

En fin, ahora mi meta es trabajar para mis hijos y comprarle un terrenito a mi papá para que él haga lo que quiera, porque aunque siempre fuimos tan pobres, yo a mi papá lo quiero mucho, porque nos enseñó a respetar a los demás y creer en Dios.

|||||||||||||||||

I'll tell a bit of my life. I'm from Chiapas. My childhood was really sad. There were ten of us kids, and I was the only girl. My mom was really strict with me. At six years old, I learned to make tortillas by hand. My mom burned my hands once because I couldn't do it, and that's how I learned. But my mom hit me a lot. When my dad would get home from work, I would complain, but he didn't defend me. He loved my brothers more because they were boys and I was a girl. My dad may not have loved me. So this really sad childhood I had is not what I want for my kids. I don't want to raise them the way I was raised. But you know, even though my mom and dad have always been hard on me I learned how to do a lot of things, like how to work and be responsible. I started working at age nine. I worked and I went to school. But I felt really alone. Because I slept at the house where I worked, and my mom just came once a month to collect my wages, and she didn't leave me anything for myself to take to school. The person whose house

I was working at used to give me clothes. I was grateful, but at the same time I felt really sad because when it was my birthday, no one did anything for me. I never got a birthday hug.

I got married at fifteen, thinking my life was going to change. My relationship with this person went badly wrong. He hit me a lot. Even if I was pregnant, that didn't matter to him: he'd punch me, he'd kick me. I was always afraid. When I heard him coming home, I immediately braced myself. And after he'd hit me, he'd say sorry and I'd forgive him because I always said what he wanted to hear. He was twice my age.

Time passed and he continued to hit me. We came north to Torreón and lived at his aunt's house. My suffering continued and continued. So other men wouldn't find me attractive, he used some scissors to shear my head. I never defended myself, out of fear of him. But the suffering was so great I wouldn't wish it on anybody.

I met a lady and she saw how beaten up I was, with a black eye. This happened all the time. He'd punch me, he'd kick me. Her advice to me was that I shouldn't let myself be beaten up by anyone. That same day I escaped from the house where I was living and went to the house of the lady I'd met, who offered me her house and her friendship. She told me everything was going to be okay. The man I had been living with was furious and called the police, but the woman who took me into her home told me, "Let him. This damn son of a bitch'll see how well it goes." She took me to file a complaint. There were witnesses who knew how he beat me. And the evidence was on my face of what shape I was in. He had threatened to take my kids away from me, but he lost on everything. They asked me what I wanted to happen as far as he was concerned. Me, the only thing I asked for, was for him not to bother me again, to leave me in peace.

From then on, my life changed a lot. The woman I'd met gave me permission to stay at her house. She got me a job. The nightmare went away. I worked a lot to help my children get ahead. I never thought about myself. From then on, I've been both father and mother to them.

Five years went by and I met the person who's my daughter's dad, the littlest one. But when I met him I was afraid of the same thing happening as with my first husband. He gave me time to get to know him. In the meantime, I was working to own a plot of land. I built a wooden house on it. I would say, "Humble, yes. But it's my house."

I told him, my baby girl's dad, I have two sons. Did he accept me like that? I was scared for a while because I thought maybe he might hurt them. But I told him, "If you do anything to them, I'll kill you." He told me he would never touch them. The way I feel as far as my kids are concerned is that no one is going to touch them, humiliate them, or hit them. I do a lot for them, though I feel like I'm really hard on them in terms of their education in school. But they've gotten a good education. They keep their grades up. I'll always work for them, to help them get ahead. And so long as God gives me life, I'll be there for them, because they're my priority. I'd like to be a better mother. I would love it if they became professionals with degrees of some kind, all three of them, since I couldn't. My parents are really poor and there were ten of us kids.

With my current partner, sometimes I can't endure the way things get. He's really possessive. He yells at me, and maybe he can't change at this point. I'd like for him to love me more, not be possessive of me. And not yell at me. Sometimes I think about leaving him. I put up with him because he loves my sons, who aren't his, both of them. And as long as he's good to my sons, I'll put up with him. I pray to God to give me strength.

My kids, I talk to them and encourage them. Even if I'm far away, I keep them in my mind and in my heart. I know they miss me like I miss them. Sometimes I feel like I shouldn't have gone away from them, but my sons are getting good grades and I want them to be respectable men in life. My daughter, too, who's a lovely, educated person, second to nobody.

Sometimes I feel like I'm old and have never made time for myself. It's always been about working and thinking about them. But maybe in the future I'll have all too much time.

Anyway, for now my goal is to work for my kids and to buy my dad a little piece of land for him to do whatever he wants with. Because even though we were always so poor, I personally love my dad a lot because he taught us to respect others and to believe in God.

JULIETA

Soy Julieta Payán Urías, de cuarenta y cuatro años de edad, originaria del DF Fuimos cuatro de familia, pero la etapa que más recuerdo es la que conviví con mi hermano, en la infancia. Mi mamá nos pegaba mucho. Mis padres habían tenido un accidente a muy poco tiempo de que nací. Estando mi mamá en un mercado, un camión se quedó sin frenos y se llevó ese mercadito. Yo tenía siete días. Mi hermanita tenía tres años y falleció a consecuencia del accidente. Mi mamá estaba convaleciente. Además, se le hundió un vidrio en su pierna. Mi papá sufrió quemaduras de tercer grado y mi hermanita también, más una fractura de cráneo. A mí no me pasó casi nada. Mi mamá me cubrió con su cuerpo y sólo tenía moretones.

Durante el tratamiento, a mi mamá le inyectaban morfina para el dolor. No le habían dicho del fallecimiento de mi hermanita, que no murió instantáneamente sino después, en el hospital. A consecuencia de todo eso, mi madre quedó enferma de los nervios. No me quería. Decía que por qué no fui yo la que murió y no mi hermana. Siempre me decía que estaba fea, que estaba gorda. Nos pegaba mucho y muy fuerte. En una ocasión me abrió la sentadera con el cinturón. A mi hermano le aventó la piedra del molcajete y le abrió la cabeza. Mi papá se enteró de maltrato y nos llevaron a vivir con mi abuelita y a ella a una clínica para tratarle de sus nervios.

Con mi abuelita pasé la etapa bonita de mi niñez. Yo tenía como seis años y mi hermanito tenía cuatro. Después volvimos con mi mamá y ella seguía con su mal genio. Yo esperaba los fines de semana para irme con mi abuelita, ya que estar con mi mamá no era agradable.

A los doce años, yo iba a la primaria. Desde ahí fui acosada por el papá de mis hijos, me daba mucho miedo. Siempre me vigilaba y andaba tras de mí. Así fue hasta que cumplí dieciséis años. A los dieciséis abusó de mí. Salí embarazada de mi hijo. Me amenazó si decía algo a mi papá. El hombre que me violó trabajaba para la judicial, y me amenazó con que algo le podía pasar a mi papá, o a mis hermanas más chicas, si yo lo denunciaba. Mi papá no me dijo nada, creyó que el embarazo había sido voluntario. Cuando me alivié de mi hijo, empecé a vivir con él. Él era casado y tenía dos niñas con su esposa. Cuando supo que su hijo que yo esperaba era niño, me obligó a vivir con él. Yo le tenía miedo, por eso accedí. Ya viviendo con él, yo me acababa de aliviar de mi hijo —nació con cesárea— todavía con los puntos él volvió a abusar de mí, y volví a quedar embarazada. Ese embarazo fue muy difícil, me controlaron mucho por lo reciente de la cesárea.

Yo era muy achacosa y él me pegaba. De la primera violación, creo que quedé con un trauma: en las relaciones íntimas, dejaba de respirar. A veces hasta me desmayaba. Él me humillaba, me decía cosas, que era mujer fría, pero yo no sentía nada. No me gustaba la relación, porque lo único que sentía era miedo. Una vez, tenía ocho meses de embarazo cuando tuve relaciones. Me desmayé y él me golpeó, tuve una hemorragia interna, me llevó a casa de mis papás y dijo: vas a decir que caíste de las escaleras. Me llevaron al hospital y el doctor dijo que no era caída, que era resultado de golpes. Yo nunca dije la verdad, tenía miedo. El hospital y el doctor, convencidos de que se trataba de golpes, hicieron la denuncia.

Lo detuvo la policía, pero él salió a otro día y me amenazó. Me dijo que porque me había atrevido. Ahora sí él haría algo que me doliera. Mandó golpear a mi hermano. Él creyó que lo habían matado. Lo golpearon y lo fueron a tirar a un drenaje, pero mi hermano no estaba muerto, sólo desmayado. Nosotras ya no supimos más de mi hermano. Ahora sabemos que se fue a Veracruz, anduvo vagando escondido. Hoy sabemos que está vivo, pero él continúa escondido. Con ese hecho, yo me le escapé y me fui a vivir a Playa del Carmen.

Después de que me fui, no sé cómo me encontró y me dijo que si yo quería saber dónde estaba mi hermano, que regresara con él. Con esa esperanza volví y él volvió a ser igual. Él jugaba con mi mente diciendo: "Yo te voy a decir". Vivía prisionera de él; no podía salir a ningún lado. Después salí embarazada de mi hijo más chico. Un día me pegó y me sacó desnuda para fuera. Empecé a escuchar cómo le estaba pegando también a mi hijo, él tenía seis años. Lo que hice, como él estaba bien borracho, esperé que se durmiera y me abrió la puerta mi niño. Sólo agarré el bote de leche, me vestí y me fui con mi papá. Le dije que me iba a ir, no le dije a dónde. Le dije que le iba a dejar a mi hijo y sólo iba a llevar a César.

Conocía a un compañero que era coyote. Le llamé y con mil dólares—fue en el 1998— con eso me vine a Tijuana. Ya en Tijuana, le llamé a mi amigo, que no tardó en llegar. El día que llegó, pasamos sin problema a los Estados Unidos. Entramos por "El Bordo" y él cargaba al niño. No pagué nada. La mamá del coyote era mi vecina. Sabía lo que yo sufría y por medio de ella me ayudó. Llegué con su familia. Ahí nos quedamos a vivir. Mi marido fue y les quitó a mi hijo a mis padres. De Estados Unidos organicé cómo robarle al niño a través de mi cuñado, quien fue y se lo quitó. Fue como una novela. Se lo robaron y me lo trajeron. En cuanto llegaron, yo le llamé a la mamá de él y le dije que yo tenía a mis hijos. Para él fue una humillación, una burla. El más chico quería regresar a vivir con su papá. Pero un día mi hijo, el mayor, le contó todo y cambió.

En el 2001, mi marido secuestró a mi mamá. Pidió veinte mil dólares de rescate. Salí a Tijuana a dejárselos pero nunca apareció mi mamá, hasta la fecha. Niega haber sido él, pero seguimos creyendo que fue él. Y pregunta si ya supimos de ella. Hace como dos años dijo que si quería saber de ella, que depositara diez mil dólares. Yo aconsejé a mi papá que no los diera, por la experiencia anterior.

A mí me detuvieron el primero de noviembre de 2014. Me pidieron papeles y me deportaron. Ya tenía diecisiete años viviendo allá. Me detuvieron cuatro meses en la cárcel. Estaba peleando mi caso para asilo, por violencia intrafamiliar, pero me lo negaron por las dos deportaciones que tenía. Ahora estoy aquí en el albergue. Me gustaría poder tener asilo en Estados Unidos. Ya me lo negaron. Tengo mucho miedo de regresar a México, DF. ¿Qué hacer?

⎮⎮⎮⎮⎮⎮⎮⎮⎮⎮⎮⎮⎮⎮

My name is Julieta Payán Urías. I'm forty-four years old, from Mexico City originally. We were a family of four, but the period I remember best is when it was me and my brother, when we were children. See, my mom used to hit us a lot. My parents had been in an accident right after I was born. My mom was at a market, and there was a bus whose brakes failed and it ran right over that little market. I was only seven days old. My baby sister was three and she passed away as a result of the accident. My mom was in recovery at the time. A piece of glass got lodged in her leg on top of that. My dad had third-degree burns and so did my baby sister, plus a skull fracture. I was almost untouched. My mom covered me with her body and I only had bruises.

During her treatment, they gave my mom morphine injections for the pain. They hadn't told her my baby sister had passed away. She didn't die immediately. She died afterward at the hospital. So as a result of all that, my mom became unwell psychologically. She didn't love me. She'd say why wasn't it me that died instead of my sister. All the time she'd say I was ugly, I was fat. She hit us a lot really hard. One time, she broke the skin on my rear end when she was hitting me with the belt. She threw the molcajete pestle at my brother and split his head open.[11] My dad found out about the abuse, and he took us to live with my grandma and took my mom to a clinic for psychological treatment.

With my grandma I had the happiest period of my childhood. I was about six and my baby brother was four. After that, we were back with my mom and she still had her bad temper. I would look forward to the weekends, when I could go to my grandma's house, since being with my mom wasn't, let's say, pleasant.

At twelve years old, I was going to the elementary school. Coming home, someone stalked me: my children's dad.[12] It scared me a lot. All the time he would be watching me and coming up behind me. That's how it was until I turned sixteen. At sixteen he molested me. I ended up pregnant with my son. He warned me not to say anything to my dad. The man who raped me worked for the ministerial police, and he warned me that something might happen to my dad or my younger sisters if I reported him.[13] My dad, he didn't say anything to me. He assumed I'd gotten pregnant voluntarily.

When I gave birth to my son, I started living with this man. He was married and had had two girls with his wife.[14] It was when he learned that the child of his that I had been expecting was a boy that he made me live with him. I was scared of him, that's why I agreed. So now, living with him, I had just given birth to my son—he was born by C-section, I still had the stitches—he molests me again, and I get pregnant again. That pregnancy was really difficult. They monitored me a lot because of how recent the C-section was.

I was really sickly and he kept hitting me. From the first rape, I think I was traumatized: during intercourse, I would stop breathing. Sometimes

I even passed out. He'd humiliate me, say things to me, like that I was a "cold" woman.[15] But I didn't feel anything. I didn't like being with him, because all I felt was fear. Once I had intercourse with him when I was eight months pregnant. I fainted and he beat me. I had an internal hemorrhage. He took me to my mom and dad's house and said, "You're going to say you fell down the stairs." They took me to the hospital and the doctor said it wasn't a fall; it was from being hit. I never told the truth—I was scared. It was the hospital and the doctor that came to the conclusion that I'd been hit and put in the complaint.

The police arrested him, but he was out in a day, and he threatened me. He said since I'd disrespected him, now he really was going to do something that would be painful to me. He had my brother beaten up. He actually thought they had killed him. They beat him up and then they went and threw him in a ditch. But my brother wasn't dead; he was just passed out. My sisters and me didn't hear from my brother again after that. Now we know he went to Veracruz, traveled around, in hiding. We know he's alive, but he's still in hiding. Well, after he'd done that to my brother, I got away from him and went to live in Playa del Carmen.

After I left, he found me somehow and told me to come back to him if I wanted to know where my brother was. I went back because of that hope, and he went back to being the same as always. He would play with my mind by saying, "I'm going to tell you." I was his prisoner; I couldn't leave or go anywhere. After that, I wound up pregnant with my youngest son. One day, he hit me and took me outside the house naked and left me there. I started hearing him hitting my oldest son too. He was six. What I did was, he was really drunk, so I waited for him to fall asleep and then my little boy opened the door for me. All I did was grab the milk, get dressed, and go to my dad's house. I told him I was going to leave; I didn't tell him where. I told him I was leaving my oldest son with him and just taking César.[16]

I knew someone, a friend, who was a *coyote*. I called him, and I took a thousand dollars with me—this was in 1998—took that with me and came north to Tijuana. In Tijuana I called my friend, who didn't take long to get there. The day he got there, we went over to the US with no trouble. We went in through "El Bordo," him carrying my little boy.[17] I didn't pay a thing. His mom used to be my neighbor. She knew what I was going through, so through her, he helped me. I went to his family's house; that's where we stayed for a while. My husband went and took my oldest son away from my parents. From the US, I came up with a plan to steal his little boy from him through my brother-in-law. He went and took him away from him. It was like a soap opera. They stole my son from his father and brought him to me. As soon as they arrived, I called his mom and told her I had my kids. He'd been humiliated, tricked. The younger one used to want to go back and live with his dad. But one day, my older son told him everything, and that changed.

In 2001, my husband kidnapped my mom, asked for two thousand dollars' ransom. I came south to Tijuana and left it for him, but my mom never reappeared, right up till today. He denies that it was him, but I still believe it was him. And he asks if we ever got word of her. About two years ago he said if we wanted word of her, to deposit ten thousand. My advice to my dad was not to pay it, given the previous experience.

I was detained on the first of November 2014. They asked for my papers and they deported me. I had been living there for seventeen years. They held me for four months in jail. I was fighting my case and asking for asylum, based on domestic violence, but they denied me based on the two deportations I had. Now I'm here in the shelter. I'd like to be able to get asylum in the US. They already denied me. I'm really afraid of going back to Mexico City. What should I do?

5

Separated from Family

Introduced by María Engracia Robles Robles, ME

After being in the United States for fifteen years, a father came to the Kino Border Initiative in Nogales, Sonora, Mexico in July 2017, with this heartrending experience:

> I was held in jail [in the United States] for a month and a half. At the end of April, while I was detained, my wife gave birth to my little girl that she was pregnant with. By then I was gone. On May fourth, [my wife] died. They are still looking into the causes. She may have gotten a virus at the hospital. I asked to be by her side during her last moments, and to be with my children, but I was denied. And here I am now, deported. I have seven children, all of them young, and the state took them. I can't even describe what I'm feeling.

Sadly, feelings of absence, confusion, and helplessness are paradigmatic for the thousands of people who are separated from their families through detention and deportation. Someone who is deported has to deal not only with being expelled from the United States, but also with losing friends, employment, possessions, house, and home. For many, however, the most painful blow is the separation from family. Family members share living spaces, feelings, care, things, and life's little rituals; that is, they weave together the most intimate dimensions of their daily lives. Humans construct families in different ways around the world, based on biological ties or other happenstance that brings people's lives together. Although its structure and members may vary, a family, at its core, is the most intimate grouping that human beings create.

Someone who goes through this separation feels deep rejection and existential crisis. For someone who is away from loved ones—who often happen to be US citizens—trying to find their way in Mexico is an extremely bewildering process. Paradoxically, the expulsion from the United States, disconcerting on its own, separates individuals from family, the very people who would be most able to offer love and support to get through such difficult moments.

The terrible consequences of separation go beyond loneliness and isolation; they also impinge on the legal realm. When a parent or guardian is deported, they can lose legal guardianship in just a few months by not responding to summonses to appear before judicial authorities. In those situations, contact between parents and children is impeded by the difficulty of tracking down family members who are detained or deported and by the lack of coordination between state-level child protective service agencies, who are in charge of minors during legal proceedings, and the US Department of Homeland Security (DHS). Adults' loss of essential legal rights triggers, for the minors, a stint in foster care or adoption, the latter resulting in lifelong legal annulment of the family.

But those are not the only unfortunate consequences. In a perverse twist, forced separation, already painful, can cause more suffering by providing urgent motivation for someone to try to return covertly in order to be reunited with their family. Some people are ready to do anything and to take any risk. They cannot be at peace and cannot stop fighting until they attain their goal. A mother I know made over fourteen attempts. In the end her tenacity was rewarded and she was able to rejoin her children in the United States, but countless people do not attain the reunification they seek.

Those who remain in the United States also suffer frustration and hopelessness after losing the anchors of their lives. If they are children, they need their parents' affection and protection all the more. Having parents torn away is as cruel a fate as that of a sapling stunted in its first years of growth. The laws that protect children acknowledge this: "The child, for full and harmonious development of his or her personality, should grow up in a family environment, in an atmosphere of happiness, love, and understanding."[1]

The special protection that children need is recognized not only in social and moral norms but also in legal agreements, such as the Convention on the Rights of the Child, which was written and signed by the United Nations and came into effect in 1990. It states that "the child, by reason of his physical and mental immaturity, needs special safeguards and care, including appropriate legal protection, before as well as after birth . . . against all forms of discrimination."[2] Critically, the US government has yet to become a signatory to or ratify the agreement.

It is clear that children are the ones who deal with the darkest consequences of their parents being deported. They feel insecurity, resentment, and trauma as they find themselves cut off and without parental support, isolated from family, going down a path that leads to a difficult future. These minors will grow up suffering the trauma of separation and orphanhood, sheltered, if they're fortunate, in a relative's home.

The apparently obvious solution of simply bringing one's children along in order to avoid separation is not a silver bullet either. Some parents do that, but taking children out of the place where they have grown up and where they were born, in many cases, means risking them losing their rights as citizens, feeling lost, or facing a series of crises and frustrations, which could have long-lasting negative impacts on their lives. A child has a right to grow up in the country in which he or she was born.

Our family nurtures our life and gives us the strength to work, strive, suffer, and make sacrifices. In Mexican and Latin American societies, we believe deeply that our family is key to enjoying and fully living life. Our family is the engine that pushes us to strike out and make progress. A forcible separation from our family can destroy the meaning of life and stamp out the very reasons for being alive. It can be a source of frustration and hopelessness and exacerbate mental illness. "I have suicidal thoughts, I feel depressed, desolate, anguished, hopeless," confessed a man who was deported and separated from his children in October 2017. A deported man named Orlando Lozano said that same month, "Anguish, anxiety. [It's a] pain that doesn't hurt but throbs in your heart from having to be away from the people you love the most." It could be said that these people survive but drag a dead weight of emptiness, nostalgia, sadness, loneliness, and deep loss, not to mention resentment toward the legal system.

How important is family unity in order to have a full life? Pope Francis considers it vital. He describes it as an essential component, together with faith in God, to "keep on taking risks for the good of the family, dreaming and building a life that has this sense of home, of family."[3]

ALBA

Soy Alba, originaria de Guerrero. Emigré a los Estados Unidos a la edad de veinte años porque quería trabajar, ya que en mi pueblo las únicas posibilidades son ser secretaria en la presidencia o bibliotecaria, trabajos que sólo con palancas se consiguen. Podría trabajar en algo muy común en el pueblo, que es ayudar a barrer o lavar trastes. Pero me pagarían, en aquel entonces, veinte pesos al día. Hoy pagan cincuenta pesos.

Cuando emigré, el primer intento no fue fácil. Lo hice por Agua Prieta, Sonora. En ese tiempo, sacaban a los migrantes de inmediato cuando nos agarraban. Me sacaron en la noche, pero había los llamados cholos, quienes nos asaltaron, nos esculcaron todo y nos quitaron lo que llevábamos. Esa noche me quería regresar, pero iba con una amiga más fuerte que yo y me animó a hacer otro intento. Salimos. Caminamos toda una noche y llegamos. Nos mandaron a Phoenix y de ahí a Utah. Allá viví por once años. Me casé, tuve tres hijas que son las que tengo ahora, de ocho, diez y trece años. Mi matrimonio, en un principio, fue todo bien. Después, hubo problemas. Pero, en general, podemos decir que fue un matrimonio normal.

Mi mamá sufre presión alta, tiene colesterol y sólo le funciona un pulmón. Cuando le sube la presión, es tan elevada que ella puede quedar inconsciente. Ante esa situación, una vez que se puso muy mal mi mamá, le dijo a mi hermana que aunque pasara algo, ella quería que nos quedáramos en Estados Unidos, que no viniéramos a verla. Eso me dolió mucho y fue cuando decidí venir. En el 2011, me vine con mis tres hijas, porque ellas, además de que mi mamá estaba enferma, querían conocer a su abuelita. Estuve de agosto hasta abril con mi mamá, nueve meses. Decidí regresar a los Estados Unidos. Salimos mis hijas y yo juntas de Guerrero, pero ellas agarraron avión para Utah y yo para Hermosillo. Como ciudadanas, se podían ir sin problema.

Yo venía con un coyote conocido. Hice el intento por Agua Prieta. Me agarraron. Lo volví a intentar y lo logré, pero anduve perdida toda la noche. Me lastimé un pie, estuve tres noches sola porque no me recogían. Después estuve una semana con una familia. Me recogieron los que me iban a llevar a Utah, pero dijeron que tenían más personas en un departamento, me movieron a ese lugar. No nos recogieron. Pasó el día, seguían entrando personas, los vecinos posiblemente nos delataron. El caso es que llegó la policía, llamó a Migración y nos deportaron. Todo mi logro estaba perdido.

Hace más de un año, estuve aquí en Nogales en este albergue, intentando volver a cruzar. Una señora me iba a pasar por la línea. Le di adelantados veinte mil pesos que me pidió. Agarró el dinero y luego se escapó. Para esas fechas yo llevaba gastados como treinta y cinco mil pesos, más o menos. Yo, antes de venir a México, tenía mis ahorros. Trabajaba en un restaurante. Hasta ese momento me moví con mi dinero, pero ya se me había terminado. Me fui a trabajar al DF ya que mi esposo, como sabía que yo tenía mis ahorros, nunca me mandó, sólo para los boletos de las niñas. Trabajé un año en el DF en una casa, con una familia judía. Eran buenas personas. Me pagaban siete mil quinientos pesos al mes y ahí comía y vivía.

La familia tenía dos niños. Yo era la cocinera pero había otra chica que cuidaba a los niños. En el 2013, decidí volver a intentar.

En ese tiempo, alguien le mandó chismes a mi esposo y él tuvo un cambio conmigo. No entiende la situación que vivo. Como él no sabe lo difícil que está ahora para entrar, me culpa, porque dice que si no me voy, es porque no quiero. Se ha movido de casa para que no lo encuentre. Ya se movió como a cinco casas diferentes, no me quiere contactar con mis hijas y ellas mismas se muestran, especialmente la mayor, resentidas conmigo. No me quieren hablar, me responden sólo con un "sí", un "no". Eso me angustia y con más ímpetus deseo llegar.

Entré de nuevo por Agua Prieta. Me agarraron en cuanto crucé la barda, todavía colgada con la cuerda del muro, pero ya no me dieron tiempo de regresar a México. Hice el esfuerzo pero no pude. Me amenazó la Patrulla Fronteriza con cortarme la cuerda. De ahí me llevaron a la corte y me castigaron con setenta y cinco días de cárcel. Como Florence es cárcel normal, me trasladaron a Eloy —cárcel de migración— y ahí estuve trece meses encarcelada. Pedí asilo y por eso me alargaron el tiempo.

Estoy regresando aquí a México a los dieciséis meses. Yo quería una oportunidad, que me dieran una fianza. Cuando estaba en la apelación del asilo, me deportaron. En resumen, no me oyeron. Me esposaron y dijeron: "Vas para afuera".

Después de tanto luchar por regresar, sin conseguirlo, ya no persigo vivir en Estados Unidos, sino recuperar a mis hijas, traérmelas. La verdad, no entiendo el cambio de mi marido. Necesito un abogado para quitárselas. Pero [*pausa*] dinero, ¿de dónde? No tengo recursos para pagarlo. Necesito ir, para desde allá, poder hacer este trámite.

En momentos me siento desolada, sin ver posibles salidas, sin esperanza. Hice una solicitud para nueva apelación. No he recibido la respuesta. Si esta falla, no sé lo que voy a hacer.

|||||||||||||||||

I'm Alba. I'm from Guerrero originally. I emigrated to the US at age twenty because I wanted to work, and in my town the only opportunities were to be either a secretary in the town hall or a librarian—jobs you have to have connections to get. I *might* have been able to do a type of work that's not at all common in small towns, which is helping sweep and wash dishes, but they would pay me, back then, a dollar twenty a day.[4] Now they pay three.[5]

When I emigrated, the first attempt wasn't easy. I did it through Agua Prieta, Sonora. During that time, migrants were getting taken back out immediately, as soon as we were caught. I got taken out at night, but there were some of those "thugs," and they held us up, frisked us completely, and took away what we had.[6] That night I wanted to go home. But I was with a friend who was stronger than me and she encouraged me to make another attempt. We headed out. We walked an entire night and got there. They sent us to Phoenix and from there to Utah. And that's where I lived for eleven years. I got married, had three girls, which is all the children I have right now. They're eight, ten, and thirteen years old. As far as my marriage goes, initially it went great, later there were problems, but overall let's say it was a normal marriage.

My mom suffers from high blood pressure, she has cholesterol, and only one of her lungs works. When her blood pressure goes up, it gets so high that she can end up passing out. And knowing that, my mom told my sister, once she got really sick, that even if something happened, she wanted us to stay in the US, not to come and see her. That was really painful and it was when I decided to come. I arrived in 2011, with my three girls with me, because aside from my mom being ill, they wanted to meet their grandma. I was there from August to April with my mom, nine months. I decided to go back to the US. We left Guerrero together, my girls and me, but they caught a plane to Utah and I took one to Hermosillo. Being citizens, they could go with no trouble.

I came with a *coyote* people knew. I made an attempt at Agua Prieta. I got caught. I tried again and made it, but I was lost all night, injured my foot. I was alone for three nights because it took them that long to pick me up. After that I was with a family for a week. I got picked up by the people who were going to take me to Utah, but they said they had more people in an apartment, so they moved me there. They didn't pick us up, the day dragged on, more people kept coming in . . . it's possible that the neighbors turned us in; in any case, the police showed up, called Immigration, and we got deported. So everything I'd gained was lost.

More than a year ago, I was here in Nogales, in this shelter, trying to get across again. A lady was going to get me through the port of entry. She asked for twelve hundred dollars in advance, which I gave her.[7] She grabbed the money and then took off. By this point, I had spent about twenty-one hundred dollars, more or less.[8] Before coming to Mexico I'd had my savings from working in a restaurant, and until this moment I'd traveled on my own dime, but now I'd run out of money. So I went to Mexico City to work, since my husband knew I had my savings and so never sent me anything except for the girls' tickets. I worked in Mexico City for a year, doing housework for a Jewish family. They were nice. They paid me 450 a month and I ate there and lived there.[9] There were two children in the family. I was the cook but there was another girl who took care of the children. In 2013, I decided to try again.

During that time, someone sent some gossip to my husband and there was a change in him toward me. He doesn't understand my current situation. He doesn't know how hard it is right now to get in, so he blames me: he says if I don't leave it's because I don't want to leave. He's moved house so I can't find him. He's moved about five times by now. He doesn't like to let me talk to my daughters, and they themselves act resentful toward me, especially the oldest. They don't like to talk to me. I say something to them and they just say, "yeah," "no." It really upsets me and it makes my desire to get there even more fierce.

I entered again through Agua Prieta. They caught me as soon as I got over the fence, when I was still hanging from the wall by the rope, but they didn't give me any time to go back to Mexico. I made the effort, but I couldn't. They threatened to cut the rope, the Border Patrol did. From there I was taken to court and given a punishment of seventy-five days in jail. Florence is a normal jail, so after the seventy-five days they transferred me to Eloy—an immigration jail—and I was imprisoned for another thirteen months there. I asked for asylum, and that's why they lengthened my time.[10]

Now I'm returning here, returning to Mexico, sixteen months later. I wanted a chance, wanted them to give me a bond.[11] They deported me while I was doing my asylum appeal. Basically, they ignored me. I was handcuffed and told, "You're out of here."

After this whole struggle to go back, and not achieving it, I'm not going to pursue living in the US anymore, I'm going to pursue getting my daughters back, bringing them here. Honestly, I don't understand the change in my husband. I need a lawyer to take them away from him. But, with what money? I don't have assets to pay for a lawyer. I need to go there to be able to do this process from there.

There are times when I feel dismal, hopeless, unable to see a way out. I applied for a new appeal. I haven't received the answer. If this one fails, I don't know what I'll do next.

ESTRELLA

Soy Estrella. Tengo treinta y cuatro años de edad. Emigré a los Estados Unidos en marzo de 2001. Nos fuimos mi esposo y yo porque nos casamos y vimos que no teníamos posibilidad de construir un hogar debido a la pobreza, ya que el salario en Chiapas es de sesenta y nueve pesos diarios. Eso es ahora, antes era menos. Esto en la actualidad equivale más o menos a cuatro dólares por día.

En Estados Unidos tuve tres hijos, los que ahora tengo: una niña de catorce años, un niño de doce y la más pequeña de ocho años. Dejé a mis padres al migrar y nunca los había vuelto a ver. Yo estaba pendiente de ellos, porque tampoco tienen de que vivir, pero yo no podía venir. Hace cuatro meses, en septiembre, sin saber lo difícil que es ahora entrar, y ya teniendo quince años sin verlos, mi papá me llamó un día y me dijo que viniera. Que él estaba perdiendo la vista y quería verme. El tiene ochenta años. Me vine y me traje a los niños, porque se oye de la dificultad para pasar, y por si no pudiera regresar fue que me los traje.

Estando en México, los niños empezaron a enfermarse: se llenaron de ronchas, se enfermaron del estómago, su cuerpo se llenó de granos, especialmente la niña pequeña. En Chiapas hay demasiados zancudos y desde que llegamos, tenía granos, se desangraba y lloraba. Decía que se quería ir a su casa. Ella sentía que estaba fuera de ella. Después, los metí a la escuela. No sabían bien el español y diario iban llorando. La chiquita no entendía el español escrito. Iba a dejarles su comida y ella me pedía que me quedara a comer con ella, porque no había mesas para comer como en Estados Unidos. La niña menor era la que más sufría. Además, en las escuelas de Chiapas, no hay aire acondicionado ni ventiladores y el clima es caliente. Yo sé que era difícil para ellos, se acostumbraron a las comodidades y yo, ahora, no podía darles eso. Además, por eso de la Reforma Educativa, hay muchos problemas en las escuelas. Días y hasta semanas que no hay clase y todas esas semanas los niños están en la casa, sin avanzar en la educación. La escuela en donde estaba mi hija ya en secundaria, como el maestro no sabía bien el inglés, él pedía a ella ayudarlo. Los papás se enojaron y dijeron que, si ella seguía ayudando al maestro, iban a ir a sacarla de la escuela.

Por todo esto, yo sufro mucho. Es mi país, pero mis hijos no estaban acostumbrados a él. Además, mis papás están sin medicina y yo no puedo ayudarlos. Por eso decidí mandar a mis hijos y yo intentar irme tras ellos. Dije a mi esposo que me iba a regresar y mandé a mis hijos por delante. Un primo vino y se los llevó. Nosotros vivimos en Carolina del Norte. Mi marido tiene buen trabajo. Siempre hemos pagado impuestos, no pedimos ayuda al gobierno, es el seguro para ellos. Yo limpio casas.

Ahora que hice el intento de entrar, me fue mal. Tengo miedo de hacer otro intento. Me dieron cinco años en que no podré entrar legal y no sé qué voy a hacer. No quisiera entrar, porque si me agarran, ya me dijeron que me van a dar veinte años. Tal vez la gente piense que es muy fácil volver a traerme a mis hijos, pero yo, que ya estuve aquí viviendo la dificultad con ellos, sé que no es fácil.

Yo pediría a las autoridades y al Señor Presidente [Obama] hacer lo que se pueda para evitar estas tragedias, que están costando tanto dolor, tantas lágrimas, tantos males a las familias. Me gustaría que se pusieran en nuestro lugar y escucharan su corazón de padres. No pierdo la esperanza en que haya un cambio a nuestro favor.

Que Dios nos bendiga a todos.

IIIIIIIIIIIIIIII

My name is Estrella. I'm thirty-four years old. I emigrated to the United States in March of 2001. It was me and my husband who went, because we got married and saw that we had no chance of building a home, because of poverty, the wage in Chiapas being sixty-nine pesos a day. That's now; before, it was less. It's equivalent to about four dollars a day currently.

In the US I had three kids, all the kids I've had so far: a fourteen-year-old girl, a twelve-year-old boy, and the littlest, an eight-year-old girl. I left my parents when I migrated, and after that I didn't see them. I did look out for them, because they don't have anything to live on, any more than we did there, but I couldn't come and see them. Then four months ago, in September—not knowing how hard it is to get in now, and having gone without seeing them for fifteen years—my dad called me one day and told me to come. He was losing his sight and wanted to see me. He was eighty. I came back, and I brought my children with me. Because you hear about the challenges of getting through, right, so in case I couldn't go back, I brought them with me, that's why.

Once we were in Mexico, my children started to get sick: they were covered in rashes, they had stomach illnesses, their skin was covered in bites, especially my little girl. In Chiapas, there are way too many mosquitoes, and from the minute we got there she had bites on her. She'd bleed a lot and she'd cry. She'd say she wanted to go home. She felt like she was away from home. After that, I put them in school. They didn't know Spanish very well, and every day they'd go to school crying. The little one didn't understand written Spanish. I would go and take them their lunch and she would ask me to stay and eat with her, because they didn't have tables to eat at like in the US.[12] The youngest was the one who suffered the most. Also, the schools in Chiapas don't have air conditioning or even fans, and the weather is hot. I know it was hard for them—they had gotten used to having all the amenities and now I couldn't give them that. Also, because of the Education Reform thing, there are a lot of problems in the schools: days or even weeks with no classes, and all that time the children are at home not making any progress in their education.[13] My daughter was in junior high, and at the school where she was, the teacher didn't know English well, so he would ask her to help him. The parents got angry and said if she kept helping the teacher, they were going to take her out of the school.

All of this is really painful for me. It's my country; but my kids weren't used to it. Also, my mom and dad didn't have health care and I couldn't help them. That's why I decided to send my kids and try to get there after them. I told my husband I was coming back and sent the kids ahead. A cousin came and took them. We live in North Carolina. My husband has a good job, we've always paid our taxes, we don't ask the government for help. My income is our insurance for my parents.[14] I clean houses.

Just now when I made the attempt to enter, it went badly. I'm afraid to try again. They gave me a five-year bar on entering legally, and I don't know what I'll do next. I wouldn't like to enter now, because if they catch me, they already told me they'll give me a twenty-year bar. I don't know, maybe people think it's really easy. I can just bring my kids to Mexico with me again. But I was already there once and faced the challenges with them, and I know it's not easy.

I would just ask the authorities and the president [Obama] to do whatever can be done to prevent these tragedies, which are causing families so much pain, so many tears, so much harm. I'd like them to put themselves in our place and listen to their own hearts as parents. I haven't lost hope that there will be a change in our favor.

God bless us all.

MARISOL

Soy Marisol, originaria de Puebla. Provengo de una familia pobre. Desde los diez o doce años tuve que ir a las casas a lavar trastes, barrer, ayudar en algo para apoyar a mis papás. A veces sólo recibía comida a cambio. Otras veces le daban a mi mamá un dinerito, poco. Fuimos a la escuela. Terminé la secundaria. A los diecisiete años, me desesperé de no poder tener suficiente para ayudar a mis padres y estudiar y me quise ir a los Estados Unidos. Fue difícil la entrada. Sufrí mucho. Fueron tres intentos los que hice y en uno de esos nos asaltaron y robaron todo el dinero.

En Estados Unidos trabajé. En el primer año conocí al que hoy es mi esposo, que es de Puebla. A los dieciocho años me junté con él. Yo no quería tener un bebé luego, pero él sí quería. Tuvimos una niña, la primera. A los seis meses de edad la tuvieron que operar. Se creía que era un tumor canceroso. Costó treinta mil dólares, pero como era nacida allá, el estado cubrió los gastos. Todo salió bien. En el 2006 nos casamos al civil. En el 2007 nació mi segunda niña. Nació por cesárea, de cuatro kilos. También el estado pagó. Ellos defienden a los ciudadanos. Lo hacen por ellos, no por nosotras, indocumentadas. Todo pasó bien. Como mi plan era tener niño y niña, no me quedé conforme y quise tener otro bebé. Fue niño. Él nació en el 2010. Ahora tiene cuatro años.

Mi mamá siempre decía: "Hija, ¿por qué no vienes a México a verme?". Yo le explicaba del miedo para regresar y no poder cruzar la frontera.

Me dieron la licencia para manejar, sin Seguro Social. Después las personas ya no pudieron renovar su licencia, porque la ciudad exigía tener el Seguro Social. En un poblado pequeño —ya cuando tenía mis tres hijos, mi niña se iba sola a la escuela— a mis niños los tenía que llevar al preescolar, de ahí me iba a trabajar.

Me habían parado sin licencia y me dieron un *warning*. No debía manejar. En la siguiente vez que me pararon, el policía vio que era mexicana. [Mi hija mayor iba conmigo]. Rebasé el límite de velocidad porque llevaba prisa. El policía me detuvo y me pidió papeles. Me preguntó si mi hija era mexicana o americana. Yo le dije que era nacida allá. Dijo él: "Que se baje aquí y a usted me la voy a llevar arrestada". Mi hija se asustó y empezó a llorar. Yo le dije: "Háblale a tu papá. Dile que me detuvieron y me llevan a la cárcel". Me esposaron. El policía llamó a Migración. Al llegar a la cárcel ya me estaban esperando. Me interrogó en tono amenazante: "¿Por dónde cruzaste? ¿Cuándo cruzaste?" Checaron mis huellas. Vieron que ya tenía tres echadas fuera. Además, ya no debería haber manejado por el *warning*.

De la cárcel ya no salí. No pude llevar nada de mi casa. Ni ropa, ni siquiera decirles adiós a mis hijos. En un día desaparecí para todos. Yo no quise que mis hijos me vieran encarcelada, como criminal, sin entender las cosas. Además, no los podría tocar. Mi esposo pagó seiscientos dólares para que saliera, pero no pude hacer nada. Me fueron trasladando de cárcel en cárcel, esposada de pies, manos y cintura como criminal, en la misma situación que un narcotraficante o suicida. Me tuvieron tres semanas. Me echaron a México por Tamaulipas a las diez de la noche. Me sentí muy mal. Solo traía mi anillo, mi celular, una medallita. Ni ropa ni dinero. En Tamaulipas llegué a un refugio para migrantes donde me ayudaron. Me dieron ropa. Estuve unos días. Me iban a ayudar con el pasaje hasta Puebla, pero no tenía CURP. Tuve que llamarle a mi esposo para que me depositara dinero.

Con las manos vacías llegué a Puebla. Me esperaban. Me alegró mucho volver a ver a mi mamá después de diecisiete años. Estuve un mes con ella. Creyendo que iba a ser fácil volver a entrar, me vine el 8 de noviembre, porque el 15 es cumpleaños de mi esposo y el 13 de diciembre cumpleaños de mi hija. Esperaba esos días ya estar allá. Desde entonces ando aquí rodando como hoja arrastrada por el viento. Mis hijos, los pequeños, piensan que vine a Puebla a visitar a su abuelita, pero ya me piden que regrese. ¿Y cómo explicarles?

Llevo tres intentos: dos por Naco y uno por aquí por Nogales. En el segundo intento me dieron un mes de cárcel. Por la vía legal no puedo hacer nada. Para ellos soy criminal.

Mi esposo allá tiene buen trabajo. Ya tiene como diecinueve años en él. Hace cinco años murió su mamá y no quiso venir. La mamá había dicho que no vinieran, que ayudaran al papá porque se iba a necesitar, pero que no vinieran.

Ahora yo estoy aquí. Después de diecisiete años, sin trabajo, sin familia, sola, muy triste sin saber qué toca hacer. Nunca planeamos nada. No tenemos casa en México. ¿Qué hacer? ¿Otro intento? ¿Hacer que se venga mi esposo con mis hijos a México?

Esta vez llevo gastados más o menos veinte mil pesos. Voy a hacer el último intento. Un agente me dijo: "¿Y a usted por qué la deportan? Tiene hijos aquí". Y él decía que no estaba de acuerdo, que era una injusticia, pero él tenía que cumplir la ley.

En la confusión de búsqueda de lo que toca hacer, son muchas las dudas. Quisiera que alguien me dijera qué es lo mejor. Es grande la incertidumbre y muchas preguntas cruzan por mi mente: ¿Dónde estarán mejor mis hijos, allá o acá? ¿Cuál es el bien para ellos? Si me los traigo, van a perder todos sus derechos. ¿Me lo echarán en cara en un futuro? Si mis hijos no se vienen, él estará muy ocupado con el trabajo y mis hijos. Yo sola, pensando en ellos, ¿no me iré a deprimir? ¿O será mejor dejar a mi hija, la mayor, allá y traerme a los dos más pequeños? Mi esposo tiene allá un buen trabajo. ¿Podrá encontrarlo en México? Y con los bajos salarios que aquí pagan, ¿para qué nos alcanzaría? Si me traigo a mis hijos y él trabaja allá, ¿podrá sostener dos casas? Nunca prevenimos esta situación y en México no tenemos nada. Él, ¿se conservará fiel a mí si yo no vivo con él? ¿Buscará otra mujer?

||||||||||||||

I'm Marisol, from Puebla originally. I come from a poor family. From the age of ten or twelve on, I had to go to people's houses and wash dishes, sweep, help out. It was to support my mom and dad. Sometimes I only received food in exchange. Other times they gave my mom a little money, not much. We went to school. I finished junior high. At seventeen, I got fed up with not being able to come up with enough to help my parents and study, and I chose to leave for the United States. It was hard getting in. I suffered a lot. It took three attempts, and on one of them, they held us up and stole all our money.

In the US, I worked. The first year, I met the person who is now my husband. He's from Puebla. At age eighteen I moved in with him. I didn't want to have a baby right then, but he did. We had a girl, our first child. When she was six months old she had to have an operation. They thought it was a malignant tumor. It cost thirty thousand dollars, but since she was born there, the government covered the expenses. It all turned out fine. In 2006 we got married officially. In 2007 my second baby girl was born. I had a C-section. She was nine pounds. Again, the government paid for it. Their thing is protecting citizens. They do it for them, not for us undocumented mothers. Everything went fine. But my plan had been to have a boy and a girl, so I wasn't satisfied yet and chose to have another baby. It was a boy. He was born in 2010. Now he's four.

My mom was always saying, "Honey, why haven't you come to see me in Mexico?" I kept explaining to her that I was scared of going back and not being able to get across the border.

I got a driver's license, without having a Social Security number. After that, people couldn't renew their license anymore because the city started requiring you to have a Social Security number. After I had all three kids, living in a small community like we did, my oldest daughter would get to school on her own, but my babies I had to take to preschool. From there, I'd go to work.

I had gotten pulled over once without a license and given a warning.[15] I wasn't supposed to drive. The next time I got pulled over, the officer saw I was Mexican. [My oldest daughter was with me.] I'd gone over the speed limit because I was in a hurry. The officer detained me and asked for my papers. He asked me if my daughter was Mexican or American. I told him she was born there. So he says, "Have her get out here, and you I'm arresting and taking with me, ma'am." My daughter got scared and started crying. I told her, "Call your dad. Tell him they detained me and they're taking me to jail." I was handcuffed. The officer called Immigration. When we got to the jailhouse, they were already waiting for me. The agent questioned me in a threatening way. "Where did you cross? When did you cross?"[16] They checked my fingerprints. They saw I had been thrown out three times. Besides that, I shouldn't have been driving because of the warning.

From that point on I never left jail. I couldn't go get anything from my house, not clothes, not—not even say *goodbye* to my kids. In one day I disappeared from their lives. I couldn't let them see me imprisoned, like a criminal, when they didn't understand how things are. I also wouldn't be able to touch them. My husband paid six hundred dollars for me to get out, but I wasn't able to do anything. They kept transferring me from jail to jail, shackled hand, foot, and waist like a criminal, treated the same as a drug trafficker or a suicide risk. They kept me for three weeks. They threw me out of the country through Tamaulipas at ten o'clock at night. I felt awful. The only things of mine I had were my wedding ring, my cell phone, and a little necklace, but no clothes and no money. In Tamaulipas I got to a migrant shelter where I got help. They gave me clothes there. I was there for a few days. I was going to get help with bus fare to Puebla, but I didn't have a CURP.[17] I had to call my husband and have him deposit money for me.

I got to Puebla—empty-handed. They were waiting for me. It made me really happy to see my mom again after seventeen years. I spent a month with her. Thinking it was going to be easy to get back in, I came to the border on November the 8th, because the 15th is my husband's birthday and December 13th is my daughter's birthday. I was hoping to be there by those dates. I've been here ever since, going back and forth like a leaf yanked by the wind. My kids, the little ones, they think I came to Puebla to visit their grandma, but now they're asking me to come back. How do I explain it to them?

I've made three attempts so far, one through Naco and one through here, Nogales. On the second one they gave me a month in jail. By the legal route, I can't do anything. As far as they're concerned I'm a criminal.

My husband, he has a good job there; he's been there nineteen years. Five years ago his mom died and he decided not to come. She had told him and his brothers and his sisters not to come; to help their dad, because it was going to be needed, but not to come.

Right now, here I am here. Seventeen years later, no job, no family, alone, really sad because I don't know what the right thing to do is. We never made any plans. We don't have a house in Mexico. What should I do? Try again? Have my husband and my children come to Mexico?

This time I've spent about twelve hundred dollars so far. I'm going to make my last try. An agent told me, "Why are they deporting *you*? Don't you have kids here?" And he kept saying he didn't agree with it, it was an injustice, but he had to do what the law said.

In this whole confusing search for the right thing to do, there are so many questions. I'd like someone to tell me what's best. There's so much uncertainty, and a lot of different things go through my mind: Where will my kids be better off, there or here? What's in their best interest? If I bring them here, they're going to lose all their rights. Will they throw that back in my face sometime in the future? If my kids don't come to me, then my husband's going to be really busy with work and the kids. What about me, alone, thinking about them, won't I get depressed? Or will it turn out best if I leave my daughter, the oldest, there and bring the two littler ones here? My husband has a good job there. Would he be able to find one in Mexico?

And with the low wages they pay here, what would we able to afford? If I bring my kids here and he works there, will he be able to support two households? We never foresaw this situation, and in Mexico we have nothing. What about him, will he stay faithful to me if I'm not living with him? Will he look for another woman?

6

Clandestine Border Crossings

Introduced by David Hill

With any international or long-distance travel, you make your arrangements, as far as possible, for arriving at your destination before you leave home. You focus on your destination. Only secondarily do you think about the legs of the journey and the means of travel for each.

Crossing borders is always significant, and in any journey that involves crossing into the United States, that crossing is certainly a significant part. Along the Mexico-US border, there are fifty official crossing points, "ports of entry," clustered in twenty-nine cross-border urban and semiurban areas— border cities and towns, fed by major roadways. Between and beyond, the 1,954-mile border consists of huge stretches of sparsely inhabited land, low deserts, and confounding mountains, not to mention the Rio Grande.

For documented US citizens, who have virtually unconditional freedom to cross back and forth using the ports of entry, passage is safe, convenient, and relatively dignified. For northbound Mexicans and Central Americans, on the other hand, even a tourist visa (which is far more accessible than an immigrant visa; forget about an immigrant visa) is out of reach without a fairly high degree of economic and social standing. To get a tourist visa, one must prove to the US immigration authorities that one's life is comfortable enough that one has no reason to emigrate and thus only wishes to cross temporarily, for pleasure.[1] For a relatively privileged minority, this is the case.

What about a poor person? If a poor person has a purpose for traveling to the United States, it is likely to be more compelling than just pleasure. It might be to escape poverty and violence, to provide for one's family, to be with the family one has in the United States, or a combination of the three. To such a person, to precisely such a person, legitimate travel through the official ports of entry is refused, with extremely narrow exceptions.

For such would-be international travelers, there is a different itinerary. Denied the simple opportunity to buy a bus ticket or a plane ticket to their destination, they turn to other forms of passage. They do what poor people always do when unable to access the legitimate market in a service or a good: they turn to the illegitimate market. Hence the phenomenon of underground travel, more commonly known as people smuggling.

Imagine you are such a person. Your odyssey will consist of much, much more than the brief act of stepping over the international boundary (the part that is punishable by law). How will you make your way northward to the border? How will you cross into US territory? And once there, how will you get where you are going? All with a minimum of exposure to extortion, sexual assault, impacts on your physical health, being held against your will, being implicated in illegal activity (beyond the illegal crossing itself), detention by the authorities, financial losses, and lost time?

The poorest reach the border region by riding freight trains. Others come by bus. On the Sonora-Arizona border, where the *testimonios* in this book were collected, common destinations where you might start a border crossing are Altar, Caborca, Sásabe, Sonoyta, Nogales, and Agua Prieta—towns you have probably never been to before and don't know anyone in. You might have left your home in Mexico or Central America already in the company of a travel guide you hired to get you all the way to your destination: the full package. Once you reach the border region, your guide uses their connections in the local smuggling networks to arrange your passage. Or you might travel to the border on your own and look for a good guide once you get here. Either way, they will tell you when, where, and how you will cross the border. Just like with legitimate travel, routes are highly defined and your movements as a traveler are highly controlled. You will pay a variety of fees, including travel expenses, *cuotas* (tolls) charged by drug cartels for use of their territory, and the guide's fee for your actual crossing—all but the last in advance; thousands of dollars in total. You will likely end up in debt.

A couple of notes about terminology are in order. The people-smuggling organizations and the drug-smuggling organizations, though they have certain links, are distinct; the words "mafia," "narco," and "cartel" always refer to drug-smuggling organizations. Drug smuggling is far more profitable than people smuggling. It's the mafia that owns and regulates cross-border territory, which is so valuable and so crucial to its business that it kills people simply for using it without its permission. It's the mafia that has, to borrow a term from the US Border Patrol (USBP), "operational control" over the territory. This is why your guide needs to pay a *cuota* to the mafia for your passage. In terms of the abuses people suffer, some are at the hands of the mafia and some are at the hands of guides.

As for the word "migrant": not everyone who participates in underground border crossing should really be called a migrant. Some of the people who cross the border are not migrating to the United States but instead are carrying a backpack of contraband, usually marijuana. Getting that backpack across the border is a job they are doing for the mafia, and when it's done they will cross back. On the Arizona-Sonora border, backpack carriers tend to be recruited from the adjacent Mexican states of Sinaloa, Durango, and Sonora itself. Like the migrants, they are poor people, trying to provide for their families. One sometimes hears migrants express a certain envy of backpack carriers; they see that they are better equipped, have experience and support, and have more success in evading Immigration (USBP) and getting where they're going—in short, that they get a better deal. Some backpackers were previously migrants, people whose original intention was to migrate; many people who are migrating also agree (or are forced) to carry a backpack of contraband, just the one time, because they can't afford the crossing fee. Many guides, too, start out as migrants. So these identities can overlap. A neutral term that encompasses migrants, backpack carriers, and guides is "border crossers."

Now to get across the international boundary itself. Just as black-market goods always try to emulate the legitimate article, underground travel has traditionally cleaved as close as possible to the ports of entry in the cross-border urban areas where legitimate crossings occur. The most legitimate-like crossing is, of course, through the port of entry itself, on foot or by bus. In years past, when border security was much more casual, this could be as simple as waiting for the lone customs agent to fall asleep. Today, it involves overtly posing as a legitimate traveler: either by pretending to be someone else using their ID or by carrying a fake visa together with your ID.

If that is not your guide's plan, then you may find yourself either (1) climbing the border wall in one of the cross-border urban areas or (2) hiking for days across open terrain well away from these areas.

In the 1990s, intensifying border security targeted the cross-border urban areas.[2] The years that ensued saw mass hiring of USBP agents, buildup of fences, installation of cameras, use of unmanned drones, and powerful stadium lighting in urban areas.[3] In 1993, USBP's El Paso Sector implemented *patrol saturation*—lining up dozens of agents just north of the border in the urban core of El Paso—and called it Operation Hold the Line. The San Diego Sector followed suit with Operation Gatekeeper in 1994 and the Tucson Sector with Operation Safeguard later that year.

One consequence of this quasi-militarization of the border has been a massive increase in death and suffering.[4] In 1994, a ten-foot fence made of surplus military gear was erected along the international boundary in Nogales, and it had an immediate effect: an epidemic of broken bones and other injuries from falls.[5] Seventeen years later, this barrier was replaced with a thirty-foot wall, more sheer in design, which increased the rate of injuries beyond what had come to be the normal rate.[6] Despite the risk, many people continue to cross by jumping the wall—and continue to be injured or even killed in the process—rather than face a long trek across the open desert, which is the main alternative.[7]

The trend of pushing cross-border traffic into the wilderness had a dramatic effect on the Arizona stretch of the border: it is much less populated overall than the California and Texas sections, where the initial buildup was concentrated, and so this desert became a major crossing area.[8] People hike across it in groups, led by a guide, and walk for days to reach a pickup point, past the USBP checkpoints on every highway. The Sonoran Desert, which covers most of the Sonora-Arizona border region, is now a vast graveyard. Every year about 150 bodies of border crossers are processed by the Pima County medical examiner, but many, many more lie forever unstumbled upon, lost in this expanse, dispersed and consumed. There is fierce heat during the long summer (as high as 119 degrees) and deep temperature plunges at night due to the low humidity that turn deceptively mild winter days into freezing nights (the temperature drop can be as much as 40 degrees). It is impossible to take enough water with you to last the journey. Water sources are sparse, and they are all contaminated, often by cattle dung laden with *E. coli*. Those who drink from them develop stomach illness and diarrhea, ending up more dehydrated than before. It is also easy to get turned around and lost in the Sonoran Desert, particularly in its more hilly and mountainous regions, where the trails get more winding and landmarks are harder to keep in sight. These are the remotest parts of the desert, and they are ever more trafficked, because the same dynamic that began in the 1990s continues: first the urban areas were closed off, pushing traffic out into the wilderness, and now the easier, more direct wilderness routes are being closed off, in favor of ever more remote and treacherous routes.

There is no single experience of clandestine crossing. Every *testimonio* is different. A recurring theme, however, is *abandono*: perhaps no one attempts to cross the border, successfully or unsuccessfully, without having to leave something or someone behind or being left behind themselves.[9] As a counterpoint, some of the most striking parts of these accounts are the little acts of kindness, even of solidarity, on the part of other border crossers and of border residents toward someone who has been left behind.

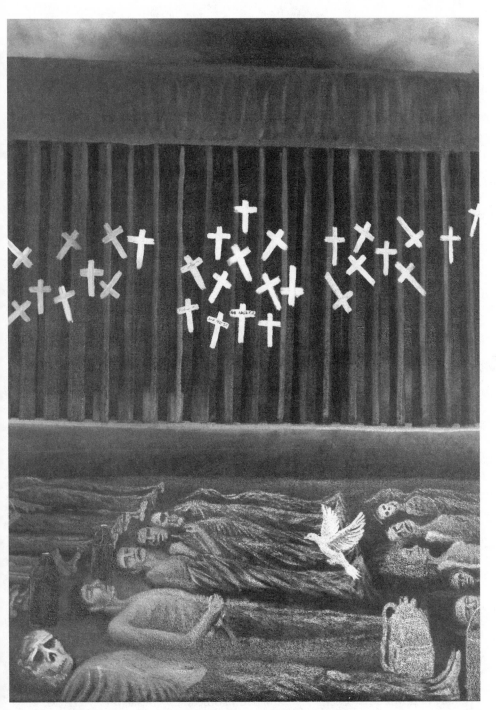

Graveyard in the desert. José Luis Cabrera Sotero.

A migrant is overcome with heat and exhaustion. José Luis Cabrera Sotero.

NAYELI LIZETTE

Soy Nayeli Lizette Frías Reynoso, de Toluca, Estado de México. Queríamos ir a los Estados Unidos. Hablamos con Isaías para que nos recomendara a alguien que nos pasara. Él nos brindó su ayuda y contactó a la Sra. Josefina, "La Chepa". Ella es de pelo castaño, ondulado, corto a los hombros, gordita, alta. Siempre trae un bolso en el brazo izquierdo color azul con rayas blancas. Llegamos y ella nos recibió en la terminal Estrella Blanca. Fue por nosotros. Me dijo cómo era y las características de cómo iba vestida. Me dijo: "Me sigues".

Lo primero que hizo fue meternos a la tienda Ley. Entramos y dijo: "Deja la maleta en el guardaequipaje". Luego dijo: "Voy a salir yo, tú vas por tu maleta y luego me sigues". Fuimos a un Oxxo y ella ahí se quedó y nos mandó a pagar una habitación en el Hotel Sta. Cecilia. Está al lado del Oxxo. De la central, como a dos o tres cuadras está el Oxxo. Ella dijo: "Pagan una habitación y allí voy yo". Entramos y al momento, llegó ella. Ya habíamos hecho un trato con ella, que le íbamos a dar quinientos dólares cada uno. Cuando ella llegó, dijo que no, que eran dos mil dólares cada uno, es decir, cuatro mil dólares. En eso, quiso hablar personalmente con los familiares para convencerlos. Llegaron al acuerdo de que pagarían tres mil dólares por los dos. Ella dijo que se los depositaran a Verónica Marta Ramos Zayas. A ella se le depositaron mil dólares. Y otra era Águeda Esmeralda, otros mil. Primero quinientos y otros quinientos. Y le entregamos en efectivo veintiún mil pesos.

Al hotel llegamos el domingo como a las ocho o nueve de la mañana y estuvimos hasta el martes a las ocho de la noche que nos sacó de allí. Ella llegó y nos dijo: "Va a venir una Suburban negra por ustedes. Yo ya me voy. Voy a andar por aquí cerca". Ella dijo: "Bueno, nos vemos. Cuídense".

Llegó la Suburban negra al Oxxo. Nos subimos a la camioneta, donde iban cinco hombres, chavos como de unos 25, 27, 22 años. Iban armados. Nos subimos. Íbamos con toda la certeza de que ellos nos iban a cruzar. Nos pidieron todo: identificaciones, celular, prendas. Nos llevaron a una casa, no conocemos dónde, caminamos unos cinco minutos, a lo más. La casa era con un portón y luego gradas para abajo. Había muchos cuartos. Nos metieron a un cuarto. Había unos veinte hombres, todos drogándose, fumando mariguana. Hablaban de mochilas con droga. Unos lavando camionetas, limpiando sus fusiles, hablando de negocios y no sé qué. Nos meten a un cuarto. Había unos siete hombres y nos dicen: "Métanse aquí, no tengan miedo. Somos buenas personas, nosotros los vamos a cruzar". Luego mi esposa entró en shock de nervios, lloraba. Ante eso, uno de ellos dijo: "OK. Ella está mal, los llevo a un hotel". Nos llevaron al Hotel Campo Santo, como a uno o dos minutos, en la misma Suburban negra. Allá mucha gente tatuada, hombres tomando, mujeres prostitutas. Le dijo a una: "Mami, me los cuidas". Le dicen Perla y nos echaron llave por fuera.

Antes de irse, nos dijo que nos comunicáramos con nuestra familia, para pedir tres mil dólares más por cada uno. Ya ahí nos dijo que La Chepa nunca nos iba a pasar, que no trabaja ni con la mafia. Ahí empezamos a hablar a la familia lo que estaba ocurriendo. Nos habían entregado todo, absolutamente todo. La familia dijo que no confiaban, que buscáramos como escaparnos. Al siguiente día, le hablamos a uno que dijo que se llamaba Riki. A esa Chepa le dice mamá y dijeron que ellos la conocían desde que estaba chiquita. Que ella no les daba dinero, que sólo los utilizaba. Ellos declararon que eran de la mafia.

Al siguiente día, le llamamos y le dijimos que no teníamos a nadie que nos ayudara y que no teníamos dinero. Él dijo: "Aguanten, a ver si llego, para que hablemos bien de eso". Llegó con dos chavos más. Dijo: "A ver, ¿cómo está la cosa?" Le dijimos: "No, pues no tenemos dinero y nuestra familia no nos quiere ayudar. Están molestos con nosotros". Él dijo: "¿Qué piensan ustedes hacer?" Y le dijimos: "Queremos regresar a nuestro pueblo. Ya no queremos saber nada de ella". Él dijo: "Se van a ir o les pago un taxi". Nos subió en un taxi y él pagó al taxista. Y nos llevaron a la central de Estrella Blanca.

Estando ahí, llegaron dos hombres diciéndonos que venían de parte de La Chepa. Como a las dos horas, llegaron otros dos con el mismo tema. Nosotros les decíamos que no la conocíamos, que estábamos esperando. La tercera vez, como a las nueve, llegó un chavo como de diecisiete años. Hablaron con el guardia y de ver esto, el taxista se nos acercó y habló conmigo y me dice: "Oye, ustedes no pueden estar aquí. Corren mucho riesgo. Si tú confías en mí, yo te llevo a un albergue para que pasen ahí la noche". Yo le dije que no podía confiar en él, porque no lo conozco y que estamos espantados. Él me dijo que confiara en él, que él me llevaba y que no me iba a cobrar. Y me dio su número de teléfono. Nos llevó al albergue como a las once de la noche. Eso fue antenoche. El día de ayer no salimos del albergue, tuvimos mucho miedo. Ahí nos quedamos. El chamaco, Riki, insistía en que quería saber qué le habíamos dicho a La Chepa. Le dijimos que no tuviera miedo, que no los íbamos a denunciar. "Está bien, confío en ustedes". Todo esto fue lo que nos pasó.

||||||||||||||||

I'm Nayeli Lizette Frías Reynoso, from Toluca, in the State of Mexico. We wanted to go to the United States.[10] We talked to Isaías to get him to recommend someone who would get us through. He offered to help us and contacted Señora Josefina, "La Chepa."[11] She's brunette, kind of wavy hair down to the shoulder, chubby, tall. She always carries a purse on her left arm, blue with white stripes. We arrived and she met us at the Estrella Blanca terminal. She came to pick us up. She told me what she looked like and how she was dressed.[12] She told me, "You follow me."

The first thing she did was take us in the Ley store.[13] We went in and she said, "Leave your suitcase at the baggage check." Then she said, "I'm going out first. You go get your suitcase and then you follow me." We went to an Oxxo, and she stayed there and sent us out to rent a room at the Hotel Santa Cecilia. It's next door to the Oxxo.[14] About two or three blocks from the bus station, that's where this is. She said, "You guys'll rent a room and I'll come there." We went in, and she got there right away. We had already made a deal with her before. We were going to pay her five hundred each. When she got there, she said, no, it was two thousand each. So, four thousand dollars. At that point she decided to talk to our family members directly, to convince them. They came to an agreement that they'd pay three thousand dollars for both of us. She said for them to send it in the name of Verónica Marta Ramos Zayas. They sent a thousand dollars to her, and another name was Águeda Esmeralda, another thousand. First five hundred and then another five hundred. And we gave her twenty-one thousand pesos in cash.[15]

We had gotten to the hotel on Sunday at around eight or nine in the morning and we were there until Tuesday at eight o'clock at night—that's when she took us out of there. She got there and told us, "There's a black Suburban that's going to come for you. I'm off. I'll be around, not far from here." She said, "Okay, see you later. Take care of yourselves."

The black Suburban arrived at the Oxxo. We got in and there were five men in there, kids, maybe 25, 27, 22 years old. They had guns. We got in. We were very clear that it was them who was going to take us across. They asked us to give them everything: IDs, cell phone, clothing. They took us to a house, we don't know where; it took us about five minutes at most to get there. The house had a gate and then stairs that went down and down. There were a lot of rooms. They put us in one of them. There were about twenty men in the house, all taking drugs, smoking marijuana. They were talking about backpacks with drugs in them. Some were washing trucks, some cleaning their rifles, some talking business, who knows what. So they put us in a room. There were seven men there, and they told us, "Get on in here, don't be scared, we're nice people, it's us who's going to take you across." Then my husband went into a state of shock. He was crying. When that happened, one of them said, "Okay. The lady's not well. I'll take them to a hotel." They took us to the Hotel Campo Santo, about one or two minutes away, in the same black Suburban. A lot of people there with tattoos, men drinking, women working as prostitutes. He said to one of the women, "Honey, you take care of them for me." They call her Perla. Our door was locked from the outside.

Before leaving, he told us to call our family and ask for three thousand dollars more each. And then he told us that La Chepa was never going to get us through, that she doesn't work with the mafia even. Then we started calling our family, telling them what was happening. They had already sent us everything, absolutely everything. They said they were feeling distrustful now and told us to look for a way to escape. The following day, we spoke to someone who said his name was Ricky. He referred to La Chepa as "sweetie," and he and his friends said they had known her since she was a little girl. They said she never gave them money; she just used them. They announced that they were from the mafia.

The following day, we called him and told him we didn't have anyone who could help us and we didn't have money. He said, "Hold on, let's see if I can get over there so we can talk about this right." He arrived with two other kids. He said, "Let's see, where are we at?" We told him, "Well I mean we don't have money and our family doesn't want to help us. They're upset with us." He said, "What are you guys thinking of doing?" And we told him, "We want to go home. We want nothing more to do with her." He said, "Go ahead and go. Or I'll hire you a taxi." He put us in a taxi and he paid the driver. And we were taken to the Estrella Blanca station.

While we were there, two men arrived and came up to us saying they were there representing La Chepa. About two hours later, two others came with the same message. We just kept saying we didn't know her, we were waiting for a bus. The third time, about nine o'clock, it was a kid who came, seventeen years old or so. He and his friends went over and talked to the security guard. And as soon as he saw that, the taxi driver came up and said something to me: he said, "Listen, you two can't stay here. You're in a lot of danger. If you trust me, I'll take you to a shelter where you can spend the night." I told him I couldn't trust him because I didn't know him and we were freaked out. He told me to trust him; he'd take me and wouldn't charge me. And he gave me his phone number. He took us to the shelter at about eleven at night. That was the night before last. Yesterday we didn't leave the shelter, we were too scared. We stayed there. That kid Ricky kept insisting he wanted to know what we'd said to La Chepa. We told him not to be scared; we weren't going to report them. "That's fine, I trust you guys." This is what happened to us, all of this.

NOMBRE RESERVADO / NAME NOT PROVIDED

Nos tiramos un día en la mañana por el desierto de Sonora. Íbamos más de seis personas. Nos acompañaba un muchacho, que es el que conocía el camino. Sólo dos llegaron de los seis que íbamos. Pero en muy mal estado. Me acaban de decir que parece que dos están muertos, y dos en muy mal estado. A otro, no lo encuentran.

Nos cargamos cada uno con cinco garrafones de agua y una mochila con comida. A veces, en el camino, llegábamos a donde el ganado bebe agua. En algunas de esas represas no podíamos llegar porque había mucha Migra. Teníamos que irnos a los cerros para sacarle la vuelta a la Migra y lo que teníamos que avanzar en un día, se convertía en dos días. El consumo de agua se aumentaba. Caminábamos toda la noche, hasta las once de la mañana o doce del mediodía. Dormíamos unas horas, si es que podíamos dormir por el calor. Y de las tres o cuatro en adelante y toda la noche seguíamos caminando. Teníamos que dormir en las horas de más calor, por lo que a veces no podíamos ni dormir. Llegábamos a las represas, tomábamos agua rápido, avanzábamos y dormíamos unas dos, tres horas lejos de la represa. Estaban muy retiradas unas de otras y por lo caliente del sol, la arena del desierto, en algunas llegábamos y ya no había agua. Teníamos que seguir así sin el agua. Yo caminé como ocho días. Luego, al bajar por un cerro —yo llevaba la comida de otro compañero que ya iba muy mal— al pisar una piedra se me rodó y me lastimé el tobillo. Y no pude decir nada porque el guía ya iba molesto. Y venía lastimando al compañero porque ya iba muy cansado y no quería dejarlo.

Nunca se dicen los nombres de los que vamos. Nos llaman "el Nayarit", "el Sinaloa", "el Sonora". Se les llama por su estado, no por el nombre. Nunca usamos nombres. De ese modo, no hay más afecto. Así, sin conocer el nombre, cuando uno se cansa y hay que dejarlo, no sientes pena, no hay afecto, porque no conoces su historia. Y si alguien muere, no hay más dolor que dejar a uno de quien nada sabemos. Los únicos que sí se conocían bien eran los de Oaxaca. Dos de ellos, uno que está muerto y el otro muchacho que no lo encuentran porque no lo quiso dejar.

Ya en la cuesta abajo, me empezó a lastimar el pie. Yo fui el primero que me quedé. Después de que me lastimé, caminamos toda la mañana. Pero a otro día, caminé unas tres horas y ya no pude. Me quedé en una arboleda porque ya no pude. Me dejaron agua y me dejaron poquita comida. No sé qué lugar era. Pero sé que llegué a una reserva. Pero no sé qué parte es. Yo caminé como trece días en total. Después que me quedé, yo me subí a un cerrito. Ahí pasó un muchacho de México y me regaló un galón de agua. Con eso, cuando el sol cayó, yo me subí a un cerrito y vi unas luces de un pueblo. El que nos llevaba nos dijo que por ahí cerca había una reserva.

Yo había hecho un par de muletas de postes de madera seca. Hice una fogata y con el mismo fuego las corté a la medida que las ocupaba. Y con la ropa que yo llevaba le puse para que no me lastimara la axila. Caminé media noche, pero no avanzaba mucho. Caminé como pude. Invoqué a mi

Migrants trek in open desert near the border fence. Wenceslao Hernández Hernández.

(*Opposite page*) View of the Pajaritos Mountains. East of Nogales, looking east. Avery Ellfeldt.

Dios, aunque nunca he sido muy creyente en Dios, pero le pedí y a otro día empecé a caminar. No sé cómo, pero empecé a caminar despacito.

Caminé, caminé más y más. Ya para cuando el sol cayó, ya había caminado como ocho horas. Con molestia, pero caminaba. Las luces ya no las miraba, pero me ubiqué y me eché a caminar en esa dirección. Caminar y caminar. Se miraban cerca las luces, pero caminaba y no me rendía, no llegaba. Me mojaba la cara y caminaba. Llevaba como medio litro de agua. La poquita agua, nada más me remojaba los labios. Me quedaba como medio litro. Pero la cuidé para no morirme de sed.

Por fin llegué. Crucé la carretera y entré al pueblito. No había gente. Pero llegué como a una escuela en construcción. No había agua. Busqué alguna llave, pero no encontraba. Encontré una que es donde reventó la tierra en el jardín y ahí abría la llave y la cerraba. Ahí dormí. No quería entregarme a la Migra. Quería llegar a Phoenix. Tomé mucha agua y me mojé la cara. Había una pequeña casita y no había gente. Ahí me dormí

un rato. Llegaron unos muchachos como de una reserva y ellos me regalaron unas salchichitas. Les hablé. Ellos muy amables, me regalaron agua
y comida. Sabritas, jugos, un galón de agua. Lo miré que fue a sacar el
celular y le pedí que no llamara a la policía. Me quedé sólo, como dos, tres
horas. Cuando llegó Migración, como que llegaron a recoger materiales de
construcción.

||||||||||||||||

We took off one morning through the Sonoran Desert.[16] There were more
than six people in all who went. A guy went with us as our guide, the one
who knows the way. Only two people arrived out of the six in my group. But
in really bad condition. They just now told me that it looks like two are dead
and two are in really bad condition. One they haven't found.

Each of us loaded up with five big jugs of water and a backpack with
food in it. Sometimes along the way we'd get to places where there's water
that cattle drink. Some of the water supplies we couldn't get to because there
was a lot of Immigration. We had to go up in the hills to dodge Immigration, and the amount of progress we were supposed to make in one day
turned into two days. Our water consumption kept going up. We were walking all night until eleven in the morning or twelve noon. We were getting a
few hours' sleep a day, *if* we could sleep for the heat. And then from three or
four o'clock onwards, and all night long, we kept walking. We had to sleep
during the hottest times of day, which is why sometimes we couldn't even
sleep. We'd get to the water supplies, drink water fast, make some progress,
and sleep for maybe two or three hours, a ways off from the water supply.
They were really far away from each other, and from the heat of the sun,
and all the sand, at some of them we'd get there and there wouldn't be any
water left. We had to keep going like that, without water. I walked for about
eight days. Then, going down a hill, I was carrying the food of one of the
guys I was with who was in really bad shape, and I stepped on a rock and it
rolled and I hurt my ankle. And I couldn't say anything because our guide
was already annoyed: he'd already been insulting that guy because he was
really tired and I was refusing to leave him.

Names are never spoken, the names of the people who go. They call us
"Nayarit," "Sinaloa," "Sonora." You call people by their state, not by name.
We never use names. That way, you don't get too attached. So when one
guy gets tired and you have to leave him, you don't know his name and you
don't feel sorry. There's no attachment because you don't know his story.
And if someone dies, the only pain is the pain of leaving someone none
of us knows anything about. The only ones who did know each other well

were the guys from Oaxaca. There were two of them. One is dead and the other is the guy they haven't found, because he refused to leave him.

So on the downhill, my foot started to hurt. It was me who was the first one to stay behind. After I got hurt, we walked all morning, but the day after, I walked three hours or so and I couldn't do it anymore. I stayed behind in a circle of trees because I couldn't do it anymore. They left me water and they left me a little bit of food. I don't know where it was. But I know I got to a reservation.[17] But I don't know what area it is. I walked about thirteen days in all. After I stayed behind, I got up on a little hill. A guy came by who was from Mexico City and he let me have a gallon of water. So when the sun went down I got up on a little hill with that gallon of water and saw some lights from a town. Our guide had told us there was a reservation right around there.

I had made a pair of crutches, out of dry sticks of wood. I made a fire and used it to cut the crutches to the length I needed them. And from the clothes I had with me, I put something there so it wouldn't hurt my armpit. I walked for half a night, but I didn't make much progress. I walked as best I could. I called on God, even though I've never been a big believer in God, but I prayed to him for help and the next day I started to walk. I don't know how, but I started to walk, slow and careful.

I walked. I walked some more and some more. By the time the sun went down, I'd walked about eight hours. Not comfortably, but walking. I wasn't watching the lights anymore, but I got my bearings and headed off walking in that direction. Walking and walking. The lights looked close by, but I kept walking and not giving up. Not getting there. Wetting my face and walking. I had about a half a liter of water on me. The little bit of water I had, just wet my lips, that's it. I had about a half a liter left. But I conserved it, so I wouldn't die of thirst.

Finally I got there. I crossed the highway and went into the little town. There were no people. But I came to, like, a school that was under construction. There was no water. I looked for a tap or something, but I wasn't finding any. Then I found one, it was where the soil was broken open in the lawn. So I opened the tap there and then I closed it again, and I kept doing that. I slept there. I didn't want to turn myself in to Immigration. I wanted to get to Phoenix. I drank a lot of water, wet my face. There was a little house with no people. I fell asleep there for a little while. Then some guys arrived, reservation-type people, and they gave me some little sausages to eat. I talked to them, you know. They very kindly gave me water and food. Bags of chips, juices, a gallon of water, you know. I saw him go to take out his cell phone and I asked him not to call the police. I stayed there alone, maybe two or three hours. When Immigration got there, it was like someone had come to pick up construction material.

ÉRIKA

Mi nombre es Érika. Soy originaria de Guanajuato, madre de dos hijos, separada de mi marido. Mi educación fue de sólo primaria. Quise emigrar a los Estados Unidos, porque en México no encontraba cómo sostener a mis hijos y mis padres están emigrados allá, en los Estados Unidos. Primero envié a mis hijos y, gracias a Dios, llegaron a su destino, sanos y salvos.

Llegué a Nogales para saltar el muro. Antes tuve una mala experiencia con el coyote, que me quiso violar. Ya para cruzar, me subieron por una escalera y estando arriba del muro, debía deslizarme por el poste para caer al otro lado. El coyote empezó a presionarme de que me apresurara, antes de que fuera a llegar la Migra. Con la prisa, los nervios alterados, el miedo, me destanteé. Se me fue un pie y caí desde arriba, hasta el suelo. De inmediato me di cuenta que no sentía las piernas. Otro compañero, que ya había saltado —éramos dos los que estaban saltando— me decía que me moviera hacia el barranco para que no nos fuera a encontrar la Migra. Yo no podía. Estaba llorando de dolor y no me podía mover.

El que iba conmigo no entendía mi situación y la gravedad de mi caso, me arrastró para esconderme. Eran las 12:30 de la madrugada. Yo pedía al compañero que llamara a la Migra, a la policía, a quien fuera para que me auxiliaran. Él, sintiéndose ya adentro, me dijo que con pena me dejaba, pero que él tenía su plan de llegar y no podía acompañarme. Dijo que tenía grandes necesidades y no quería echar a perder su plan. Yo le insistía que sólo llamara un auxilio para mí. Pero él se fue y me dejó sola. Nunca llamó a nadie por el temor de ser atrapado.

En la soledad, sin poder moverme y con el dolor intenso, yo gritaba sin parar, pidiendo auxilio. Me parecía imposible que, cuando yo necesitaba que pasara la Migra, no llegaba. Fueron cinco horas y media de espera con intenso dolor, angustia, desesperación en medio de la soledad. El tiempo que transcurrió me pareció una eternidad. La causa de mi dolor era porque estaba fracturada de la columna. No supe si algún tiempo perdí el conocimiento, pero sí recuerdo que fue una noche terrible. En algún momento pensé en rodarme hacia el barranco para que ya terminara mi vida sola, en aquella situación y sin auxilio de ningún tipo.

A las 5:30 de la mañana, pasó la Migra. Me llevaron al hospital en Tucson. Me intervinieron para ponerme una placa en la columna. Los doctores decían que era un milagro que pudiera mover las piernas. A los ocho días de la cirugía, me sacaron del hospital y me deportaron. Los dolores eran muy fuertes todavía. Al salir de Estados Unidos, estando en migración mexicana, me tuvieron mucho tiempo sin ninguna atención. Por fin, me llevaron al hospital regional donde no me hicieron nada. Yo seguía con muchos dolores. Me veía sola en Nogales, sin conocer a nadie para pedir auxilio, con el dolor.

Ante esa realidad, el único teléfono que tenía era el del coyote. El que ocasionó mi caída al cruzarme, el mismo que había intentado violarme antes de cruzar, del que me defendí como pude con golpes y amenazas de denunciarlo. Era pues la única persona de quien tenía número de teléfono. Le llamé y pedí que fuera e hiciera algo para que me atendieran. Él fue al hospital general, donde hay mala o ninguna atención, me sacó de ahí y me llevó a un hospital particular, el Hospital del Socorro, atendido por las Hermanas Mínimas. Yo le dije que me llevara a donde me atendieran, ya vería la forma de pagar. Llevo un mes hospitalizada. Estoy dada de alta, pero no puedo salir, porque mi papá no ha pagado. Es más, ni le he pasado la cuenta porque tengo pánico de hacerlo. Temo mucho su reacción cuando sepa la cantidad.

Mi situación, después de operada, no es nada halagadora. Puedo dar algunos pasos apoyándome, pero necesito rehabilitación para volver a caminar con normalidad. Posiblemente pierda también toda la dentadura porque traigo brakets y, al caer, se me aflojaron todos los dientes. No he visto dentista, pero según me han dicho los doctores, es posible me los tengan que sacar.

||||||||||||||||||||

My name is Érika. I'm from Guanajuato originally. I'm a mother; I have two kids; I'm separated from my husband. My education is just through sixth grade. I chose to emigrate to the United States because in Mexico, I couldn't find a way to keep my kids fed. And my parents are emigrants there, in the United States.[18] First I sent my kids and, thank God, they arrived safe and sound.

I came to Nogales to jump over the wall. Before I did, I had a bad experience with the *coyote*. He tried to rape me. To get across, they had me go up a ladder, and when I was on top of the wall I was supposed to slide down the post to land on the other side.[19] The *coyote* started pressuring me to hurry up before Immigration came. Between being rushed, nervous, and scared, I got mixed up, one of my feet slipped, and I fell from the top all the way down to the ground. I immediately noticed I couldn't feel my legs. Someone I was with who had already jumped—it was two of us who were jumping—he kept telling me to move toward the ravine so Immigration wouldn't find us. I couldn't. I was crying from the pain and I couldn't move. He didn't know how seriously injured I was, and he dragged me along the ground to hide me. It was 12:30 at night. I kept asking him to call Immigration, the police, whoever, to come and help me. But now that he was inside, he told me that he felt bad about leaving me, but he had a plan to get where he was going and he couldn't stay with me. He had major needs to deal with and he wasn't willing to throw away his plan. I insisted to him that he call for some help for me, that's all. But he went away and left me alone. He never called anyone because he was afraid he would get trapped.

I was alone, I couldn't move, and the pain was intense, so I kept yelling and didn't stop, asking for help, help. It seemed impossible to me that right when I needed for Immigration to come by, they weren't arriving. It was a five-and-a-half-hour wait, in intense pain, feeling anxious and desperate, all alone. The time that went by seemed like an eternity. The reason I was in pain was because my spine was fractured. I never knew if I lost consciousness for any amount of time, but I do remember it was an awful night. At one point, I had the thought of rolling myself toward the ravine to go ahead and end my life, considering that I was by myself, in the situation I was in, and there was no help of any kind.

At 5:30 in the morning, Immigration came by. They took me to the hospital in Tucson. They did a procedure to put in a plate in my spine. The doctors kept saying it was a miracle I could move my legs. Eight days after the surgery, they took me out of the hospital and deported me. The pain was still really bad. After leaving the US, when I was in Mexican Immigration, they kept me for a long time without any medical care.[20] Finally they took me to the local hospital, where no one did anything. I still had a lot of pain. I felt like I was alone in Nogales, not knowing anyone I could ask for help. And in pain.

Given that that was the reality I was facing, the only number I had was the *coyote*'s. The person who caused my fall in the process of crossing me. The same person who had tried to rape me before that. The one I defended myself from any way I could, punching him, threatening to report him. I mean, he was the only person I had a phone number for. I called him and asked him to come and do something so they'd give me some care. He came to the general hospital, where the medical care is bad to nonexistent, and got me out of there and took me to a private hospital, the Hospital del Socorro. The Little Sisters provide the care there.[21] I told him to take me wherever I'd get care, I'd figure out how to pay afterward. I've been hospitalized for a month so far. I've actually been released—but I can't leave, because my dad hasn't paid. In fact, I haven't even shown him the bill because I'm terrified to. I really dread his reaction when he finds out how much it is.

As far as how I'm doing since the operation, it's not exactly pretty. I can take a few steps by myself with crutches, but I'll need physical therapy to walk normally again. I may lose all my teeth too, because I have braces, and when I fell, all my teeth got loosened. I haven't seen a dentist, but from what the doctors have told me, it's possible that they'll have to come out.

NOMBRE RESERVADO / NAME NOT PROVIDED

Estuve diez días en el desierto. El desierto a nadie se lo deseo. A nadie le deseo que cruce en estas fechas el desierto. Quizás el desierto es fácil para gente que ya tiene práctica, va y viene y son días. Pero la gente que no estamos acostumbrados a caminar cerros, barrancas, caídas, todo eso . . . tiene un momento que pisa uno tierra americana. Desde ahí se corre peligro por tanto animal que hay, tanta insolación, tanta soledad, tanto peligro con los narcos. Ya el temor no es a la Migra, sino a los narcos. Entonces fue algo difícil. Íbamos ocho y de los ocho yo me quedé. Fui el único. No querían que me quedara. Me quedé por ya no poder caminar por como traía los pies. Imagino que el calzado no era adecuado, pero es lo que los polleros nos imponen. Ellos dicen cuál calzado. Al cuarto día yo me ampollé. Me salieron ampollas, pero me las curaron con merthiolate. Pero ahí mismo se me hicieron ámpulas. Este miércoles van a ser quince días. Hoy es el cinco de junio.

Yo duré ocho días con ellos caminando y dos más solo. Llegó un momento en que yo les dije que ya no podía. En un cerro hay un pozo de agua. Yo les dije que ahí me dejaran. Que ahí me quedaba yo, que de hambre no me moriría, pero de sed sí. Ellos temían que yo los delatara. Decían: "Venimos en un grupo". Pero yo decía: "Es que ya no puedo". [*Solloza*]. Me decían: "¿Seguro?" Yo decía: "Sí, yo mañana me entrego a la Migra, se lo prometo". El guía me dijo: "No te voy a reportar, ni nada, pero no te entregues ahora". Me trató bien. [*Llora*]. Lo que más duele es que ya estaba por llegar. Ya habían sido ocho días de sacrificio. El guía lloró conmigo. Me dijo: "Te cuidas", y se fueron.

Ellos me dejaron como a las once de la mañana. Ahí me quedé tirado. Como a las cinco de la tarde, bajó otro grupo que llegó a tomar agua. Pero yo para esa hora ya me había mojado la cabeza, como pude saqué agua y algo me reanimé, porque yo ya no podía caminar. Ya había llevado algunos golpes. En el cerro, las barrancas. [*Muestra los rasguños, la piel rasgada*]. Y llegó el grupo. Eran hondureños. Uno de ellos me dijo: "Amigo, usted tiene que seguir adelante". Le dije: "Ya no puedo, amigo". "Sí, va a poder". Me lavó, me echó una pomada en los pies para adormecerme el dolor y me dijo, "Sube ese cerro y el pueblo que veas, a la casita que veas, llegas. Ahí le van a dar comida y lo van a ayudar. Pero no se quede aquí". Esas palabras y la pomada me dieron fuerza. Él me dio calcetines. Se quitó su playera y me la dio. Todo eso que hizo por mí me dio fuerza.

Subí el cerro como pude, porque yo iba con esa mentalidad de que ellos me habían ayudado y yo tenía que responder. Como a las seis de la tarde, yo pensé que tenía que bajar, porque ¿qué iba a hacer solo, arriba? Y como era de bajada, no me fue tan difícil como la subida. En eso vi muchas luces y ya me animé. Pero estaba lejísimos. Yo me guié por esas luces y caminé desde las seis de la tarde hasta las doce de la noche, seis horas. No llegaba. Me tiré y caí dormido. Escuchaba los coyotes. Me levanté como a las 4:30 de la mañana y seguí. Por fin llegué a un lugar, Santa Rosa. Ahí llegué como a la una de la tarde. Ya tenía dos días sin comer. Llegué con un señor mexicano. Me dio de comer. Me dio sandía y me dijo: "Vete a los matorrales y te quedas allá. Ya cuando esté clarito, te vienes para decirte cómo te vas a ir". Le agradecí, me dio agua y me fui a acostar a los matorrales.

El señor me permitió bañarme ahí fuera. Me dio ropa. Y me dijo: "Síguele! Vas a llegar. Nada más pasas esas luces del retén y ya de ahí se divisa Phoenix, Arizona". Pero yo sentía que ya no podía. Él me estuvo ayudando. Me fui y como a la una me quedé dormido. Me levanté temprano, pero yo no podía. Me encontré con unos indios y el indio me decía: "Tú puedes, síguele". Me dijo que no llamaba al doctor porque él llamaría a Migración, pero yo sentí que no podía. Y entonces tomé la decisión de que llamaran a la ambulancia para que me llevaran. A mí no me siguió la Migra. Me atendieron, me lavaron, me dieron medicamento y de ahí ya llamaron a Migración. Me llevaron a Phoenix y la Migra me trató muy bien. Me hablaban para darme el medicamento a sus horas y mis medicinas.

A las cuatro de la mañana me trasladaron a otro módulo y ahí yo llegué para preguntarme mi nombre y para dónde iba. Él me dijo que me iba a encerrar. Yo pregunté, ¿por qué? Pedí hablar con el Consulado Mexicano para saber cómo le iba a hacer sin dinero. Ellos dijeron que acá ellos me iban a ayudar.

Y así está mi historia. Y lo que quiero es irme. Irme para México. Allá tengo dos hijos: un hijo y una hija. El hijo es profesionista. Para eso fui a Estados Unidos, para darles estudio a mis hijos. La necesidad hace que uno pueda hacer grandes proezas.

||||||||||||||||

I was in the desert for ten days. The desert is something I wouldn't wish on anyone. I wouldn't wish it on anyone to cross the desert at this time of year. The desert might be easy for people who already have practice; they go back and forth and it takes days. But the people like me who aren't used to hiking through hills, canyons, climbs and drops, all of that . . . you have a moment where you set foot on American soil. From then on you're in danger from all the animals around, all the sun exposure, all the isolation, all the danger from the drug traffickers. The thing to be scared of isn't Immigration now; it's the drug traffickers. So it was pretty hard. There were eight of us who went, and out of those eight, it was me who stayed behind. I was the only one. They didn't want me to. I did because I couldn't walk anymore because of how my feet were. I suppose it was the wrong footwear, but that's determined by the *coyotes*: they tell you what shoes you're going to wear. By the fourth day I'd blistered up. I got blisters on my feet. But someone treated them for me with Merthiolate.[22] But then I got blisters underneath the blisters. This Wednesday it'll be two weeks. Today is June the fifth.

I lasted eight days walking with them and two more on my own. A moment came when I told them I couldn't do it anymore. On a hillside, there was a watering hole. I told them to leave me there. I told them that's where I was staying, me. Told them hunger wouldn't kill me, but thirst, yes. They were afraid of me turning them in. They kept saying, "We came as a group." But I was like, "I just can't do it anymore." [*Sobs.*] They kept saying, "Are you sure?" I said, "Yes. Tomorrow I'll turn myself in to Immigration, I swear." The guide said to me, "I'm not going to report you, I'm not going to do anything, but don't turn yourself in right now." He treated me well. [*Cries.*] What hurts the most is that I was just shy of getting there. It had been eight days of sacrifice already. The guide cried with me. He told me, "You take care of yourself," and they left.

They left me there at about eleven in the morning. I stayed there, lying down, stuck. At about five in the afternoon, another group came down. They came to get water. But before they got there, I'd wet my head, drawn water as best I could, and perked myself back up a bit. Because at that point I wasn't able to walk. I'd already taken a bit of a beating. In the hills, the canyons. [*Shows the scratches on his skin.*] So this group came. They were Hondurans. One of them said to me, "My friend, you have to keep going." I said to him, "I'm just not able to anymore, my friend." "Yes, you'll be able to." He cleaned me up, threw some ointment on my feet to numb the pain for me, and he told me,[23] "Climb that hill and whatever town you see, whatever little house you see, you're going to get there. They're going to feed you and they're going to help you. But don't stay here." Those words and the ointment gave me strength. He gave me socks. He took off his T-shirt and gave it to me. All these things he did for me gave me strength.

I climbed the hill as best I could, because now I had the attitude that they had helped me and I had to live up to it. At about six in the evening I thought, I have to go down, because what am I going to do on my own on top of this hill? It was downhill, so it wasn't as hard for me as the climb. Right then, I saw lots of lights, and I perked right up. But it was really, really far away. I pointed myself in the direction of those lights and walked from six in the evening to twelve at night, six hours. I wasn't getting there. I collapsed and fell asleep. I could hear the coyotes during the night. I got up at about 4:30 in the morning and kept going. Finally I got somewhere, a place called Santa Rosa. I got there at about one in the afternoon. I hadn't eaten for two days. I came to a Mexican gentleman's house. He gave me something to eat. He gave me watermelon, and he told me, "Go in the bushes, and you're going to stay there. When it's good and bright, you're going to get yourself back here so I can tell you which way you're going to go." I thanked him, he gave me water, and I went to lie down in the bushes.

The gentleman allowed me to bathe outside there, gave me clothes. And he told me, "Keep it up! You'll get there. You just go past the lights from that checkpoint and then you'll be able to make out Phoenix from there." But I kept feeling like I couldn't do it anymore. He was helping me. I left, and at about one I fell asleep. I got up early, but I couldn't do it. I met some Indians and one of them told me, "You can do it, keep it up." He told me he wasn't going to call a doctor because they would just call Immigration, but I felt like I wasn't able. And so I made the decision for them to call an ambulance to come and take me away. In my case, Immigration didn't follow me. The medics treated me, cleaned me up, gave me medication, and then called Immigration from there. I was taken to Phoenix and Immigration treated me really well. They would call me to come up when it was time to give me the medication, and they'd give me my other medicine then too.

At four in the morning I was transferred to another unit. I went up so they could ask me my name and where I'd been headed. The guy told me he was going to lock me up. I asked, "Why?" I asked to talk to the Mexican consulate, to find out how I was going to manage it without money.[24] The consulate people told me they would help me here in Nogales.

And that's my story. And what I want to do now is leave. Go to Mexico City. I have two kids there, a son and a daughter. My son is a professional with a degree. That's what I went to the US for, so my kids could get an education. Need enables a person to do tremendous feats.[25]

LETICIA

Soy Leticia Elizabet Chávez Navarro, originaria de Toluca, Estado de México. Tengo veintiún años de edad. Decidí ir a los Estados Unidos a trabajar porque quiero un futuro mejor para mis padres y para mí. La situación que he vivido ha sido de pobreza extrema. Mi mamá está enferma de diabetes.

Me recomendaron a un pollero, con la idea de que él me llevaría hasta allá, pero al llegar a la frontera él me entregó a otro compañero de él. Esto fue en Altar, el día seis de julio del presente año. Ese día inició mi proceso. Me tuvieron en Altar cinco días en casa de un señor. Yo entregué mil dólares para la mafia, para la comida ahí y para entrar al desierto. El dinero me lo prestaron mis primos en Estados Unidos.

Entramos al desierto. Estuve dos días caminando, después me enfermé del estómago, luego me dejó el pollero. Me dijo que no podía estar esperándome, eso porque yo ya estaba sin fuerza para caminar. Deponía y tenía diarrea. Me abandonó. Yo empecé a caminar sóla. Caminé como diez días. Yo me sentía muy triste, con miedo, especialmente en la noche. Viví lluvia. Tenía frío porque mi ropa estaba mojada. Caminaba y se me secaba. Dormía en el monte, en algún lugar plano, para evitar que hubiera animales. No tenía nada de comida. Sobreviví a base de agua y de fe en Dios. Rezaba, le pedía a Dios y sentía un alivio en el corazón.

Lo que yo caminaba era hacia México, equivocadamente, porque yo quería llegar a los Estados Unidos. De repente, ya estaba yo en la línea. Dios sabe por qué pasan las cosas. Ya terminando los diez días, como a las ocho, me alcanzó un grupo. Yo no confiaba en ellos y no quise hablar. Ellos sí querían ayudarme, pero me vieron muy mal y por eso ya no me llevaron. No querían que me quedara a medio desierto y me dieron comida y agua y me orientaron hacia donde caminar.

Caminé todavía dos días y finalmente encontré a un señor. El señor me ofreció [*pausa*]. Yo estaba sentada, había mucho calor. Él me encontró y me llevó a su casa. Me dijo que no me iba a hacer nada, que en casa estaba su familia. Fue a traer su carro porque iba en un caballo. Me llevó a su casa. Ahí habló con el Grupo Beta para que fueran a buscarme. Caminé con el Grupo Beta casi una hora para llegar hasta aquí. Llegando, me llevaron al hospital y me inyectaron. Ya no podía ni ver la comida, me daba náusea.

Yo llegué aquí a Nogales el viernes, veinticinco de agosto. Yo no tenía teléfono, ni celular ni reloj. No sabía qué día era, a qué hora me levantaba, en qué fecha estaba. Nada. Me llegaba mucho sueño. Me tiraba, me dormía y la verdad no supe si pasaban varios días.

‖‖‖‖‖‖‖‖‖‖‖

My name is Leticia Elizabet Chávez Navarro and I'm originally from Toluca in Mexico State. I'm twenty-one years old. I decided to go work in the US because I want a better future for my parents and myself. Extreme poverty is the life experience I've had. My mom suffers from diabetes.

I had a *coyote* recommended to me. The idea was that he'd take me all the way to the US, but when we got to the border, he turned me over to a buddy of his. This was in Altar, on the sixth of July of this year. That was the day my trial began. They kept me in Altar for five days at a gentleman's house. I handed over a thousand dollars to pay for the mafia, for the food there, and to enter the desert.[26] The money was lent to me by my cousins in the US.

We headed into the desert.[27] I walked for two days. After that, I got a stomach illness, then the *coyote* left me. He told me he couldn't keep waiting for me, which he had to do because I didn't have strength for walking anymore. I was vomiting and having diarrhea. He left me behind. I started to walk by myself. I walked about ten days. I was feeling really sad, scared, especially at night. There was rain. I'd get cold because my clothes were wet. I'd walk and that would dry me off. I slept on the ground, somewhere flat so there wouldn't be animals. I didn't have any food at all. I survived off of water and faith in God. I'd pray, I'd ask God for help, and I'd feel some relief in my heart.

The walking I was doing was toward Mexico, which was by mistake, because what I wanted was to get to the US. Suddenly I was at the border. God knows why things happen. At the end of those ten days, at about eight o'clock, there was a group that caught up to me. I didn't trust them and refused to speak. They did want to help me, but they saw I was in really bad shape, so that's why they didn't take me with them. They didn't want me to get left behind in the middle of the desert. They gave me food and water and showed me the right direction to walk in.

I walked yet another two days and finally, I ran into this gentleman. He offered me [*pause*] I was actually sitting down, it was really hot, and he came across me and invited me to his house. He told me he wasn't going to do anything to me; his family was right there. He went to get his car, because he was on a horse. He took me to his house. From there he called *Grupo Beta* so they'd come and find me.[28] I walked with *Grupo Beta* almost an hour to get here. When I finally did, I was taken to the hospital and given injections. I was at the point where I couldn't even look at food, it made me feel sick.

I got here, to Nogales, on Friday, August twenty-fifth. I didn't have a phone. No cell phone and no watch. I would get up in the morning and not know what day of the week it was, what time of day, what the date was. Nothing. I kept feeling really sleepy. I'd lie down and go to sleep, and honestly, for all I know, days and days would go by.

7

Abuses by Government

Introduced by Joanna Williams

I n the current discourse about immigration control in Mexico and the United States, it is taken for granted that authorities are in place in order to enforce laws and that by doing their job efficiently they ensure safety and justice. Furthermore, the reigning narrative is that it is migrants who bring disorder to US society. However, our daily experience at the *comedor*, and the collection of *testimonios* before your eyes tell a different story. In fact, it is agents of law enforcement themselves—police officers, US Border Patrol (USBP) agents and Immigration and Customs Enforcement (ICE) agents, among others—who exploit migrants' vulnerability and create an atmosphere of insecurity.

These testimonies contain very serious instances of physical, emotional, and verbal abuse. These attacks hurt and cause harm. However, when considering the seriousness of these abuses and their lasting effects, we should also examine the landscape of impunity that fosters a culture of abuse by the powerful. Be it a blow, an insult, extortion, or denying a request for medical assistance, these abuses add up to the clear message to migrants that they are powerless and worthless.

Throughout their journeys, migrants encounter many sources of abuse. Central American migrants who flee their villages or cities may be stopped by their country's own police or military officers, who may keep them from leaving the country. As they traverse Mexico, they have to avoid checkpoints and raids by *Instituto Nacional de Migración* (INM) agents. Exploiting migrants' vulnerability and irregular migratory status, INM officers extort them by threatening to detain or deport them. Other municipal, state, and federal police agents, and even trained security agents (who have no legal authority over migration issues), take advantage of migrants' defenselessness in order to extort them or physically assault them. In 2019, Mexico deployed the National Guard, which was supposedly tasked with promoting security but has in fact harassed migrant shelters and used excessive force against groups of migrants, including women and children.[1] Sometimes, either by looking the other way or by actively participating, National Guard agents are complicit in allowing migrants to be held up or kidnapped by organized crime.

Beyond the hardship they have already suffered on the way through Mexico, migrants from Mexico, Central America, and other places then have to risk agents' power abuses within the United States. Crossing the desert means coming across USBP agents in remote places, away from cameras, where agents can engage in physical and verbal abuse with impunity. Between January 2010 and July 2020, 109 people died as a consequence of interactions with Border Patrol agents, and only one case resulted in criminal charges being brought against the perpetrating agent.[2] When migrants are in US government custody, they have few possibilities of making complaints about abuses without facing retaliation, and there is no political will to investigate abuse allegations. Likewise, deaths that occur during long-term ICE detention—mostly through medical neglect—do not result in legitimate investigations.[3] Sixty-five percent of long-term detention centers are controlled by private companies, which are not held to the same transparency regulations as government entities. This arrangement also allows the government to sidestep any need for accountability. Throughout their whole journey through Central America, Mexico, and the United States, migrants are constantly exposed to abuses by authorities.

Abuses are not isolated incidents but, rather, well-documented, systemic challenges. Estimates based on a survey of migrants who were deported to Nogales show that one out of every three people detained while crossing the southwest US border (408,870 people in 2016) suffered abuse at the hands of Border Patrol agents.[4] One factor contributing to this high rate of abuse is that the number of USBP agents doubled between 2003 and 2011. In 2017 there were 19,437 agents, many who joined the agency without fulfilling the necessary requirements for the position.[5] Although the number of agents has remained mostly stable since 2012, those agents with little training or issues in their applications, who joined the agency during its growth spurt, continue to work there. Just as important, however, is the culture of abuse and disregard for migrant lives within the agency. These attitudes were dramatically exposed with the revelation of a secret Facebook group in which

Border Patrol agents regularly posted racist and sexist comments, even dismissing the deaths of migrants.[6] While the rhetoric of the Trump administration has exacerbated this cultural issue, its existence predates the Trump presidency. The Homeland Security Advisory Panel points to these cultural concerns in its 2016 review of Customs and Border Protection (CBP) abuse, urging the agency to promote a "culture of transparency."[7]

In Mexico, too, the problem is structural. Approximately 99 percent of the crimes committed in Mexico against migrants from Central America and other regions go unpunished, which shows the inefficiency of the government—especially the *Procuraduría General de la República* (Attorney General's Office)—when it comes to investigating crime.[8] The rate of abuse of migrants by Mexican authorities in particular has gotten worse since the implementation of *Programa Frontera Sur* (Southern Border Program) in 2014, which is a means for the US government to partly finance Mexico's migration control.[9] The incidents of abuse continue unabated because there are no accountability mechanisms. Fewer than one in twelve migrants who suffer abuse by USBP tries to file a complaint. Most of them say that while they were detained, they never received information about how to do such a thing.[10] Even when they do manage to lodge a complaint, 96 percent of these result in no action taken against the agent.[11] Out of 214 complaints filed between 2009 and 2014 regarding Border Patrol abuse or mistreatment of migrant children, only one agent was disciplined.[12] In Mexico there are human rights commissions tasked with investigating abuses by authorities, but of the 1,617 complaints received by the *Comisión Nacional de los Derechos Humanos*, or National Commission for Human Rights (CNDH), between December 1, 2012, and June 15, 2015, only four resulted in recommendations to the institutions that were accused of human rights violations.

All of these risks to migrants are compounded by their marginalization. In Mexico and the United States migrants face discrimination and racism from citizens themselves, who support officers who commit abuses or who at least stand by and allow the abuse to happen. Migrants don't have the necessary social or political clout to resist. Despite this, they often risk their well-being in order to struggle against this impunity using the minimal tools at their disposal, such as staging hunger strikes inside detention facilities. Their courage against the obstacles they face is admirable.

Mexican and US residents should take migrants' example and courage to heart and assume their roles as participants in society. They must recognize not only their responsibility for the actions of their government, but also their power within the work that must be done to change these structures. We can meet with or call our representatives in each country to demand that the system be reformed. We have the ability and freedom to publicly show our disagreement with the status quo by staging demonstrations in the streets or through campaigns in the media. We are deeply dissatisfied with these injustices. The migrants who chose to share their stories did so because they believe a different world is possible. We hear them, and we are with them.

NOMBRE RESERVADO / NAME NOT PROVIDED

Entramos al desierto un día martes ya en la tardecita. Empezamos a caminar y a caminar. Éramos ocho personas, puros hombres. Empezamos a caminar, a caminar y ya habíamos caminado como dos días. Pero de ahí donde nos quedamos, ya no caminamos, porque el terreno estaba muy caliente. Había mucha Migra vigilando a los alrededores y a cada rato pasaba un helicóptero. Vimos que pasaban unos jeeps, de los verdes de la Migra, y recorrían el terreno. El helicóptero pasaba por arriba de una brecha que había cerca de nosotros.

Después de los dos días que caminamos, nos quedamos allí en un cerro. Como estaba muy caliente allí a los alrededores, dos días no caminamos y nos tuvimos que esconder y estuvimos hablando de qué íbamos a hacer, ni modo que nos regresáramos para atrás. Ya de allí, era un sábado como a mediodía que empezamos a caminar, caminar, caminar. Caminamos como entre cuatro o cinco horas. Empezamos a caminar y cruzamos una brecha. Ya estaba ocultándose el sol, ya fue que nos avisaron que habían visto polvo de aquel lado, el polvo que levantan los jeeps al pasar. Nos escondimos, pero ya nos habían localizado, porque había una cámara y meramente estábamos pasando por enfrente de la cámara, una cámara que estaba un poco retirada, yo creo que esa nos detectó.

Y al rato, como en unos diez minutos, ya fue que llegó el helicóptero. Ya nos localizó el helicóptero y se puso arriba de nosotros. Los demás, mis compañeros, se echaron a correr para regresar a donde estábamos. Lo que hice yo fue que me agaché y pensé que iban a lograr escaparse los demás compañeros. Pero nada. Ya cuando me di cuenta, estaban como a menos de cinco metros, allí los tenían todos esposados y yo, por mientras, estaba todavía en el suelo, sin correr, sin nada. Ya no hice nada yo.

Y ya lo que hicieron los *armis*, porque así los conocen, dicen, son los que nos agarraron a nosotros pues, son los armis (soldados). Llegaron en unos jeeps que cargan todo terreno. Ya de allí, agarraron el teléfono y nos empezaron a grabar y traían amarrado a un perro. Ya que habían agarrado a mis compañeros, yo estaba tirado en el suelo, boca abajo. Ya de allí, ellos sacaron su teléfono. Todavía tenían amarrado al perro. Y ya fue que soltaron al perro, le dieron la orden al perro y fue que el perro me atacó y supe que era una orden porque había un compañero de nosotros que hablaba inglés. Él se puso a discutir con ellos, por eso, y yo le pregunté qué les estaba diciendo. Y él me dijo que les estaba reclamando, porque ellos le dieron orden al perro de que te atacara y por eso lo soltaron a propósito, me dijo. No era para que te mordiera, sino que le dieron la orden ellos. Y mientras estaba yo gritando, queriendo defenderme, cuando veo que me iban a disparar si le hacía algo al perro, cortaron cartucho. Si ya veía que me iban a disparar, ya nomás me quedaba gritar. Y me decían: "Levanta las manos, alza las manos". Y viendo al perro destrozando mi pierna pues y ya casi como cinco minutos que habían pasado. Ya cuando se cansaron de grabar y ya fue que llegaron y me quitaron al perro. Y me grabaron y tomaron fotos y aparte ellos traían cámaras en la frente, todos. Eran como unos siete los que nos agarraron, todos camuflajeados. Y lo único que me di cuenta fue del número de la perrera, era la 14067, ese era el número. Y el rostro de ellos, sé que sí me acuerdo, pero tendría que verlos otra vez. Si los veo, sí los identifico.

Y eso pasó en el desierto y nos llevaron a donde ellos, a Ajo, no sé qué nombre tenga. Hay una oficina de ellos allí en medio del desierto, ya fue que me llevaron. Cuando llegué, ya fue que cortaron mi pantalón y vieron la herida y todavía una risa y vinieron sus demás compañeros de ellos y empezaron a tomar fotos. Que una foto para el Facebook y risa y risa ellos y empezaron a burlarse y todavía me dicen: "Sabes que, te vamos a tomar una foto, pero con una sonrisa". Y así humillándome. Y todavía le dije a ellos: "Es bonito humillar a las personas". Y ya fue que le bajaron tantito, ya me empezó a curar uno de ellos. A lavarme nada más, no a curarme. Nomás a lavar donde estaba el polvo y todo y me puso una venda.

Ya fue entre las doce o la una que nos llevaron hasta Yuma, donde nos toman las huellas. Creo que es Yuma. Ya me empezaron a tomar las huellas y me tuvieron allí encerrado. Yo pedía para que me llevaran a un hospital y ya buscaron a uno y me hizo más o menos una limpieza ahí. Yo lo que quería era ir al hospital, porque es peligroso. Imagínate si se llega a infectar, me destruye toda la pierna porque el perro me arrancó un pedazo.

Ya como a las cinco de la mañana me llevaron a un hospital. Vi la hora, porque había un reloj allí, creo que en Tucson. Me atendió una doctora, ya la doctora les dijo que por qué a esa hora. Me dieron un brazalete. Lo que me interesaba era que me quitaran el dolor porque me dolía bastante. Y pues que no se fuera a infectar. Allí estuve menos de una hora. Ya la doctora me dio algo para el dolor y me inyectó contra el tétanos, me recetó unas pastillas. No me acuerdo del nombre de la doctora, pero quedé registrado allí. La cita quedó en que me iban a presentar otra vez al día siguiente, porque la doctora intentó costurarme, ya que la herida estaba muy abierta. Pero no había piel para que se cerrara. Lo que les dijo la doctora fue: "Tráemelo para mañana para ver cómo está la herida y si no se ha infectado". Me regresaron a Yuma. Allí donde estaba yo encerrado les decía: "Tengo otra cita con la doctora. Necesito ir al hospital". "No, aquí mismo te lo lavamos", me dicen. Llegó uno del *armi* y ya me empezó a lavar. Y como sea, me lo amarró con una venda y ya me la dejó así.

Ya dentro de dos días, para presentarme a corte, así me llevaron. Me esposaron de las manos y de los pies, así con la pierna hinchada. Allí me dijeron que iba a ver al consulado mexicano. Les dije a mis compañeros: "Ya está, les voy a decir para que hagan algo". Y le dije al del consulado: "Sabes qué, me mordió un perro que me echaron y mi pierna esta delicada. ¿Qué puedo hacer?" le digo. Y me dice el del consulado: "No, pues ahorita vemos tu caso". Ni siquiera le puso atención, porque había mucha bulla de los compañeros. Habíamos como quizá como treinta. Ya luego dijo: "Siguiente", como que traía prisa. Y quedo pendiente y le digo: "Qué, ¿le digo al juez para que se pueda hacer algo del caso?" "Si quieres", me dice. "De todos modos dile para que lo tome en cuenta". Es todo lo que me dijo.

Ya de ahí me asignaron un abogado defensor, ya fue que le dije que qué podía hacer. Le expliqué lo del perro. Me quité la venda, le enseñé la herida y todo eso. "No, olvídate de eso", me dice.

Tú tienes un delito que es delito mayor, que te pueden aplicar de dos a veinte años de cárcel, así que es mejor. Esa es la mala, que tienes un delito mayor. Pero hay una buena. Podemos descartar lo que es delito mayor y lo podemos poner como delito menor, porque no puedes comprobar de que tú entraste legalmente aquí a los Estados Unidos. Por lo tanto, cada vez que te pregunte el juez, di que sí. Di que sí y di que sí y declárate culpable y se acaba tu asunto. Y ya eso de la herida, solito se va a curar, es lo único que puedo hacer por ti.

Pues ya nadie me apoyaba, ni el consulado, ni el abogado, ya durante la corte tuve que declararme culpable. Ya de allí, ya nos sentenciaron.

Llegamos al CCA. Te desnudan. Ya me revisaron todo. Ya pasamos a un hospital. Ya cuando llegamos a Florence, allí me asignaron para ir al hospital. Allí empezaron a hacerle limpieza otra vez a mi pierna. Primero vi a una doctora, fue quien me empezó a hacer limpieza otra vez. Checó como estaba. Ya me recetaron medicamento y ya me sentí un poco mejor. Pero desde que me mordió el perro hasta que me atendieron en Florence, ya habían pasado como cuatro días. Pero en Florence tuve que insistir mucho de que quería ver a un doctor. "No, que aguántate", me decían, "es un proceso que tienes que hacer". Por tu ropa te asignan tu celda. Pero no soy yo al único que ha mordido el perro, hay otras personas que tienen mordeduras graves allí en Florence. Hay también personas con disparos en la pierna. No sé por qué pero allí están. Unos están intentando pelear su caso, pero si peleas tu caso allí adentro, ellos te retienen allí más tiempo, te sentencian más tiempo. Cada vez que te llaman a corte, no te sentencian. Te posponen y te posponen. Allí está un hondureño. Él tiene un disparo en la pierna. Está peleando su caso y allí esta. Ya lleva como cuatro cirugías. Yo lo único que quiero es que los oficiales que hicieron esto se hagan responsables, porque me lo hicieron de maldad, haz de cuenta, para humillarme. Porque no puse resistencia. No me fui contra ni uno de ellos. No golpeé a ninguno de ellos, nada. Por eso tienen la grabación que tienen en la frente, traen una cámara en la frente.

llllllllllllllllll

We headed into the desert on a Tuesday, late in the afternoon. We started to walk and walk and walk. There were eight of us, all guys. We started to walk and walk and walk, and before you know it we'd walked about two days. But from the spot where we stopped, we didn't walk any further, because the area had a lot of heat.[13] There was a lot of Immigration on the lookout all around, and every so often, a helicopter would fly over.[14] We noticed that some of those green Immigration guys' jeeps kept going by, they were doing patrols of the area.[15] The helicopter kept flying over a dirt road that was close to us.

After those two days of walking, we stayed put, on a hill. Since it was really hot all around there, for two days we didn't walk, we had to hide, and we were talking about what we were going to do. Forget about going back the way we came. It was a Saturday at about noon when we started out from there. Walking, walking, walking. We walked for maybe about four or five hours. We started walking again, and we crossed a dirt road. The sun was starting to go down and that's when they told us they'd seen dust over on that side, the dust the jeeps raise when they go by.[16] We hid, but they'd already located us, because there was a camera, and we were just barely passing in front of this camera just then. This was a camera that was a little ways back from the trail. I think it was what picked us up.

And in a little while, like ten minutes or so, that's when the helicopter got there. The helicopter located us and got on top of us. All the guys I was with took off running back to where we were before. What I did was duck down. I ducked down and I said to myself, they're all going to manage to escape, all the guys I was with. But not at all. When I looked up again they were less than five or so yards away. They were all handcuffed there, and in the meantime I was still on the ground, not running, nothing. *I* didn't do anything at that point.

And what the armies did—that's how people know them, call them, that's who arrested us, okay, the armies.[17] They came in some jeeps that are all-terrain. So at that point they grabbed their phones out of their jeeps and started recording us. And they had a dog with them; he was tied up. Since they'd caught the guys I was with, I was staying flat on the ground, face down. They grabbed their phones out of their jeeps. They had the dog tied up still. And that's when they released the dog, gave the dog the command, and that's when the dog attacked me. I found out it was a command because one of the guys I was with spoke English. He started yelling at them about it, and I asked him what he was saying. And he told me, "I was complaining to them because they ordered the dog to attack you," and "that's why they released him, it was on purpose," he said. "There was no reason for him to bite you except that they gave him the command." And all this time I was yelling, trying to defend myself, and then I see that they're ready to shoot me if I do anything to the dog. I heard them cock their guns. Once I could see they were ready to shoot me, the only thing left for me to do then was yell. And they kept telling me, "Hands up, hands in the air." And they could see the dog ripping my leg to shreds, okay, and by then maybe five minutes or so had passed. And after they got tired of taking videos, that's when they came up to me and took the dog off me, and they took some videos and pictures of me. And they had cameras on their foreheads too, all of them. There were about seven of them, the ones who caught us, all in camouflage. And the only detail I caught was the patrol truck's number: it was truck 14067; that was the number.[18] And their faces, I *know* I remember them. I'd have to see them again though. If I see them, I *will* be able to identify them.

So that's what happened in the desert and then they took us to their place in Ajo, I don't know what it's called. There's an office they have there in the middle of the desert; that's where they took me. When I got there, what happened was they cut my pants off and looked at the wound, and they're still laughing, and all the other agents came over and started taking pictures. Like "a picture for Facebook," and laughing, laughing, laughing, and they started making fun of me. They wouldn't stop; they said, "Hey, you know what, let's get a picture of you, but with a smile this time." And stuff like that, humiliating me. And I finally said to them, "It's nice to humiliate people, isn't it." And they finally toned it down a little bit. One of them finally started to treat my wound. Clean it, that's all, not really treat it. Just clean where there was dirt and stuff, and he put a bandage on it.

Then between twelve and one, that was when they took us to Yuma. Where they take the fingerprints. I think it's Yuma. So they started taking my fingerprints, and then they kept me there in a cell. I kept asking to be taken to a hospital, so they went and found somebody and he gave me sort of a cleaning there. What *I* wanted was to go to the hospital. I mean, it's dangerous. What if it gets infected? It'll destroy the whole leg, I mean, the dog yanked a chunk out of me.

Then at about five in the morning they took me to a hospital. I saw the time because there was a clock there. It was Tucson I think. A doctor looked me. Then the doctor asked them, why only now? They put a bracelet on me. What I was concerned about was getting them to do something about the pain, because it hurt a whole lot. And to keep it from getting infected, obviously. I was there less than an hour. The doctor gave me something for the pain and a tetanus shot, prescribed me some pills. I don't remember the doctor's name, but I'm in their records. The follow-up plan was that they were going to have me show up again the next day, because the doctor tried to sew me up, since the wound was wide open, but there wasn't enough skin for it to be able to close. What the doctor said to them was, "Bring him back to me tomorrow so I can see how the wound is and if it's gotten infected." They took me back to Yuma. I kept telling the people there where I was locked up, "I have another appointment with the doctor. I need to go to the hospital." "No, we're going to clean it for you right here," they told me. One of the army guys got there and started to clean it. Then he wrapped a bandage around it in a random way, and he just left it like that.

Then, before two days had passed, they took me like that to appear in court. They shackled my hands and feet, even with my leg swollen up like it was. That's where they told me I was going to see the Mexican consulate. I told the guys I was with, "There you go, I'm going to get them to do something about this." And I said to the consulate guy, "Hey, you know what, I got bitten by a dog that they sicced on me and my leg is in delicate condition right now. What can I do?" And the consulate guy says, "Oh, yeah, we'll take a look at your case in a second." He didn't even pay attention. There was a lot of racket from the guys I was with. There were maybe like thirty of us.[19] And then he said "Next," like he was in a hurry. And I was still waiting for an answer, so I asked him, "So, like, do I tell the judge, so he can do something about my situation?" "If you want to," he says. "Tell him anyway so he'll take it into consideration." That's all he said to me.

Then from there I was assigned a defense lawyer, so then I asked him what I could do. I explained about the dog. I took off the bandage, showed him the wound and everything. "No, forget about that," he says to me,

> You've got a felony, which means they can give you two to twenty years
> in jail, so it's better if you forget it. That's the bad news, that you have

a felony. But there's good news. We can dismiss the felony charge and we can call it a misdemeanor.[20] Because you can't prove you entered the United States legally, right? For now, every time the judge asks you something, say yes. Say yes and then say yes and then plead guilty and this is all over. And as far as the wound goes, it'll heal all on its own. It's all I have to offer you.

Well, so nobody supported me, not the consulate and not the lawyer. Then during the hearing I had to plead guilty. Then from there we were sentenced.

We got to CCA.[21] They make you take all your clothes off. So they inspected me all over. Then we went to a hospital. Right when we got to Florence, they assigned me to go to the hospital right there. They started doing another cleaning of my leg. First I saw a doctor. She was the one who started doing the cleaning. She checked me over, then prescribed me some medication and then I felt a little better. But from the time I got bitten by the dog to the time they took care of me in Florence, about four days had passed by then. But in Florence I had to insist a lot that I wanted to see a doctor. "No, sit tight," they'd tell me. "It's a process you have to go through." They assign you your cell based on your clothes. But I'm not the only one that's gotten a dog bite; there's other people with serious bite wounds there in Florence. There's also people with bullet wounds to the leg. Who knows what for, but there they are. Some are trying to fight their case but if you fight your case while you're inside, they hold you there for longer, they sentence you for longer. Every time you're called to court, they don't sentence you. They postpone and postpone. There's a Honduran guy there. He has a bullet wound in the leg. He's fighting his case and he's still there. He's had about four surgeries so far. Me, all I want is for the officers who did this to take responsibility for this, because they did it to me for evil, let's say. They did it to humiliate me. Because I never resisted. I never went against a single one of them. I never hit any of them. Nothing. That's why they have the recording that they have on their forehead. That's why they have a camera on their forehead.

ROGELIO HERIBERTO

Soy Rogelio Heriberto Montes de Ruiz. Nací en México el veintiocho de agosto de 1978. A los quince años, me llevaron a Estados Unidos. Entré a la edad de quince años en 1993. Ahora tengo treinta y siete años. Diecisiete de vivir allá.

Estaba en proceso de arreglo para residencia y permiso para trabajar, que ya tenía. Esto se me cortó por no haberme presentado a una corte. Fue omisión de mi abogada, que no me avisó y ni se presentó ella. Sin esperarlo, un día después del juicio, llegó la policía y me arrestaron. El juez me deportó.

El día veinticuatro de octubre de 2014, un amigo y yo decidimos brincar la muralla por Nogales, Sonora. Eran como las siete de la tarde. Brincamos. Después de treinta y cinco o cuarenta minutos de caminar, nos rodearon dos oficiales de Migración en motocicleta. Uno era anglo. El otro hispano, hablaba bien el español. El agresivo fue el güero. Alto, corpulento, como de veintisiete años. El latino, estatura mediana, hispano. Hablaba perfecto el español y el color de la piel era como del nuestro.

Nosotros estábamos escondidos en una mancha de zacate chiquita. Ellos habían entrado por el lado oeste de Nogales. Los oficiales se iban acercando más y más, hasta que nos encontraron. Uno de ellos le dijo al otro: "Ya los encontré". Como yo los miré cerca, me puse de rodillas con las manos en la cabeza. Uno de ellos me dijo que pusiera las manos en la cabeza. Yo lo obedecí. Pero en ese momento, otro que venía por un lado corrió hacia mí para golpearme con sus rodillas en mis costillas del lado derecho. Yo nunca quise correr. Nunca estuve parado, porque si ven mi golpe, estaría en mi cadera si hubiera estado de pie. Con el golpe me tiró al suelo. Yo no podía respirar. Lo que él hizo fue poner su bota sobre mi cabeza para que no me moviera, haciéndome tragar tierra y zacate. Mi amigo, quien estaba acostado aún, porque no lo dejaron levantar, les dice: "¿Por qué lo golpean tan feo si él no está haciendo nada?" En ese momento me levantan a mí del cuello y a él lo levantan también y el oficial que me golpeó se va con él enojado a gritarle y diciéndole que él nos podía matar, porque estábamos en su terreno.

Después de habernos esposado, el oficial que me golpeó a mí le dijo a mi amigo que cuando viniera el sargento Covarrubias, le iba a quitar las esposas para pelear con él. Los peores insultos que puedan imaginar, nos los dijo golpeándonos, echándonos su saliva en la cara con insulto, amenazas, burlas. Cuando llegó el sargento Covarrubias con su patrulla, el güero cambió la historia, diciendo que me resistí al arresto. Yo lo entendía porque entiendo inglés. Ellos pensaban que yo no entendía nada.

Después de eso, el sargento Covarrubias nos subió en su camioneta para trasladarnos a las oficinas de Migración. En el transcurso del camino, el sargento me pregunta cómo fueron los hechos. Yo le dije la verdad, le dije que viera dónde tengo el golpe. Que si yo hubiese estado parado o intentado correr, el golpe lo tendría en mis caderas, no en las costillas.

En eso llegamos a la oficina de Migración. El sargento Covarrubias, latino, se baja de su camioneta. Abre la ventanilla de mi lado y se pone del lado de mi ventanilla. Es ahí donde me dice que puedo poner un reporte en contra del oficial. Que él iba a llamar la atención al oficial, al mirarme que no pude bajarme de su camioneta. Cuando el oficial que me golpeó mira que no me pude bajar, se ríe y el sargento Covarrubias le hizo saber que sí me había roto las costillas.

De ahí nos trasladaron en una van que llegó por nosotros a otra oficina de Migración, donde fui llevado a una clínica con un doctor. Ahí el doctor me examinó y me dijo que estaba quebrado de dos costillas. Me dijo que no podía ponerme yeso, que las costillas sanaban de por sí, pero en el reporte que me dieron, solo pusieron que estoy golpeado. De ahí fuimos trasladados, un lunes trece de octubre, a Tucson, Arizona, donde me entrevistó Asuntos Internos, quienes me pidieron una declaración. Me tomaron datos, me grabaron y me tomaron fotos de mi costado derecho. Ellos me dijeron que podía agarrar un abogado y que ellos iban a investigar mi caso.

De ahí, el martes once de noviembre del 2014, tenía corte. Le comenté mi caso al consulado mexicano de Tucson, fue una señorita, quien me dijo que tenía que decir lo que me pasó a mi abogado y a la juez que me iba a sentenciar. Así lo hice. La juez tomó nota. Reforzó el que podía agarrar un abogado. Ahí me puso la juez la sentencia de un mes en Florence, Arizona. En todo ese mes no me checaron, sólo me dieron pastillas para el dolor. Yo pedía que me sacaran radiografía, pero nunca me la sacaron. El golpe me afectó la cadera, no camino como antes. La señorita de Migración ya nunca respondió las llamadas.

||||||||||||||||||

My name is Rogelio Heriberto Montes de Ruiz. I was born in Mexico City on August twenty-eighth, 1978. At fifteen, I was taken to the US. I entered at fifteen years of age, in 1993. Now I'm thirty-seven. Seventeen years I lived there.

I was in the process of settling my status to get residency and a work permit. I already had the work permit. It got cut because I didn't show up at a court date. It was my lawyer's oversight—she didn't let me know and didn't even show up herself. I didn't know it until the police came for me, one day after the trial, and arrested me. The judge deported me.

On October the twenty-fourth of 2014, a friend and I decided to hop the wall near Nogales, Sonora. It was about seven at night. We did the jump. After walking for twenty-five or forty minutes, we were surrounded by two Immigration officers on motorbikes.[22] One was Anglo. The other one was Hispanic and spoke good Spanish. The aggressive one was the blond one. Tall, stocky, maybe twenty-seven years old. The Latino was medium height. Spoke perfect Spanish and his skin color was about the same as ours.

We were hiding in a patch of grass, not a very big one. They had entered from the west side of Nogales. The officers kept getting closer and closer until they found us. One of them said to the other one, "I found them."

I saw them get close, so I got on my knees with my hands on my head. One of them told me to put my hands on my head. I obeyed him. But just then, another one of them coming from a different direction ran at me and gave me a knee in the ribs on my right side. I never tried to run. I never stood up, I mean, if you look at where my injury is, it would be on my hip if I'd been on my feet. He knocked me to the ground with that knee. I couldn't breathe. What he did then was put his boot on my head to keep me from moving, making me swallow dirt and grass. My friend, who was still lying down, because they didn't let him get up, he says to them, "Why are you hitting him so bad if he's not doing anything?" Just then they pick me up by the neck and they pick him up too and the officer who hit me, he goes over to him all mad and yells in his face and tells him he can kill us if he wants to because we're on his turf.

After they'd handcuffed us, the officer that hit me said to my friend that, when Sergeant Covarrubias came, he would take his handcuffs off for him, so he could box with Sergeant Covarrubias. And he insulted us, the worst insults you could imagine, while hitting us at the same time. Getting his spit in our faces, while spouting insults, threats, taunts. When Sergeant Covarrubias got there in his patrol truck, the blond officer told a different story, saying I resisted arrest. I understood what he was saying because I know English. They thought I didn't understand anything.

After that, Sergeant Covarrubias put us in his truck and took us to the Immigration office. Along the way, the sergeant asks me how it all happened. I told him the truth. I told him to look where my injury is, I said if I'd been standing up or tried to run, I'd have the injury on my hip, not in the ribs.

At that point we arrived at the Immigration office. Sergeant Covarrubias, who's Latino, he gets out of the truck. He opens my window and stands on that side. That's where he tells me I can make a report against the officer. That he was going to personally reprimand the officer, now that he saw how I couldn't get out of the truck by myself. When the officer who hit me saw how I couldn't get out, he laughed and Sergeant Covarrubias told him that he had in fact broken my ribs.

From there they transferred us in a van that came and took us to another Immigration office. I was taken to a clinic there that had a doctor. The doctor there examined me and told me I had two fractured ribs. He told me he couldn't put a cast on it, the ribs would heal by themselves. But in the report they gave me, they just put that I was injured, not how. From there we were transferred to Tucson, Arizona; it was a Monday, October the thirteenth. I was interviewed there by Internal Affairs. They asked me to make a statement. They took down details, recorded me, and took pictures of my right side. They told me I could get a lawyer and they were going to investigate my case.

From there, I had a court hearing on Tuesday, November eleventh, 2014. I mentioned my case to the Mexican consulate of Tucson.[23] It was a young woman. She told me I had to tell my lawyer what happened to me and also tell the judge that was going to sentence me. So I did that. The judge made a note. She stressed that I could get a lawyer. Then she gave me a sentence of one month in Florence, Arizona. In that whole month, they didn't check me over, they just gave me pain pills. I kept asking them to take an X-ray, but they never took one. This injury has affected my hip; I can't walk like before. The young woman from the consulate never did return my calls.[24]

NOMBRE RESERVADO / NAME NOT PROVIDED

Llegamos al estado de Sonora y nos pararon. Veníamos en el autobús cuarenta y cinco personas. Exigieron un recurso económico para dejarnos pasar sin hacernos ninguna revisión. Muchos de nosotros traíamos poco dinero y les dijimos que no traíamos para aportar. Querían 250 pesos por persona. Unos empezaron a darlo y como muchos no queríamos, empezaron a bajar a todos pidiéndonos identificaciones, credencial con fotografía. Muchos mexicanos, aunque se identificaban, decían que eran centroamericanos.

Después que bajaron a todos, nos empezaron a meter dentro de una "capilla" uno por uno y nos exigieron que sacáramos todas las pertenencias que llevábamos en las bolsas. Después de poner las pertenencias sobre la mesa, se dirigían hacia las cosas. Tomaban nuestra cartera y tomaban el dinero que ellos querían. A uno de mis compañeros que traía suficiente dinero, le tomaron ocho mil pesos y lo amenazaron. Le dijeron que ellos eran parte de la mafia y que si los reportaba, lo iban a matar. Así fueron diversos robos. A mí sólo me tomaron quinientos pesos porque era lo único que traía.

También llegó una mujer de la PGR y ella se encargó de revisar a las mujeres, que eran como doce mujeres. Las formó en una fila y las esculcó, tocándolas. Después metían de una por una en una camioneta Cherokee azul, sin placas. Las cuestionaban y a una parte de ellas, les quitaron recursos y las agredieron verbalmente.

Venían tres personas de Centroamérica. Ellos tuvieron que pagar diez mil pesos por cada uno para que los dejaran pasar. Como querían pasar, los pagaron. Amenazaron que iban a llamar a Migración si no lo pagaban.

El conductor del autobús bajó y habló con la PGR diciendo que el vehículo ya llevaba más de dos horas y que el autobús estaba siendo checado y el dueño preguntaba por qué lo habían detenido por dos horas. Así fue cuando ellos nos dijeron que subiéramos y empezaron a marchar. Pero antes a mí, que conozco de mis garantías individuales y me quise defender expresando lo que dicen algunos artículos de la Constitución Política —como el 11, el 14 y el 16— y que forman parte de mis garantías individuales, ellos simplemente me empezaron a agredir y me dijeron que yo era político y que si no callaba la boca, me iban a bajar del autobús y me iban a dejar ahí. Les dije que no tenían derecho a violar las garantías individuales y me empezaron a insinuar que no era mexicano, sino de Centroamérica. No obstante que me identificaba con mi licencia de conducir y mi credencial de elector. Y me la querían arrebatar de la mano. Uno de ellos molesto, me empujó a que subiera al autobús y ordenándome que me callara la boca y que no quería saber más de mí. Con cada autobús que viene de Chiapas, se comportan así, porque suponen que vienen centroamericanos y actúan con ellos como si no tuvieran ningún derecho.

||||||||||||||||||

We got to the state of Sonora and they pulled us over. There were forty-five people on the bus. They demanded funds to let us through without submitting us to an inspection. A lot of us didn't have much money and we told them we didn't have anything to contribute. They wanted fifteen bucks per person.[25] Some of us started to give that and a lot of us weren't willing, including me, so they started taking us all off the bus and asking us for identity documents, photo ID. With a lot of the Mexicans, even though they showed their ID, they were saying they were really Central Americans.

After they'd gotten us all off the bus, they started taking us inside this chapel, one by one, and they demanded that we empty our pockets of all the belongings we were carrying.[26] After each person put their belongings on the table, they went through them. They took our wallet and they took the money they wanted. One of the people I was with had plenty of money. They took five hundred from him and they threatened him.[27] They told him they were part of the mafia and if he tried to report them, they were going to kill him. It was like that, a bunch of thefts like that. From me they only took thirty bucks because it was all I had.[28]

There was also a woman from the PGR who came and took charge of inspecting the women.[29] There were twelve women. She made them get in line and she frisked them, touching their bodies. After that they took the women one by one and put them in a truck, a blue Cherokee without license plates. They questioned them. With one set of them, they took funds away and got verbally aggressive.

There were three people from Central America on the bus. They had to pay six hundred each to be let through. They wanted to get through, so they paid it. They were threatened with having Immigration called on them if they didn't pay it.

The bus driver got off and spoke to the PGR. He told them his vehicle had been there for two hours so far and was still being checked and the owner was asking why it had been held up for two hours. So then they told us to get on, and they started leaving. But before that, well, I'm someone who's familiar with my constitutionally guaranteed rights, and I chose to stand up for myself by articulating what it says in some parts of the Constitution, like in Article 11, Article 14, and Article 16.[30] Those are some of my constitutional rights. When I did that, they only got aggressive with me and said I was an activist and if I didn't shut my mouth, they were going to take me off the bus and they were going to leave me there.[31] I told them they didn't have any right to violate constitutional guarantees, and they started insinuating that I wasn't Mexican, that I was from Central America. Despite the fact that I presented my driver's license and voter ID.[32] And they kept trying to grab it out of my hand. One of them got annoyed and shoved me onto the bus, ordering me to shut my mouth and he didn't want to see me or hear from me again. With every bus that comes from Chiapas, this is how they behave, because they figure there's Central Americans on board, and with Central Americans, the way they conduct themselves is like they didn't have any rights at all.

8

Mexico as the New Southern US Border

Introduced by Marla Conrad and Jorge A. Andrade Galindo

The US southern border has expanded south of the Rio Grande. This new, thick border stretches southward along the expanse of Mexico's territory. It lies along the Suchiate and Usumacinta Rivers, where it is conterminous with the border between Mexico and Guatemala. The physical fence on the US-Mexico boundary may provide a feeling of safety to some who are inside and signal to those outside that they are not welcome. But there are other fences, walls, borders, and buffers created through a combination of anti-immigrant threats and actions—authorized or unauthorized practices by US and Mexican government officials, harms by organized crime groups, and everyday exploitation—that are even more effective for keeping migrants away.[1] The new southern US border shows itself through the detentions at truck stops and tollbooth stations in Mexico and at the international bridges between the United States and Mexico. Here, violence and the threat of violence force migrants to take riskier routes to the United States. Enforcement of the new southern border has been strengthened by collusion between Mexican police as well as immigration and military officers and drug-trafficking cartels that target migrants for robberies, assaults, kidnappings, trafficking, and extortion. In addition, closed-door immigration policies such as safe-third-country agreements and the so-called Migrant Protection Protocols—explained in chapter 11—that force people to remain in Mexico make the new southern US border more impenetrable than any brick-and-mortar US-Mexico border wall.[2]

The southern expansion of the new border between the United States and Mexico has been achieved with the collaboration of the Mexican government. Mexican migratory policy hit a nadir in July 2014, when a decree created the *Coordinación para la Atención Integral de la Migración en la Frontera Sur* (Coordinating Mechanism for Comprehensive Attention to Migration at the Southern Border), better known as *Programa Frontera Sur* (Southern Border Program, or PFS in Spanish). This decree led to an increased number of operatives from the *Instituto Nacional de Migración* (INM) and of municipal, state, and federal police officers in order to detain Central American and other migrants entering Mexican territory. The detention of migrants increased considerably once PFS was implemented, as shown in the following data:[3]

Year	Detentions
2014	102,887
2015	158,644
2016	145,369
2017	95,497
2018	131,931

The figures are undeniable. Mexican migration policy consists of detaining every person who enters the country clandestinely in order to get to the United States. While these detentions are indeed alarming, the cruelty extends to the migrant detention centers where people are taken if detained by the INM or other agencies.[4] People taken to these places face overcrowding, unsanitary conditions, vulnerability, and sometimes even torture—both physical and psychological—by immigration agents.

In this context of increased security concerns, whereby migration is treated as a matter of national security, it becomes essential to ask: How are borders, such as the southern US border, being created? And what is the role of supposed liberal democratic states, such as the United States and Mexico, in enacting violent border policing? Throughout the years the very concept "border" has changed for those that live it every day.

The thickening and southward projection of the US border can be understood in six stages. First, Immigration and Control Act negotiations of 1986 regularized about three million unauthorized migrants and ramped up "security," or militarized immigration policing, on the US-Mexico border. Second, several "security operations" (discussed in chapter 6) implemented in the 1990s to dissuade migrants from crossing into the United States actually had the effect of pushing migration routes out of urban areas to dangerous, deserted places.[5] Third, in the wake of the 2001 attack on the

View of the Patagonia Mountains, to the west of Nogales. Avery Ellfeldt.

Twin Towers, the INS was transferred to the US Department of Homeland Security (DHS), and the border with Mexico simultaneously became a focus of anti-terrorism and anti-immigration efforts. Fourth, the increased visibility of violence in Central America that pushed thousands of unaccompanied minors in 2014, and entire families in 2018, to flee the misery in their countries has led to the hardening of the border and of US asylum policy.

As the US government has directly enacted the first four stages, it has influenced the emergence of others. The hardening of US-Mexico border enforcement has given rise to a fifth stage: harsh human smuggling regimes. As the United States doubles down on its southwest border, organized crime groups fine-tune tactics and strategies to subvert border enforcement. Militarization incentivizes sophisticated criminal action, since migrants can no longer navigate the border on their own, and makes the smuggling business more lucrative. Mexico's northern border is now controlled by organized crime, and the prices for crossing are skyrocketing. A migrant pays a smuggler, or *coyote*, who charges between US$4,000 and US$12,000, in addition to a fee (US$300–US$3,000) to whichever criminal organization controls

A family migrates together. José Luis Cabrera Sotero.

the area. These groups have their own security service that functions similarly to a border patrol; these are people who are hired to surveil the border and ensure nobody goes through without authorization. If someone has not paid the fee, they risk being seen, beaten, tortured, kidnapped, and killed. These tactics all occur in the service of controlling passage, supervising drug trafficking, and making the largest profit possible. The brutality of organized crime's control of human smuggling in Mexico acts as a further southward projection of the US border.

The sixth stage is Mexican government policies and actions, such as those from 2014 mentioned above. These include other officially sanctioned strict enforcement and extraofficial abuses of power. The risk of detention by the INM, in addition to the high costs of being smuggled through Mexico and the difficulty and dangers of the road, has dissuaded migration and increased migrant suffering.[6] Corrupt police who normally profit from the smuggling of vulnerable migrants have to come up with other schemes to make money through deception. Migrants become the victims of serious crimes and of human rights violations. Jorge is an example of someone in this situation, as he was kidnapped by federal police:

> I was held for ransom for a month. They warned us that if we left the house, there were people outside watching, and they would kill us. They didn't bring us very much food and water, and they didn't feed us every day, and when they did feed us, it was only once a day and a really small amount of food. A lot of us were beaten with planks. The people they beat the most were the ones who had cell phones or who they knew had relatives in the US. The police officers had some people who were in charge of things from day to day, and they came every so often to ask how the thing was going and find out who had given up phone numbers.
>
> Every day they threatened me and demanded that I give them some US phone numbers, because I had a five-thousand-dollar ransom to pay and that was the only way they were letting me leave.

In Mexico there are no consequences when government actors or members of organized crime groups trample human rights and dignity. Few migrants want to report the crimes committed against them. Many have difficulty identifying the location and identity of their abusers. They are mistrustful of authorities, they are afraid of retaliation, and they happen to find themselves at the epicenter of criminal activity. They do not have support structures they can rely on to file complaints and follow up on them. When they do work up the will to make a complaint, they are going up against authorities who are indifferent to injustice, and who revictimize them by looking for excuses and justifications to not investigate crimes. For example, between 2014 and 2016 federal police received 5,824 complaints from migrants in Chiapas, Oaxaca, Tabasco, Sonora, and Coahuila. There were only forty-nine convictions, which suggests that 99 percent of crimes reported by migrants are met with impunity.[7] This high rate would not be possible without the collusion of public institutions and government officials, who have allowed organized crime to take over the territory in order to run its business. Impunity for those who victimize migrants reflects the efficacy of the extended southern US border.

The fencing that stretches along the border on the boundary that divides Mexico and the United States is an expensive symbol of division. But it is one of many barriers—some visible, some not—that migrants face on their journey and that extend southward throughout Mexico, comprising the new southern US border. That this border projects this far has been observed by

US government officials themselves. In a 2012 speech, the assistant secretary of homeland security and former so-called border czar, Alan Bersin, stated plainly: "The Guatemalan border with Chiapas is now our southern border."[8] In this chapter, five migrants narrate their interactions with government authorities and organized crime and shed light on the difficulties of coming face-to-face with the new southern US border.

RIGOBERTO

Soy Rigoberto Acosta Arriaga, hondureño de Santa Rita. Tengo treinta años de edad y tres hijos. Vengo por necesidad de trabajar, para dar educación y sustento a mis hijos. Viajé en el tren pagando una cuota que me cobraban las mafias. En general he venido con pánico por todos los riesgos que se viven en el tren. Soy deportado. Mi esposa y mi niño están en Phoenix.

En Tierra Blanca, Veracruz, tomé el tren para Orizaba, Veracruz. Allí encontramos dos individuos que cobran renta por subir al tren, pero resultó que eran de los Zetas. Nos asaltaron. Dijeron: "Somos los que cobramos cuota y nos tienen que pagar cien dólares". Como no teníamos, querían llevarnos secuestrados para pedir a nuestra familia que vive en Estados Unidos. Éramos cinco los detenidos. Cambiaron de opinión y dijeron: "Váyanse, vamos a esperar al otro grupo". Ya nos habían quitado todo lo que traíamos. Al fin dijeron: "Les vamos a hacer el paro, no los vamos a secuestrar". Uno quería el secuestro, el otro no. Nos dejaron.

Fuimos para Apizaco. Llegamos a la casa del migrante y estuvimos tres días allí. Volvimos a agarrar el tren para venir a Lechería, Estado de México. Bajamos y tomamos una combi para Huehuetoca. Allí estuvimos queriendo tomar el tren. Pero por ahí pasa muy rápido. No podíamos tomarlo. Después, mejor agarramos una combi para Bojay y llegamos a una casa del migrante, pero estaba cerrada. Entonces, yo y mi amigo fuimos para la tienda a comprar alimentos. Cuando íbamos caminando hacia la tienda, encontramos al Instituto Nacional de Migración. Nos vieron y se pararon para agarrarnos. Corrimos por un lugar desierto. Nos siguieron como una hora. Más tarde, fuimos a buscar nuestras pertenencias. No estaban. Las habíamos dejado al lado de las vías. Nos fuimos caminando como un kilómetro adelante para agarrar el tren, porque andábamos huyendo de la Migración mexicana. Nos metimos en un maizal para escondernos.

Como en media hora, llegaron un grupo mentado, los Zetas, a pedir supuestamente la cuota para poder agarrar el tren. Luego llamaron a mis familiares. A todo el grupo le pidieron el teléfono, teníamos que darlo porque si no, siguen otros problemas. Ellos nos obligan a llamar para pedir la cuota, cien dólares, y luego le llamaron a mi esposa que necesitaban los cien dólares para dejarme libre. Nos tuvieron dos días en un arroyo sin comida ni agua. Era castigo para que diéramos el número y pudieran llamar. Ellos eran ocho. Ahí estaban cuidándonos. Ellos sí comían. Luego a mí me separaron porque no había pagado la cuota. Me llevaron para atrás, a Huehuetoca, con un grupo de alcohólicos y drogadictos que, supuestamente, no tienen licencia para tener ese centro. Ahí dijo el muchacho: "¿No quieres pagar? Ahorita yo le mando un video a tu mujer para cobrar mil dólares". Me iban a golpear y mandarle el video. Entonces yo dije que sí voy a cooperar. Me metieron al cuartito donde estaban todos los drogadictos. Eran como treinta. Y ellos empezaron a llamar a mi mujer y la mujer encargada de hacer llamadas le pidió ochocientos dólares. Como mi familia no mandaba nada, dijo que ya era mil quinientos dólares. Mi familia reunió los mil quinientos dólares. Como ya mi familia y yo entramos en pánico, tuvo que enviar los mil quinientos dólares. Yo no sabía que estaban pidiendo todo ese dinero, porque ella hablaba sin avisarme. Yo no sabía nada. Después, el grupo pidió quinientos dólares más. Mi familia se los mandó.

Me enviaron para Nuevo Laredo, Tamaulipas, con el grupo de los Zetas, para seguirme extorsionando. Como yo les decía que no conocía, entonces me enviaron con uno de los miembros de ellos que me venía cuidando. Nos venimos a Puebla. Después tomamos otro camión para Celaya. El que me cuidaba y yo fuimos a preguntar la hora de salida del camión para Nuevo Laredo. Entonces le dijeron que salía a las 5:30. Faltaba hora y media para salir el camión. Fuimos a comer y en una chanzá en que íbamos al mercado, yo agarré tiempo para escaparme. Me les fui corriendo. Él me seguía, pero no me encontraba porque había mucha gente. Me fui corriendo, hice llamada a mi esposa de que ya no enviara dinero, porque yo ya me había escapado.

Y me fui con un amigo a un pueblito que se llama Malpasito. Me estuve ahí una semana con él, porque yo iba con gran pánico. Vivíamos en un cuartito como veintidós. Ahora si alguien me habla, yo tengo los nervios de punta. Todo me da miedo. Apenas me estoy recuperando. Una semana estuve ahí encerrado.

‖‖‖‖‖‖‖‖‖‖‖

I'm Rigoberto Acosta Arriaga, from Honduras, from a place called Santa Rita. I'm thirty years old and I have three kids. I've come north because I need to work in order to educate and feed my kids. I traveled by train by paying the tolls that the different mafias charged me. I've generally been in a state of panic because of all the dangers you experience on the train. I'm a deportee. My wife and my baby are in Phoenix.

In Tierra Blanca, Veracruz, I took the train to Orizaba. We ran into two individuals there; they were collecting *renta* to get on the train, but it turned out they were with the Zetas Cartel.[9] They held us up. They said, "We're the guys who collect the toll, and you have to pay us a hundred dollars." We didn't have it, so they wanted to take us away, kidnap us, so they could ask our families in the US for money. There were five of us they'd stopped. They changed their mind and said, "Leave, we're going to wait for the next group." They had already taken away everything we had, but in the end they said, "We're going to help you guys out. We're not going to kidnap you." One of them wanted to do the kidnapping and the other didn't. They let us be.

We headed to Apizaco. We got to the migrant center, and we spent three days there. We caught the train again to get to Lechería in Mexico State. We got off and took a shuttle bus to Huehuetoca. We stayed there intending to get on the train. But it goes by really fast there, we couldn't get on. After that we caught a shuttle bus to Bojay instead. We got to a migrant center, but it was closed. So, me and my friend headed to the store to buy food. We were walking toward the store when we ran into the National Migration Department. They saw us and stopped to grab us. We ran through a desert area. They followed us for about an hour. Later, we went and looked for our belongings, but they weren't there. We had left them by the train tracks. We left town on foot, walked about a half a mile out to catch the train, because now we were running away from Mexican Immigration. We ducked into a cornfield to stay hidden.

About a half an hour later, a well-known group arrived, the Zetas, supposedly just to ask for the toll to catch the train. Then they called my relatives. They asked all of us for a phone number, and we had to give it up because if you don't, other problems follow.[10] They made us call and ask for the toll, a hundred dollars. Later they called my wife and told her they needed that hundred dollars to let me go free. They kept us for two days in a ditch without food or water. It was punishment so we'd give up the number and they could call. There were eight of them. They were there guarding us. They did eat. Later they separated me from the others because I hadn't paid the toll. They took me backward, to Huehuetoca, to a home for alcoholics and drug addicts. Supposedly they don't have a license to operate that center. The guy said to me, "You don't want to pay? I'll send a video to your wife right now and collect a thousand." They were going to beat me up and send her the video. So I said yes, I'll cooperate. They put me in the little room where all the drug addicts were; there were about thirty of them. And they started calling my wife, and the woman in charge of making calls asked her for eight hundred dollars. When my family hadn't sent anything, she said that now it was fifteen hundred. My family got the fifteen hundred together.

Both my family and I had gone into a state of panic by now, so they had to send the fifteen hundred. After that—I didn't know they were asking for all that money, because she was calling without telling me. I didn't know anything. After that, the group asked for five hundred more. My family sent it.

They sent me to Nuevo Laredo, Tamaulipas, to stay with the Zetas group there, so they could keep extorting me. I had told them I didn't know the area, so they sent along one of their members who had been guarding me before. We got to Puebla. After that we took another bus to Celaya. In Celaya, the guy who was guarding me took me with him to the counter and we asked what time the bus for Nuevo Laredo left. So they told him it was leaving at 5:30. There was an hour and a half before it left. We went to eat, and when there was a good moment, while we were going to the market, I grabbed the chance to get away. I took off running, away from them. He followed me for a while, but he couldn't find me because there were a lot of people. I took off running, called my wife, told her not to send any more money because I had already gotten away.

And I went with a friend to a little town called Malpasito. I stayed there for a week with him, because I was still in a huge panic. There were about twenty-two of us living in a little room. Now, if someone speaks to me, I'm on edge and irritable. Everything scares me. I'm just barely recovering now. I spent a week there in that little room.

JORGE

Salí de mi casa en Honduras el cuatro de marzo de 2015. Salí el veintidós de abril con la idea de ir a los Estados Unidos. Viajé un día y media hasta La Técnica, la cual es la frontera de Guatemala con México. De allí caminé una semana y media hasta Tenosique. Estuve un mes en la casa de migrante, esperando que pasara el tren. Fuimos de Tenosique en tren y nos paramos en diferentes lugares. Estuvimos aproximadamente veintiocho días en el camino cuando llegamos a Apizaco, Tlaxcala, que fue aproximadamente el veintiocho de junio de 2015, aproximadamente a la una de la mañana.

En Apizaco, pararon el tren nueve o más policías federales, con uniforme negro. Llevaban una chamarra con estrella en la frente y que decía "Policía Federal" en la parte de atrás. También llevaban armas largas y una pistola que llevaban en las piernas. Nos dijeron que nos bajáramos del tren, porque no podíamos ir en el que íbamos, porque llevaba químicas, y que nos iban a decir en cuál tren podíamos subir. Éramos aproximadamente diez personas. Había mucha siembra de maíz donde nos pararon, en los dos lados de las vías. Las patrullas eran carros, y habían unas cuatro patrullas.

Nos subieron a las patrullas diciéndonos que nos iban a llevar hasta donde podíamos subir al tren. Sin embargo, nos llevaron a una casa de cuatro cuartos, una sala y un baño, que está a la orilla de las vías. Estaba pintada de rosa y blanca y los balcones eran negros. Las casas en este pueblo tienen mucho terreno y esta casa tenía un campo de maíz en la parte de atrás.

Entramos a la casa y vimos unas seis personas tiradas en el piso. Los policías llevaron a las otras personas a uno de los cuartos y nos preguntaron si teníamos familia en los Estados Unidos. Nos revisaron toda la ropa, hasta que nos desnudaron. Nos quitaron nuestro dinero, y a los que tenían celular, también se lo quitaron. A mi me quitaron 130 pesos. A las personas que tenían números de personas en los Estados Unidos, los separaban. Estuve secuestrado un mes y nos amenazaron que si saliéramos, que había personas afuera vigilando la casa y que nos matarían. Nos llevaban poca comida y agua, y no nos daban de comer todos los días y cuando nos daban de comer, solo era una vez al día y muy poca comida. A muchos los golpeaban con tablas y más golpeaban a las personas que tenían celulares y que sabían que tenían familiares en los Estados Unidos. Los policías tenían a otros que estaban encargados y venían de vez en cuando para preguntar cómo iba el asunto y saber quién había dado números.

Todos los días me amenazaron, exigiendo que les diera números de teléfono en los Estados Unidos porque tenía que pagar cinco mil dólares para mi rescate, y que solo así me iban a dejar salir. Les decía que no conocía a nadie en los Estados Unidos, pero no me creían. Había unas cinco personas, las que estaban encargadas de cuidar el lugar y estaban a las órdenes de las policías. Después de un mes de estar secuestrado, logramos escaparnos varios, cuando salieron los que nos vigilaban. Pusieron llave desde afuera, pero logramos tumbar la puerta para escaparnos. Corrimos una hora y después logramos agarrar un tren ese mismo día.

||||||||||||||||||

I left my house in Honduras on March fourth, 2015. On April the twenty-second, I left to go to the United States. I traveled for a day and a half and got to La Técnica, which is the border between Guatemala and Mexico. From there I walked for a week and a half and got to Tenosique. I stayed at the migrant house for a month, waiting for the train. From Tenosique we went by train and stopped in different places. After about twenty-eight days on the road, we got to Apizaco, Tlaxcala. This was on about June twenty-eighth, 2015, at about one o'clock in the morning.

In Apizaco, the train was stopped by federal police, at least nine of them, in black uniforms, and they had a jacket on with a star on the front and "Federal Police" on the back. They were also carrying rifles, plus a pistol, which was on their thighs. They told us to get off the train because we couldn't ride on the one we were riding on because it was carrying chemicals, and they'd tell us which train we could get on. There were about ten of us. There were a lot of cornfields in the place where they stopped us, both sides of the tracks. The police vehicles were cars. There were four of them or so. They got us into the police cars by telling us they were going to take us to where we could get on the train. However, they took us to a house. This house has four bedrooms, a living room, and a bathroom and is on the side of the railroad tracks. It was painted pink and white and the balconies were black. The houses in this town are on big lots, and this house had a cornfield behind it.

We went in the house and saw six or so people on the floor. The police officers took these other people in one of the rooms and asked us if we had family in the United States. They went through all our clothes, strip searched us in fact. They took away our money, and they also took away people's cell phones if they had one. From me they took eight dollars.[11] They started separating out people who had phone numbers of people in the US. I was held for ransom for a month. They warned us that if we left the house, there were people outside watching, and they would kill us. They didn't bring us very much food and water, and they didn't feed us every day, and when they did feed us, it was only once a day and a really small amount of food. A lot of us were beaten with planks. The people they beat the most were the ones who had cell phones or who they knew had relatives in the US. The police officers had some people who were in charge of things from day to day, and they came every so often to ask how the thing was going and find out who had given up phone numbers.

Every day they threatened me and demanded that I give them some US phone numbers, because I had a five-thousand-dollar ransom to pay and that was the only way they were letting me leave. I kept telling them I didn't know anyone in the US, but they never believed me. There were five or six people who were responsible for taking care of the place and who took orders from the police officers. After a month of being held for ransom, a bunch of us managed to escape when the people who kept an eye on us went out. They locked the door from the outside, but we managed to break it down so we could escape. We ran for an hour, and later the same day we managed to catch a train.

IVÁN

Subí el tren de Ferromex en Irapuato, Guanajuato, e iba rumbo a Guadalajara. Saliendo de la estación, corrimos aproximadamente dos millas y allí es

donde me balearon. El tren se puso más despacio para que los oficiales che-
caran el tren. Primero vi dos camionetas, color azul con gris, que las alum-
braba los toletes. El tren iba debajo de un puente y vi una persona con un
farol en una mano y una pistola en la otra mano. Me comenzó a disparar.
Fueron tres tiros. Un tiro se rebotó en el fierro donde estaba sentado, otro lo
sentí rozar la cabeza y otro me pegó en la pantorrilla. A veinte minutos de
donde me balearon, me bajé, y allí había gente que me ayudó y llamaron a
la ambulancia. Había perdido mucha sangre. Fui al hospital en La Piedad,
Michoacán. Allí me atendieron, el doctor me curó y me sacaron. Me dirigí al
albergue donde había estado en Irapuato. Viajé en un camión. Llegando a la
casa de migrante, me atendieron y me llevaron al hospital, donde me dieron
una receta. Estuve en la casa de migrante por ocho días y seguí mi camino.

|||||||||||||||||

I got on the Ferromex train in Irapuato, Guanajuato, heading toward Guadalajara.[12] We pulled out of the station and covered about two miles and that's
where I was shot. The train slowed down so the officers could check the
train. First I saw two trucks. They were blue with some gray; the nightsticks
lit them up.[13] The train started going under a bridge, and I saw someone
with a lantern in one hand and a pistol in the other. He started firing at me;
there were three shots. One shot bounced off the metal where I was sitting,
another one I felt graze my head, and another one hit me in the calf. Twenty
minutes down the road from where I was shot, I got off. There were people
there who helped me and called the ambulance. I'd lost a lot of blood.
I went to the hospital in La Piedad, Michoacán. They took care of me there,
the doctor treated me, and they released me. I headed back to the shelter
where I'd stayed in Irapuato. I went by bus. When I got to the migrant house,
they took care of me and took me to the hospital. I got a prescription there.
I stayed at the migrant house for eight days and then continued on my way.

MÁYNOR

Mi nombre es Máynor. Soy de San Pedro Sula. Las cosas están muy duras allá.
No hay empleo y, si pones un negocito, las bandas te cobran cada semana
para que puedas vender. Mi esposa y yo salimos para irnos a Estados Unidos.
Sabíamos que el camino es difícil y más porque mi primo fue uno de los
que mataron en San Fernando. Cruzamos por Tecún Umán hacia Tapachula.
Como no traíamos dinero, decidimos viajar en tren. Pasamos caminando
tres días para poder tomar el tren. En el que nos subimos iba mucha gente.
En Veracruz, no recuerdo el nombre del lugar, unos maleantes, que iban

entre los migrantes, comenzaron a pedir dinero a toda la gente; se escuchaban gritos de hombres y mujeres. Cuando llegaron a donde yo estaba, me pidieron cien dólares para poder seguir viajando. Nosotros teníamos que dar doscientos, porque mi esposa también tenía que pagar. Les dijimos que no traíamos, entonces que agarran a mi esposa y la avientan a las vías del tren. A mí también me aventaron, pero yo caí a un lado. Me quedé desmayado por un tiempo y, cuando desperté, vi a mi esposa destrozada por el tren. A lo lejos me di cuenta que estaba una camioneta de policías. Como pude me paré y fui a decirles lo que había pasado. Sus uniformes eran negros y decían Policía Federal y les conté lo que había pasado y los llevé al lugar donde estaba mi esposa. Entonces me comenzaron a pegar. Sólo me acuerdo que vi cómo recogían los pedazos de cuerpo de mi esposa, los metían en una bolsa y los subían a la patrulla. Ahí me quedé tirado por varias horas. Me subí a otro tren y estoy aquí. Tengo que seguir mi viaje, porque dejamos a nuestros dos hijos pequeños (una niña de cuatro años y un niño de dos) con mi suegra. Tengo que llegar para juntar dinero para poderlo mandar y que ellos estén bien. No les puedo avisar lo que pasó, porque mi suegra tiene diabetes y se vaya a enfermar y ella es la que cuida de nuestros hijos.

||||||||||||||||||

My name is Máynor and I'm from San Pedro Sula. Things are really rough there. No one is hiring, and if you start a business of your own the gangs charge you every week, for you to be able to sell stuff. My wife and I left to go to the United States. We knew it was a difficult trip, especially because a cousin of mine was one of the people who were killed in San Fernando.[14] We crossed through Tecún Umán toward Tapachula. We didn't have any money, so we decided to make the trip by train. We spent three days walking to be able to catch the train. The one we got on had a lot of people riding on it. In Veracruz—I don't remember what the exact place was called—these crooks who were riding amongst us migrants started asking everyone for money. You could hear people yelling, regular people. When they got to where I was, they asked me for a hundred dollars to be able to continue the trip. We would have to pay two hundred, since my wife would also have to pay. We told them we didn't have it. So then they actually grab my wife and throw her onto the railroad tracks. They threw me off too, but I fell to one side. I was passed out for a while, and when I woke up, I saw my wife all torn up by the train. In the distance, I noticed there was a police truck. As best I could, I stood up and went to tell them what had happened. Their uniforms were black and said "Federal Police," and I explained what had happened and took them to the place where my wife was. So then they started to smack me. All I remember is seeing how they were picking up my wife's body parts, putting them in a bag, and putting them in the truck. I stayed there, by myself, for a long time. I got on another train and I'm here. I have to keep going, because we left our two small children (a four-year-old girl and a two-year-old boy) with my mother-in-law. I have to get where I'm going so I can save up money, to be able to send it so they'll be all right. I can't tell her what happened. See, my mother-in-law has diabetes. She'd get ill, and she's the one who looks after our children.

CRISTÓBAL

Llegué el treinta de octubre de 2015 a Nogales, Sonora, viajando en tren. Después de unos días ahí, me fui a Grupo Beta a pasar el día, después de comer en Iniciativa Kino. Durante el trayecto, un pickup color beige llegó a la cancha de básquet que está cerca a las oficinas de Grupo Beta. Atrás llevaba una máquina de soldar, un soplete y una prensa. Era una troca de trabajo. No puse atención si llevaba placas. Sólo llegó y preguntó quién era soldador y yo me ofrecí porque soy soldador y me subí con toda confianza, porque vi toda la maquinaria atrás.

En ese pickup sólo iba la persona que la manejaba. Era un hombre alto, moreno, delgado, cabello oscuro y un poco largo de atrás, porque parecía que traía el cabello largo. Vestía con pantalón de mezclilla azul y camisa a cuadros entre azul y negro y una chamarra café como destruida de las mangas, como si fuera un trabajador. Salió de ahí, de la cancha, y tomó el bulevar Colosio hacia el sur, para salir después por completo de Nogales. Fueron como veinticinco o treinta minutos de trayecto. Salimos de la ciudad, después se detuvo sobre la carretera y había puro mezquite alrededor, seguían pasando tráilers y autobuses.

El hombre se bajó y me dijo: "Ven, vamos a cambiar de carro". Atrás se había estacionado una camioneta cerrada, de color negro con vidrios oscuros. El hombre del pickup beige me tomó de la mano y me llevó hacia la camioneta negra. El acompañante del chofer de la camioneta se bajó con la cara cubierta con un pasamontañas. Era alto y robusto y tenía un arma corta; me amenazó con ella diciéndome: "Súbete a la troca, que ya te cargó la chingada." Así que me tuve que subir y ahí adentro estaban cuatro personas más con la cara cubierta; me dijeron: "Súbete, no vas a mirar ni suspirar. No hables, porque ya te cargó la chingada". Iniciaron el camino, como cincuenta minutos o una hora. Llegamos a un lugar que parecería un rancho. Había mezquite y bellotas alrededor. Había ganado alrededor. Había vacas y caballos, había un papalote para sacar agua, de esos que tienen como un ventilador arriba que, cuando hay aire, puede sacar agua. Y alcancé a ver unos cerros que estaban cerca.

Cuando llegamos al lugar, me bajaron del carro negro con la cabeza agachada. Creo que era una casa, no pude ver bien, pero afuera había dos personas encapuchadas, paradas y cuidando. Me metieron y había cuatro personas. Por su aspecto parecían ser como de Oaxaca o Chiapas, no se veían maltratados, quizá acababan de llegar. Me tuvieron ahí con ellos los tres primeros días, era un cuarto con paredes de ladrillo rojo y losa. A los cinco nos cuidaban dos personas adentro, también encapuchadas. Ellos me dijeron que no podía hablar con nadie, también me amarraron de pies y de manos con una piola.

Desde que llegué, esos dos hombres me pidieron números de teléfono para poder salir de ahí, que tenía que conseguir seis mil dólares. Querían los números de teléfono, porque ellos harían todo, que si daba los números no me iba a pasar nada, nada de lesiones ni nada, porque me pedían números de teléfono gabacho. Yo les decía que soy analfabeto, que no tengo a nadie allá. Siempre pensé que era lo último que iba a vivir yo, pensé que ya no viviría. Esos dos hombres que nos cuidaban casi no se hablaban, se comunicaban con señas y siempre traían como una regla, como de cuatro pulgadas de ancho y una pulgada de gruesa. Le llamaban la amansalocos; si volteaba a ver a alguien me golpeaban con ella en la espalda. Desde el primer día me golpearon con el amansalocos. Me pedían el número de teléfono y al decir que no lo sabía me golpeaban. Después entre ellos se decían: "Déjalo un rato para que se acuerde de los números". Después volvían a preguntarme y yo con la misma respuesta y empezaban a pegarme nuevamente estando hincado. Me dejaban otro rato, diciendo: "A lo mejor está nervioso, déjalo". Pero a cada rato volvían a golpearme.

Pasaron tres días y me metieron a mí solo a otro cuarto y me siguieron pidiendo seis mil dólares para poder irme y yo les dije que no tenía dinero y que venía a trabajar a Nogales y que no tenía nada. Me pidieron número de teléfono: "Yo no sé cómo le vas a hacer, pero vas a buscar seis mil dólares y nos darás un número de teléfono". Yo insistí que no tenía un número. Así que me golpeaban y me golpeaban con el amansalocos en la espalda, en las piernas y en los brazos. Esto era cada vez que ellos querían, varias veces al día y todos los días. Después de quince días me empezaron a forzar el brazo izquierdo hacia atrás, me lo doblaban hacia la espalda para provocarme dolor. Después de tanto forzarme, me lo lastimaron y más me hacían daño ahí, porque sabían que era más dolor. Me golpeaban feo. Se fueron cansando y hasta dijeron que iban a hacer más feria conmigo, vendiéndome en pedazos. Yo les decía que no iba a Estados Unidos, que me quedaría en México, pero ellos no creían nada de lo que yo decía.

Desde que llegué, me daban de comer frijoles pintos y arroz blanco sin tortilla, una vez al día o cada dos días. También me daban agua en latas como de chiles jalapeños. El que estaba cuidando era quien me llevaba la comida a ese cuarto, que no tenía ventanas. No había baño adentro, así que orinaba en botellas Coca-Cola de dos o tres litros que me daban, si hacía del dos me daban bolsas que después ellos sacaban. Tenía una colchoneta para dormir sobre el piso rústico y una cobija, porque hacía mucho frío. El cuarto ése sólo tenía una puerta negra de metal, que se abría únicamente por afuera. No vi la luz del sol en todo el tiempo que estuve encerrado, sólo alcanzaba a ver la claridad del día, por eso podía distinguir el día y la noche.

Logré escapar la madrugada del miércoles veintiocho de diciembre. Esa madrugada yo escuché mujeres, música y personas que estaban tomando ahí. La noche anterior me llevaron la comida muy tarde; no sé si ellos se descuidaron en su borrachera, pero la puerta quedó abierta y yo no me había dado cuenta hasta que el viento la movió, así que pude salir cuando estaba amaneciendo; aún estaba oscuro. Pude ver a varias personas, quizá seis, incluyendo mujeres, como dos o tres. Todos estaban afuera, cerca del corral de vacas. Tenían una fogata y estaban tomando. Yo salí y no me entretuve a verles. Creo que ellos no me vieron cuando me salí, así que corrí y corrí como unas dos horas, entre caminando y corriendo, tratando de alejarme lo más que pudiera. El terreno no era plano, subí y bajé unas lomitas, pasé como un arroyito. El sol salía a mi lado derecho, llegué hasta chocar con la línea de los Estados Unidos. Me metí a los Estados Unidos como unos doscientos metros, me quedé ahí como tres horas viendo si no venían atrás de mí. Después me salí y me encontré a un hombre que parece llevaba gente para el otro lado, como a nueve personas con mochila. Yo le dije que me ayudara a ubicarme y llegar a la ciudad, que me había lastimado en el Gabacho y el coyote me había abandonado. Ese hombre me dijo dónde estaban las vías del tren y qué rumbo tenía que tomar para llegar a Nogales, porque me dijo que detrás de unas montañas estaba Cananea.

Entonces opté por irme a Nogales, de ese lugar fui hacia la derecha y caminé como tres horas. El terreno tampoco era plano y también tuve que subir y bajar lomas, crucé una brecha y llegué a las vías del tren. Ahí estuve tres días esperando a que pasara el tren. Y pasó el domingo en la mañana y me pude subir porque pasó bien quedito y pude llegar a Nogales como a mediodía. Después, me fui a Grupo Beta para hacer una llamada a El Salvador. Más tarde me fui al comedor de Iniciativa Kino para buscar a la licenciada que me ayudara, pero la pude ver hasta el día siguiente y me mandaron para Agua Prieta, para poder estar en la casa del migrante. Aquí me atendieron en el Hospital General por el dolor en mi brazo. El doctor me sobó y me vendó, también me dio cremas. Me dijo que si tenía un cono-cido que sobara, que fuera, porque mi brazo está dislocado.

IIIIIIIIIIIIIIIIII

I got to Nogales, Sonora, on October the thirtieth, 2015.[15] I made the trip by train. After a few days there, I went to spend the day at *Grupo Beta* after eat-ing at Kino Border Initiative.[16] Along the way there, a beige-colored pickup showed up at the basketball court that's close to the *Grupo Beta* building. In back it was carrying a welding machine, a torch, and a press.[17] It was a work truck. I didn't notice if it had license plates or not. Just showed up and asked if anyone was a welder, and I stepped forward because I am a welder, and I got in with no reservations because I could see all the equipment in the back.

The only person in the pickup was the driver.[18] He was a tall, dark-skinned, slender man with dark hair that was a little long in the back, because it looked like he had long hair. He was dressed in blue jeans and a checked shirt, either dark blue or black, and a brown jacket with the sleeves all torn up. Like a worker. He pulled out from there, from the basketball court, and took Bulevar Colosio south, all the way out of Nogales eventu-ally. It took about twenty-five or thirty minutes; we left the city; after a while he stopped on the highway; there was nothing but mesquite all around.[19] There were still semis and buses going by.

The man got out and said to me, "Come on, we're gonna change vehi-cles." There was an SUV that had parked behind us, it was black with tinted windows.[20] The man from the beige pickup took me by the wrist and walked me toward the black SUV. A man got out of the passenger side of the SUV with his face covered with a ski mask. He was tall and sturdy looking, and he was holding a handgun, which he threatened me with. He said, "Get in the truck, you're fucked now." So I had to get in, and there inside, there were four more people with their faces covered, and they said, "Get in, and you ain't gonna be looking at the scenery and moaning. Don't talk. 'Cause you're fucked now." They got going, it took maybe fifty minutes or an hour and we got to a place; it looked like maybe a ranch. There were mesquite and acorn trees all around, there were cattle all around, there were cows and horses.[21] There was a windmill to draw water, one of those with a fan at the top that can draw water when there's wind. And I could just see some hills nearby.

When we got there, they took me out of the black truck with my head bent down. I think the place was a house, I couldn't see well enough to tell, but outside there were two people with their heads covered, standing guard.

They took me inside, and there were four people there who looked like they were maybe from Oaxaca or Chiapas. They didn't look like they'd been mistreated. Maybe they'd just arrived. I was kept there with them for the first three days. It was a room with brick walls and slab flooring. The five of us were guarded inside the house by two people, who had their heads covered too. They told me I couldn't talk to anyone. They also tied my hands and feet with cord.

From the day I got there, these two men asked me for phone numbers to be able to leave there. They told me I had to get a hold of six thousand dollars, and they wanted the phone numbers because they'd take care of the whole thing. Said if I gave them the numbers nothing was going to happen to me, no injuries or anything. Because it was *gabacho* phone numbers they were asking me for.[22] I kept telling them, I'm illiterate and I don't have anyone there. Every time I thought, this is the final moment of my life; I thought I wasn't going to be alive anymore. These two men that guarded us pretty much didn't speak to each other; they communicated with signs. And they always had this stick with them, maybe four inches wide and one inch thick, they called it the idiot tamer—if I turned to look at someone, they'd beat me on the back with it. From day one they beat me with the idiot tamer. They'd ask me for that phone number and as soon as I told them I didn't know it, they'd beat me. Afterward, one of them would say to the other, "Leave him be for a little while so he can remember his numbers." They'd ask me again later and I just had the same answer and they'd start hitting me all over again while I was on my knees. They'd leave me be for a little while again, they'd say, "He's probably stressed out now, leave him be." But every little while they'd go back to beating me.

Three days went by and then they put me in another room by myself. They kept asking me for six thousand dollars to be able to leave and I just told them I didn't have money, I came to Nogales to work and didn't have anything. They asked me for a phone number. "I don't care how you go about it, but you're going to look for six thousand dollars and you're going to give us a phone number." I kept saying the same thing, I didn't have a number. So they'd beat me and beat me with the idiot tamer, on my back, on my legs, on my arms. Whenever they felt like it, many times a day, every day. After fifteen days they started wrenching my left arm backward, twisting it behind my back, to cause pain. With all that wrenching they injured it, and then they kept hurting me in that spot, because they knew it was more painful. They kept beating me bad. They were tiring themselves out, they even said at one point that they were going to make more cash off me by selling me in pieces, but I kept telling them, I'm not going to the United States, I'm going to stay in Mexico. But they didn't believe anything I said.

From the day I got there, they would feed me pinto beans and white rice without tortillas once a day or once every other day. They'd also give me water in a jar, like a jalapeño jar. The guy who was on guard would bring me my food in that room, which didn't have windows. There was no bathroom in there, so I urinated in these Coke bottles they'd give me, two- or three-liter bottles. If I went number two, they'd give me bags to use, which they'd take out later. I had a pad to sleep on—the floor was unfinished—and a blanket, because it was really cold. That room only had one door, a black metal door, and it only opened from the outside. I didn't see sunlight in all the time I was locked in there. I could only just see how it got brighter during the day. That's how I was able to separate day from night.

I managed to escape before dawn on Tuesday, December the twenty-eighth. I woke up and heard women, music, and people who were drinking. The night before, they'd brought me my food really late. I don't know if they got careless out of drunkenness or what, but the door was open. I hadn't noticed, not until the wind moved it. So I was able to leave while it was just getting light. It was still dark out. I could see a bunch of people, six maybe, including women, like two or three. They were all outside, near the cow pen. They had a fire going and they were drinking. I walked out, and I didn't mess with looking in their direction. I don't think they saw me leave. So I ran and ran for like one or two hours, sometimes walking and sometimes running, just trying to get myself however far away I could. The terrain wasn't flat, I went up and down some little hills. And I passed a little creek bed or something. The sunrise was on my righthand side. I got to a point where I actually ran into the boundary line of the United States. I went into the United States maybe two hundred yards or so, stayed there about three hours, watching to see if they were coming behind me. After that I came back out and ran into a man who I guess was taking people to the other side, like nine people with backpacks. I asked him to help me figure out where I was and get to the city. I said I'd hurt myself on the *gabacho* side and my *coyote* had left me there. This man told me where the train tracks were and which way I needed to go to get to Nogales. Because he told me that behind some mountains was Cananea.[23]

So, I opted to leave for Nogales. From that spot, I went to the right and walked about three hours. The terrain there wasn't flat either: I had to go up and down hills there too. I crossed a dirt road and got to the train tracks. I was there for three days, waiting for the train to go by. And it did go by, on Sunday morning, and I was able to get on because it was going nice and slow. And I was able to get to Nogales by about noon. After that, I went to *Grupo Beta* to make a call to El Salvador, and later on I went to the Kino Border Initiative *comedor* to look for the lawyer so she could help me, but I wasn't able to see her until the next day. And then they sent me to Agua Prieta so I could stay at the migrant house. I got some medical attention at the general hospital here for the pain in my arm. The doctor massaged it and bandaged it for me. He also gave me some creams. Told me if I knew someone who did massages to go see them, because my arm was dislocated.

9

Deporting through Crime and Race

Introduced by Tobin Hansen

Criminalization—that is, the social and legal processes through which some people come to be perceived as harmful to the public good, or "criminal"—has facilitated expulsions and exclusions since the beginning of North American colonialism. While criminalization has persisted, aspects that render people criminal have undergone constant change. Broader notions of who belongs to local communities and the US nation—who is seen as a contributor or, conversely, undesirable—have, for centuries, fluctuated around social identities such as class, religion, race, and ethnicity. Simultaneously, social identities have shaped understandings of what makes people seem criminal or otherwise unworthy of belonging. Laws and policies become enacted based on these understandings and then themselves, over time, legitimate and normalize the membership of some people and the exclusion of others.

Historically, exclusions and removals associated with criminalization and other forms of undesirability have affected various groups. Centuries before the first formal federal deportation in 1882 marked an important moment in the rise of the immigration enforcement regime, a patchwork of exclusionary social and legal arrangements existed in local settlements and states.[1] During seventeenth- and eighteenth-century British colonialism, ostensibly to maintain "social order," laws targeted poor people deemed morally dubious and referred to as "public charges," "strolling poor people," "transients," "vagabonds," and "vagrants."[2] Such people were threatened with imprisonment and made to flee their villages in a process called "warning out."[3]

Moreover, dispossession of Indigenous people in the nineteenth century, underpinned by assumptions of Euro-American superiority, first came in the form of diminished sovereignty and then through removal policies enforced by violence. Slave laws likewise subjected Afro-descendant people to coercive movement, including removal abroad as a type of punishment and fugitive slave laws that prohibited escape from slaveholding jurisdictions.[4]

White supremacy and racial anxiety have inspired, legitimated, and normalized exclusions and expulsions.[5] During the colonial period, whiteness became conflated with emerging Anglo-American social, political, and economic dominance. Since then, various strands of nativism have become rooted in racialized xenophobia. People from different parts of the world have been seen as inferior; issuing from backward civilizations; and threatening to the racial, cultural, and moral "purity" of the United States. Anti-Asian, anti-Black, anti-Arab, and anti-Latinx racisms have motivated harsh restrictions on the entry of migrants, beginning with the Chinese Exclusion laws of 1882 and 1892. The explicitly race-based 1917 Immigration Act and 1924 National Origins Quota Act established numerical quotas that imposed austere limits on migration from Africa, Asia, and Arab regions as well as southern and eastern Europe, while encouraging migration by "white" western Europeans.[6] The Immigration and Nationality Act of 1965 set more uniform national quotas but strictly limited migration from Latin America, a region that had not been previously targeted for restrictions.[7] Given the long history of Mexican workers being recruited to work in US agriculture and other industries, there was a well-established practice of work-related migration that became illegal overnight given the new restrictions.[8] This sudden, massive "illegalization" of Mexican nationals strengthened race-based stereotypes associated with "illegality" and racialized Mexicans.[9]

In recent decades, as federal US immigration statutes have become race neutral on their face, social and migratory control has increasingly focused on crime, illegality, and punishment.[10] As a result, numbers of so-called criminal alien deportations have soared, disproportionately of nonwhite people, particularly nationals of Mexico and Central American countries.[11] In 1986, the Immigration Reform and Control Act (IRCA) instituted expeditious removals of "criminal aliens," catalyzing the Criminal Alien Program, which facilitated identification and removal of noncitizens in prisons and jails.[12] In 1996, The Antiterrorism and Effective Death Penalty Act (AEDPA) and Illegal Immigration Reform and Immigrant Responsibility Act (IIRIRA) had various effects. These new laws expanded police cooperation with immigration officials, reduced certain waivers and judicial reviews of deportation (e.g., based on existing social and cultural ties in the United States), created more mechanisms for fast-track deportations and mandatory detention for many people, and expanded the categories of crimes that render people deportable.[13] These new measures meant in practice that factors that historically were taken to reflect belonging, such as time living in the United States, or family and community ties, often could not be considered.

Situating people within the reductive category "criminal" has, for the hundreds of years since colonial contact, been a useful tool for signaling who is thought to be dangerous, Other, and not to belong. This can be seen from the system of "warning out" to the rise of mass deportation in recent decades. But the severe measure of expelling from national territory noncitizens deemed criminal, made possible when a 1917 federal statute for the first time rendered noncitizens deportable for crimes committed in the United States, reflected a draconian shift in the treatment of "criminals."[14] Actual deportations under this new criminal status provision, nevertheless, remained relatively uncommon for much of the twentieth century. Not only were there generally low incarceration rates in the United States and low immigration enforcement capacity, but also vagueness surrounding which crimes made people deportable.[15] The ramped-up crime control of 1986 and beyond invigorated the migratory control apparatus in terms of apprehensions, personnel, equipment, and budget. This watershed year marked the convergence of mass incarceration and mass deportation. The provisions in IRCA and, ten years later, the AEDPA and IIRIRA, have led to record numbers of so-called criminal alien deportations—expulsions of people convicted of a misdemeanor or felony crime—in recent decades. While the US government deported 2,318 "criminal aliens" throughout the entirety of the 1970s, it expelled 4,385 in 1987 and 33,951 in 1997.[16] By 2019, the yearly figure was up to 150,141.[17] The US Department of Homeland Security (DHS) boasts that "ICE remains committed to directing its enforcement resources to those aliens posing the greatest risk to the safety and security of the United States."[18] This glosses over the fact that the top categories of "criminal charges and convictions" arrests by ICE's Enforcement and Removal Operations, comprising 55 percent of total offenses, are for "Traffic Offenses—(DUI)," "Traffic Offenses," "Dangerous Drugs," and "Immigration."[19] More serious crimes, such as "Homicide" and "Kidnapping" (together comprising 0.8 percent of total offenses), are further down the list, at 25 and 26. Moreover, there is ample social scientific evidence that higher immigration is associated with lower crime rates and that immigrants are less likely to engage in criminal behavior than the native born.[20]

The focus on prosecuting would-be border crossers for illegal entry and illegal reentry—misdemeanor and felony crimes, respectively, according to federal statute—has also intensified criminalization. Since 2005, many

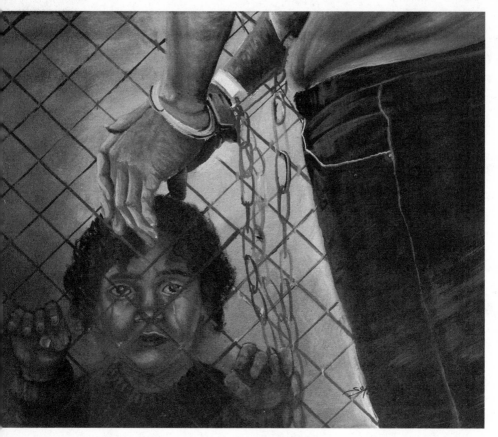

Criminalization, restraints, and a cyclone fence separate loved ones. José Luis Cabrera Sotero.

apprehended Mexican-national border crossers who in the past would merely have been returned to Mexico are prosecuted under Operation Streamline (as outlined in chapter 1); serve federal sentences in the range of thirty days for illegal entry or, in the case of illegal reentry, a few years; and now have criminal records and formal orders of deportation that make any future applications for lawful entry extremely unlikely to be granted.[21]

The intensification of the expulsions of "illegals" and "criminals" during the last few decades was not inevitable but rather a result of the nativist desire to solve the so-called migration problem, underpinned by centuries of overt and implicit racial exclusions. For many in the United States, migrants represent a shadowy and nefarious threat to society. The criminalization of noncitizens, through legal mechanisms and vilifying discourse, has been an effective means of bringing about their expulsion. The punitive measures of the criminal justice system—and its jails, courts, and prisons—are deemed an insufficient penalty, and deportation becomes an additional sanction. The experiences of criminalization, as recounted in the *testimonios* below, reveal how immigration enforcement is inflicted upon some noncitizens. For Gerry, after struggling with drug use and spending time incarcerated, difficulties in Mexico compound his hardship. And for Mike, after a prison sentence in the United States, also for drug use, the additional process of deportation becomes a sort of double punishment. Last, Rafael's short *testimonio* demonstrates how his very treatment by authorities—who use handcuffs and leg restraints to effectuate his deportation—communicates criminality. Although deportation is nominally a civil procedure, declared by the Supreme Court to be an administrative and not a punitive action, Mike, Gerry, and Rafael's experiences of deportation and its consequences are worse than any criminal punishment they face.

GERRY

My name is Gerardo. Everyone calls me Gerry. I was born in Nogales, Sonora, in 1977. When I was three years old, my dad left us. He just ran out. So my mom kind of ran away. It was like 1980 when we got to Tucson. We had this place in Tucson, off East Ajo Way. I don't have a lot of memories from when I was that age. But we were so poor in Nogales. The first time I wore shoes was in Tucson!

I don't really remember that time, but we must have been so happy to be in Tucson. Coming from here [Nogales] and having nothing, it must have been great. Later on, we moved to Santa Rita Park.[22] That's where I grew up. I went to school there and everything.

I tried to be a good kid. I did everything my mom said. She would tell me, "Mijo, you've got to do things right and work hard. And don't ever take anything that isn't yours." And I don't. I was a good kid. I learned all that stuff. If I have a friend and they let me into their house, I would go in and would never take nothing. 'Cause if I take something one time, then you're gonna think that I'm going to take something again and you won't invite me back. I just think you have to do things the right way. If you're gonna do something, do it and do it right.

So I was good. My life was good. My dad taught me how to work construction. He can build anything! He would work on these houses and make them so good. He showed me how to join pieces together the right way. My dad was so good. He taught me how to do all that stuff right.

I was doing real good up there until I got into those pills. Those pills is what messed me up. And I started doing bad, started messing up there. So I went to prison for two years. The two years I did in Buckeye wasn't really hard time.[23] I never got into gangs. That wasn't my thing. I just wanted to do my time and get out of there.

When I knew I was gonna get deported, I started getting *nervios*, bad.[24] You know, I was like this.[25] I couldn't relax, I couldn't sleep. I was eating a lot. That was the only thing I could do, was just eat a lot from all the *nervios*. I didn't know Mexico, and I didn't know what was gonna happen to me here when I got dropped off. I think the *nervios* is maybe how I got diabetes. You know, from being afraid. And then I got deported. That was in 2002, but I still remember every detail. I can tell you everything about it. I was deported to Nogales. It was so hard. It's hard for me to talk about. You know, to talk about it *me da vergüenza*.[26] The stuff that I did, and that I got deported.

Here the cops treat you the way that they see you. So, like, if you're dressed perfect you wouldn't have no problem. But I look kind of crazy. They look at me and think a lot of things. I was staying at this abandoned house, up by Las Mesas bar, at the top of the *cerro*.[27] And the cops came by. I guess they were hungry or something and I was eating. I had this plate and they came up and saw that I was eating. They said they were gonna take me for my 36.[28] I said, "No way! I'm not doing anything. I'm just eating." But they arrested me. I didn't fight. They just took me away, and the food was right there. They must've taken it then.

You shouldn't resist [arrest]. You can't yell at the cops; that just makes them madder. You have to do what they say and just keep calm. Out here in front of everyone, they just try to look respectful. [But privately] I've been hit by police and I've been kicked by police. I've been spit on by police down here. They hit me so hard one time in the ribs. Damn!

MIKE

My dad was born and raised in Navojoa, Sonora, and my mother is from Nogales, Sonora. I have three brothers and one sister. I was born in 1974. In 1977 we moved to Phoenix.

I grew up in Central City in Phoenix. It's a Black neighborhood and we were the only Mexicans. It was a tough neighborhood. We got picked on and got jumped. School was hard. I didn't speak English when I started kindergarten. My best friend was Martín. My dad was a musician. He played music in bars and worked at a shoe store for a long time. All of my cousins and everyone are US citizens.

I started getting into trouble when I was thirteen or fourteen. We had a riot [fight] at school, the whole school year. At school we were tired of getting pushed around and we would fight. We also started stealing, like bikes and skateboards. We would take them down to the cruising scene on Central Avenue. We go there and that's where everything was happening. First it was bikes and skateboards. Then we would buy weed, then beer. We were just fourteen or fifteen years old, but sometimes we sold the stuff we stole so we had money. We'd see people and ask them to hook us up.[29] They ignored us until we pulled a Benjamin out of our pocket and then they'd be like, "What do you need?"[30] Back then, you could get hooked up and have a blunt or a beer, right there on Central. The cops knew us, but that wasn't even a problem.

I got caught stealing. I was on probation when I was seventeen, so I couldn't leave the house. But I didn't get along good with my dad at that time. We would get in fights over stupid stuff. I would get frustrated and I would go to my friend's house. My probation officer told me I couldn't leave though. He was cool and didn't violate me.[31] When I was seventeen years old, I went to a halfway house.[32] I was there for seven months. There was people from all over Arizona there, a lot of people with no friends or family. We were all troublemakers. We formed our own little clique.[33] We were all together: whites, Mexicans, and Blacks.

I was smoking weed and using other drugs. I went to county [jail] and then prison for the first time in 1995, until 1997. I had a pen pal when I was in prison. Her name was Stephanie. I actually met her through a friend. He had a girlfriend and I asked him if she had any friends. So Stephanie and me would write. We met after I got out and we got together. When I was in prison my parents would visit once every three months or so. It was really far for them to travel so they couldn't visit more often. I didn't cry about being in prison. I mean, I got myself in that situation. And it was only two years. I had a friend in there. A real good friend that watched my back. We played cards, played chess. Now in prison there's more gangs and it's more racial.[34]

Stephanie and I had our daughter in 1999. I would have arguments with Stephanie then just go stay at my parents' house. I worked as a plumber and I was trying to get into the union. I was training. I worked on a project for quite a few months. I was still young too. But I started using glass.[35] It started just on weekends. But then I would use it on weekdays, too. I would have fights with Stephanie. I knew she didn't want me to be high. I would smoke weed and come back a few hours later. After prison, I started doing commercial painting. Things were good with Stephanie. Things were great until I drank too much. We would go to the movies or to Olive Garden. I would take her there on Mother's Day. But I was using glass and we were having problems.

I had to take UAs through my PO [Parole Officer].[36] I thought everything was fine. I found out later that I had two dirty UAs in a row. But I didn't know after the first one. In 2009, my PO told me that she could help me with Immigration, because she had a friend in Immigration.[37] She would visit me on Thursdays. And she showed up at the house on a Wednesday. I was like, "What the heck?" There were two black Suburbans across the street. I didn't think nothing of it. But then the ICE agents started walking over to me. I couldn't believe she did that. They say, "You're coming with me." I said, "Why? What did I do? I didn't violate my probation or anything." I was in immigration detention for nine months.

I look at it like I got screwed twice by the system. I did time for my crime. I paid my debt to the society I grew up in. I tried to fight my case. I even went to BIA.[38] When I went before the judge, he asked if I had fears [about deportation to Mexico]. I said, "Yeah! I have no place to stay, no family, no way to get a job." He said, "No, not that type of fear. Do you have fear of death?" I was like, "Yeah! I'm afraid of dying from hunger in the streets!" But he deported me.

People here think you have money just because you're a deportee. They see you're from the States. I called my bro Lucas last week and I told him I was hungry, that I didn't have anything to eat. He was mad at me because I didn't let him know before. I felt bad because I'd asked them for money before and they said they didn't have it. I feel bad asking. They have their life, their house on that side [the US side of the border].

My dad calls me all the time. He asks if I'm okay. He says that I won't get a job. He says, "Apply over here, apply over there. There's a place where I worked when I was a kid." He says, "You're not applying yourself." It's not that. It's just that it's hard. I did get a translation job, because Bobby [another deportee] has a friend that's the manager at a company. It was really hard and I couldn't catch on since they deal with medical supplies and stuff. It was a lot of medical language.

RAFAEL

Mi nombre es Rafael Lugo Domínguez. Fui deportado de USA y me hicieron sentir como un verdadero criminal. Cuando me pusieron las esposas en las manos y en los pies me sentí muy humillado. No soy un criminal. Estoy en contra de las esposas.

||||||||||||||||

My name is Rafael Lugo Domínguez. I was deported from the US. They made me feel like a real criminal. I was so humiliated when I was put in handcuffs and leg shackles. I am not a criminal. I'm against using handcuffs.

10

Deported from Home

Introduced by Tobin Hansen

I s deportation a return home? The popular conception in the United States
is that yes, it is. When people are seen as criminals and laws are passed
that make more people deportable, as discussed in the previous chapter,
deporting people "back home" seems to some like a good idea. The experiences of deportation receive little consideration or, perhaps, are imagined as
a homecoming: a reunification with family and a return to a local community, to a country of legal nationality, and to a familiar culture and language.
That is often not, however, the way it plays out. Experiences of deportation
are diverse. In many cases, legal nationality—what a birth certificate indicates about legal membership and implies about belonging to a culture and
geographical territory—does not line up with social ties and cultural identity. This chapter explores those mismatches. It considers how home is made
over time in the places people live, irrespective of legal nationality. Here, we
explore why ramped-up immigration enforcement in the US interior, far
from the country's borders, has increased deportations *from* home.[1] Moreover, the chapter illuminates the consequences—disorientation, lack of
government documents, unemployability, vulnerability to violence, family
separation, and a profound sense of loss—of being deported from home.

Home is made over time. It is not merely a dwelling where you live
between walls, under a roof. It is also a powerful metaphor for the place
where we belong, where it is natural and normal to carry out our lives, where
we feel rooted. People born in Mexico who go to the United States and
live there for decades, as in the case of many deported people who have

become stuck in Nogales, develop strong bonds to people, local ways of life, and to the US nation itself. These bonds are especially reflected in the lives of those who migrate to the United States as children. Belonging has interpersonal, cultural, and linguistic dimensions and is tied to individual and collective memory. If someone grows up in a Phoenix or Los Angeles neighborhood, or in another Arizona or California town, they might speak more English than Spanish or Indigenous language and know more history about Abe Lincoln and George Washington than Benito Juárez and Miguel Hidalgo. And in those US communities, people make home through connection with others and everyday contact, the intertwining of lives and identities, and sharing in a sense of mutual existence.

Many noncitizens call the United States home. Deep social and cultural ties are interwoven over the lengthy periods that people live in the country. One survey demonstrated that those born in Mexico and deported between 2009 and 2012 had lived an average of 8.8 years in the United States.[2] According to data collected in 2018 of Mexican nationals deported to Mexico, 82 percent had lived in the United States for more than three years and 42 percent more than ten years.[3] More remarkably, of all Mexican nationals living in the United States in 2013, fully 77 percent had lived there for at least ten years, whereas in 1990 that was the case for 50 percent.[4]

By what means are longtime US residents expelled, then? US immigration laws—more draconian since the 1980s, as examined in the previous chapter—have created more obstacles to legal regularization.[5] Many longtime residents, even those with US citizen family members, jobs, and extensive community ties, are not eligible for legal residence without having to spend ten years waiting outside of the country, potentially separated from family and far from home. Moreover, border militarization has interrupted the circular migration patterns that became normalized over hundreds of years. Paradoxically, in many cases this traps people *in* the United States.[6] Harsh border policing has reshaped the possibilities for people to enter the United States and work, return to Mexico sometime later, and then enter the United States again. In effect, the hardened border ensures that more people remain in US territory because exits to Mexico produce the risk of future crossings or the weight of perpetual exile. And the US government's focus on immigration enforcement is not confined to the country's borders but also takes place in the interior. In 2019, 137,084 of all US Department of Homeland Security immigration-related arrests, or 27 percent of the total, were not of people trying to cross a border into the United States but of people living in the country.[7]

Some deported people—including some who gave *testimonios* in the previous and the present chapters—carry taboo associations with drug use, gang membership, and incarceration in US prisons. The *testimonios* presented

An artistic self-portrait behind bars. A loved one laments separation over years in US prison, under watchtower surveillance. Deportation is imminent, to a Nogales depicted as drug-filled and violent. Alain Ojeda.

here are not representative of all deported people. More importantly, this chapter seeks to challenge moral valuations that consider criminalized Latinx men as less worthy of physical and social belonging and perceive them as dangerous threats, when taboo associations garner derision for white US citizens but are not equated with the need to banish them from national territory. Belonging developed over time, even when it is cultivated within the oppositional spaces of gangs and prisons, does not diminish the fact that it exists.

Deportation from home is associated with several compounding social, financial, and psychological hardships.[8] Cultural disorientation derives from lack of familiarity with local and national histories, ways of communicating, popular culture (such as music and movies), and civic culture (e.g., holidays and government operations). It engenders the feeling of being perpetually out of place and, as some deported longtime US residents have told me, "like you're on Mars" or "on the moon." There are practical implications as well. Many talk about the confusion and difficulty figuring out aspects of day-to-day life. Someone put it to me this way, saying bluntly in English: "Down here, I don't know how anything works."

Deportation to Nogales is also complicated by a lack of documents and by obstacles to accessing services. Deported people may be able to obtain birth certificates from family in the United States or by requesting a replacement from the *municipio* (town) where they were born. Receiving these documents can take time, cost money, or, in some cases, lead to a dead end when the record cannot be found. A birth certificate is a requirement for obtaining a standard identification card, known as an INE. Only then is it possible to begin the process of enrolling in *Seguro Popular* (medical insurance for people with limited means), acquiring a population registry number (known as a CURP [*Clave Única de Registro de Población*, Population Registry Code]), being hired for a job, finding housing, exercising the right to vote, or avoiding problems with local police, who extort deported people for money when they are out of compliance with a local ordinance requiring that people carry photo identification. Unfamiliarity with complex government bureaucracies compounds problems accessing documents and services. And while the Mexican government does issue a temporary ID—known as a *Constancia de Repatriación* (Repatriation Certificate)—when someone is deported, it is valid for a limited time and carrying one reinforces the stigma of deportation and can still mark someone as out of place and therefore a target.

Employment poses an additional challenge. The absence of photo identification and population registry number complicate hiring, forcing many people to seek work in the informal economy. Moreover, not having a certificate of completion from a Mexican junior high or high school can disqualify applicants from certain jobs. Simple unfamiliarity with the local economy and job opportunities and few social ties are themselves a setback. Moreover, some work skills developed in the United States have no application or yield low wages in Mexico, as is the case for restaurant work or construction.

Longtime US residents deported to Mexico also face particular vulnerability to violent victimization by organized crime mafias. Being recognizable as an "outsider" in Nogales puts deported people and immigrants at risk of kidnapping or extortion. Characteristics such as "different" clothing, hairstyles, tattoos, and accents and vocabulary in Spanish mark people as being on the move. As geographer Jeremy Slack points out, migrants in northern Mexico are targets of organized crime, even though financial hardship is presumably one motivation for their migration, because there may be family members elsewhere who can pay a ransom of several hundred or several thousand dollars.[9] Families of longtime US residents are assumed to have even greater wealth by dint of participation in the US economy, rendering "Americanized" deported people more vulnerable. Moreover, their visible "outsider-ness" is difficult to mitigate because, as some explain, you feel American, look American, and talk American.

The hardships of family separation discussed in chapter 5 are also felt by those deported after many years in the United States. Often, they have had very little, if any, contact with family in Mexico. And seeking out distant family often does not seem like a good option—some report shame at seeking out relatives only in a time of need or otherwise feel like they do not deserve the support of family in Mexico, after being out of touch for years or decades.[10]

In what ways might someone belong to a place? Political nationality and legal recognition offer certain rights and privileges. But nationality does not determine the way someone relates to their family, to a place, a community, or a nation. Although political nationality and cultural nationality often align, that is not always the case. Many—such as Larry and Ramón, whose *testimonios* are below—experience unbearable exile, deep loss, and the feeling of living in a permanent gray zone. Understanding these individuals' struggles encourages rethinking of how laws might recognize the bonds individuals have to a country that is not a country of legal citizenship and be more flexible in permitting legal residence.

LARRY

Me llamo Larry. Soy originario de Guadalajara. Tenía aproximadamente ocho años cuando mi padre llegó de Estados Unidos a México. Yo a mi padre, como quien dice, no lo conocía. Él estaba en Estados Unidos y, cada año, iba a visitar a mi mamá, que vivía en Jalisco. Somos tres hermanos: dos hermanos y yo. Mi papá nos construyó una casa con el dinero que reunía trabajando en los Estados Unidos. Gracias a que él trabajaba de carpintero, haciendo casas de madera, construyó nuestra casa. Cuando yo tenía ocho años fue que vino a México y decidió llevarnos con él, porque el dinero no le rendía en México. Éramos tres hijos y mi mamá. Muchos gastos, con los útiles de las escuelas no nos alcanzaba a calzar, vestir a todos igual. Andábamos mal vestidos.

Pues hicimos la jornada nosotros hacia los Estados Unidos. Afortunadamente hicimos como tres noches y tres días. ¡Nos agarró la Migra! Yo tenía ocho años. A mi padre lo encerraron. Íbamos nosotros —los tres hijos, mi mamá y mi papá— y otros dos vecinos del barrio. ¡Ya estábamos en Estados Unidos! Pero nos deportaron.

Mi papá, aferrado, dijo que nos volveríamos a aventar. Gracias a Dios pasamos. Llegamos a El Paso, luego a Houston, Texas, y a Oklahoma City, donde yo viví catorce años. Fui a la escuela desde cuarto grado hasta el décimo grado. Mi padre ya estaba más viejo y no creía que uno va a vivir lujos. Uno vive todo amontonado. Éramos tres y mi papá y mi mamá en un apartamento de dos recámaras. Vivíamos amontonados. La gente piensa que, por vivir en Estados Unidos, uno vive lujos, que porque sube cosas al Facebook ya es rico. No, están equivocados. Vivíamos amontonados. Y lo mismo que nos pasaba en México nos pasaba allá. Porque mi padre no ganaba mucho. Pero yo, como a los quince años, empecé a abrir los ojos, pude saber cómo iban los demás. Empecé a trabajar en los veranos, a ayudarle a mi papá, y me sentía más independiente. Ya me empezó a gustar el dinero. Empecé a agarrar mi carrito, ya hasta novia tenía y decidí salirme de la escuela. Seguí viviendo con mis padres y hasta ahora, a los veintitrés años, seguía viviendo con él, estando yo casado. Por lo mismo, porque no es fácil. Uno piensa que puede vivir solo, tener riquezas, pero no es así. Como gana uno en dólares gasta también en dólares. Y aquí estoy viendo que no rinde el dinero.

Yo tengo catorce años sin venir aquí, es más, no conozco la frontera. Y a mí la Migración ahora me dio un cheque, pero qué gano, si tengo un cheque y no lo puedo cambiar. Voy a las tiendas y no lo puedo cambiar. Ya me dijeron que voy a poder cambiarlo aquí. Y es que me aventaron sin identificación. Por lo mismo me aventaron, porque no tengo papeles ni de Estados Unidos ni de México.

Me agarraron, porque yo iba a un cumpleaños, de Oklahoma a Las Vegas, donde vive mi prima. De regreso, choqué con un tráiler y la trailera en Shamrock, Texas, le avisó a la Migra que yo era mexicano. Pues nada más por el color. Llegó la Migración y me tramitó la salida. Yo les dije que desde niño estaba allá, pero no les importó. Yo me había juntado con una americana, tengo un hijo, cumple dos años el dieciséis de septiembre de 2017. Se lo dije, pero no les importó y ahora estoy yo aquí, en un país al que pertenezco pero que no conozco. Ya hablé con el consulado mexicano y me aconsejó ubicarme por aquí cerca o allá en Guadalajara. Pero es lo mismo, no conozco a nadie. Ya no viven mis abuelos. Si vivieran, con ellos llegaba. Pero ni de aquí ni de allá. Si me voy a mi rancho, pueblo, barrio [pausa], pues mejor aquí en la frontera. Porque la verdad, sí me voy a aventar de nuevo. El consulado, o donde nos reciben, me dijo que si mi esposa viene y se casa aquí conmigo, a los seis meses ella me puede pedir. Y yo regreso allá con papeles. Pero mi padre ya es grande de edad y mis hermanas son pequeñas. No pueden trabajar. Y nomás se vence poquito la renta y los corren si no pagan. Por eso considero que tengo que ir, pasarme, porque estoy acá y necesito pagar la renta. Porque mis padres dependen de mí, ya son viejos. Por eso me siento responsable por ellos todavía.

Yo no tengo record criminal, sólo este choque. Yo no miré ni un juez, no firmé ni un papel. Pero sí puse mi huella. Yo le dije al de la Migra que no quería firmar hasta ver a un abogado. Estaba con la esperanza en la noche de que, al día siguiente, iba a llegar mi abogado, pero como a las tres de la mañana nos levantaron y me dijeron: "Te vas a tu casa". Oh, ¡qué bien! ¡Yo creí que a mi casa en Estados Unidos! Pero ahí me llevan todo esposado a subirme al camión y ya me enteré que me iban a traer para México.

Vamos a agarrar un departamento Sección 8, como ella es norteamericana. Pero esto toma un tiempo, seis meses. Ella no trabaja. Yo me crié, como quien dice, sin madre. Y yo quiero que mi hijo se críe con la mamá, para que no salga tan callejero como yo. Porque salí callejero, con mañas. En México fui vago por criarme de callejero. Pero en estos catorce años, yo arreglé mi vida. Voy a hablar con mi señora, para ver si se puede venir ella, para casarme. Quiero trabajar y mandarle dinero a mi esposa de aquí para allá. Mis padres tampoco metieron papeles, porque tenían miedo de que, al citarlos, los mandaran para acá.

IIIIIIIIIIIIIIII

My name is Larry. I'm originally from Guadalajara. When I was about eight years old, my father arrived from the United States. Me and my father—you might say I didn't know him. He was in the US, and then every year he'd come to visit my mom in Jalisco.[11] There are three of us kids, my two brothers and me. My dad built us a house with the money he saved up from working in the US. He worked as a carpenter, making wood houses, so he was able to build our house. When I was eight years old, he came to Mexico and decided to take us back with him because his money just wasn't going far enough in Mexico. It was us three kids and my mom. Lots of expenses. After school supplies, we didn't have enough for shoes and clothes for all of us equally. We were always badly dressed.

So we made the journey to the United States. We were lucky and it just took us three nights and three days. Immigration caught us! I was eight years old. My father they locked up. On the trip it was us three kids, my mom and dad, and two people from our neighborhood. We were already in the US! But they deported us.

My dad was determined. He said we were going to go for it again. With God's help, we got through. We reached El Paso, then Houston, and then Oklahoma City. I lived there for fourteen years. I went to school there from fourth grade to tenth grade. My father was getting old. He didn't believe you were supposed to live in luxury. You were supposed to live all crowded together. It was the three of us and my dad and my mom, in a two-bedroom apartment. We lived all crowded together. People think just because you live in the US you live in luxury, if you post things on Facebook that means you're rich. No, they're wrong. We lived all crowded together. And the same thing that happened to us in Mexico happened to us there, because my father didn't earn much. But when I was about fifteen, I started to open my eyes, found out how everyone else was doing. I started working during the summers, to help my dad, and it made me feel more independent. I started to like money. I was getting a hold of a little car, I even had a girlfriend, and I decided to leave school. I still lived with my parents. Right up till just now, at twenty-three, I still lived with my dad even though I was married. For the same reason, because it's not easy. You think you can live alone, have riches, but it's not true. You earn in dollars so you also spend in dollars. And I'm here and I've seen that the money doesn't last.

I haven't come to Mexico in fourteen years. I don't know the border either. And what happened to me just now is that Immigration gave me a check, but it's no good to me, having a check and not being able to cash it.[12] I've been going to all the stores and I can't cash it. Someone told me I'll be able to cash it here.[13] And the reason is they threw me out without ID. They threw me out *for* that very reason, not having papers! Neither US papers nor Mexican papers.

The reason I got picked up was because I went to a birthday party in Las Vegas, where my cousin lives. On the way back, I got in an accident with a semi in Shamrock, Texas, and the driver told Immigration that I was Mexican. I mean, on no other basis than skin color. Immigration got there and processed my departure. I told them I'd lived there since I was a little kid, but they didn't care. I had gotten together with an American girl; I have a son. He's turning two on September sixteenth, 2017. I told them all this, but they didn't care and now I'm here, in a country that I belong to but don't know. I talked to the Mexican consulate and they recommended I get a job near here or else down there in Guadalajara. But it's the same either way: I don't know anybody. My grandparents aren't alive anymore. If they were, I would go and stay with them. But there's no one either here or there. If I leave here and go to my town, farm, neighborhood—whatever you want to call it—I think I'm better off here on the border. Because to be honest, I *am* going to go for it again. The consulate, or the place where they meet us when we arrive, they told me if my partner comes and marries me here, in six months she can request me, and then I go back there with papers.[14] My father is old now and my sisters are little. They can't work. All it takes is for them to get a little behind on the rent and they'll get evicted if they don't pay. That's why I feel like I have to go, get myself through, because I'm here and I need to pay the rent. Because my parents depend on me—they're old now. That's why I feel like I'm still responsible for them, even now.

I don't have a criminal record, just this car accident. I didn't lay eyes on one judge, didn't sign one document.[15] But I did give a fingerprint. I told the Immigration person I didn't want to sign until I saw a lawyer. During the night, what I was hoping was that my lawyer would arrive the next day. But at about three in the morning, they got us up and they told me, "You're going home." Oh, great! I thought they meant Oklahoma City! But then they took me, all shackled, and put me on the bus and that's when I realized they were taking me to Mexico.

We're going to get ourselves a Section 8 apartment. She's American, so we can. But it takes some time, six months. She doesn't have a job. I grew up without a mother, you might say, and I want my son to grow up with a mom, so he doesn't turn out to be a street kid as much as me. Because I came out that way, a street kid. I had hustle. In Mexico I was a lazybones, on account of growing up a street kid. But in the last fourteen years I've straightened my life out. I'm going to talk to my lady and see if she can get here to marry me. I want to work and send money from here to my wife there. My parents never filed papers either. They were scared that when the appointment came, they would get sent over here.

RAMÓN

Soy Ramón Islas. Yo llegué a los Estados Unidos cuando tenía dos años. Soy de Nogales, Sonora, de la colonia Buenos Aires. Me llevaron allá para tener una mejor vida. Ahora tengo cuarenta y nueve años. Allá me crie. Los hijos estudiamos, nos casamos, tenemos familia allá. Yo tengo hijos hijos, ocho nietos y es lo más importante, lo más bonito de la vida. Estar con tus hijos, disfrutar la vida. Pero ahora, como van las cosas . . . Me sacaron en el 2015.

Yo fui detectado con cáncer en el 2012, cáncer de la piel. Yo pensé: van a curarlo, estando como estaba en los Estados Unidos. Pero me dijeron que tenía un tumor maligno, que andaba muy recio. Y comenzaron a hacerme operaciones. Me cortaron el dedo gordo de mi pie y me sacaron un tumor de mi pierna, muslo. Después de eso, ya se hizo peor la cosa. Comenzó a moverse más de volada. Ya se hizo peor el tumor. Se me subió al pecho y luego ya lo tuve en el cerebro. Todo esto pasó en los Estados Unidos del 2012 al 2014, cuando tuve la última cita. Dijeron: "Vamos a darte la radiación". Porque la quimioterapia ya me la estaban dando cada tres semanas. Pero que la quimio no iba a trabajar en el cerebro, por lo que me iban a dar la radiación, para controlar el cáncer y las manchas en el cerebro.

Pasó eso en noviembre de 2014. Para ese tiempo, ya tenía un año afuera de la cárcel, que me dieron un año de permiso. La federal me dio un año de permiso, para estar con mi familia y poderme tratar el cáncer. Todo bien. Me estaban dando cada tres semanas la quimioterapia, me dieron la radiación. Y todo iba bien. Pero ya se me estaba acabando el tiempo. Yo pensé: con tiempo voy a ir a la Migración, como me indicaron que fuera, y platicarles y decirles mi situación. Esperaba que dirían que todo bien, pues tú estás enfermo, tú tienes cáncer, te vamos a dar más tiempo para que estés en Estados Unidos para terminar tu tratamiento.

Bueno, pues fui y no fue así. Completamente fue lo contrario. Y lo más horrible, nunca me esperé yo estar aquí otra vez, siendo ya víctima de cáncer. Yo pensé: pues nomás voy a estar esperando que me mejore o lo que quisiera Dios. Es decir, esperando morir. Ahora estoy aquí, me deportaron. Fui a la cita de Migración a que me dieran más tiempo para cubrir mi cáncer, las radiaciones o quimioterapia, pero no sé qué pasó ahí, pero me subieron a una camioneta así, así de fácil, de un día para otro. En menos de cinco horas estaba aquí en Nogales. Ni despedirme de nadie, ni agarrar cosas, ni nada. Bueno pues, aquí estoy. Entré a Nogales el doce de diciembre de 2014. Ya son casi tres años.

Me río porque soy creyente en Dios y vivo de la oración. La gente aquí me ha ayudado mucho con oraciones, porque sin tratamientos, sin radiación, sin quimio [pausa]. Más de dos años [pausa]. Algo tiene que haber ahí, algo tiene que haber de que es un milagro. Me habían dado un año de vivir, nada más, y ya voy para el cuarto. Llevo casi tres años de vivir aquí y sin quimioterapia, ni una pastilla, pero eso no es nada, porque la oración es lo que rifa. La gente dice: "No, pos no trabaja". Estoy hablando con Él y casi no me pongo triste, no me pongo así, porque yo ando todo el tiempo solo. Andar solo en Nogales es batalloso. Yo digo que no se puede vivir. Batalloso porque es mucho, muy diferente de como a mí me criaron.

Yo estaba rentando un departamento. No tengo mi familia aquí. Tengo a un primo, un tío y una tía, pero no somos muy allegados. Realmente, yo no me pongo a pensar en la realidad de estar muy solo, porque si me pongo a pensar, me da tristeza. Yo sé que aquí tengo que luchar, para obtener las cosas que necesito tener. O platicar con personas, porque platicando, me levanta el corazón, olvido mis tristezas, me levanta el ánimo. Yo solo, porque sé que tengo que ver por mí mismo, porque sólo la oración y el poder de Dios me acompañan. Yo sinceramente creo que Dios sí trabaja. Pero vamos a seguir con la plática de cómo he vivido.

Ha sido bien difícil obtener cosas, cosas que se requieren para vivir. Porque teniendo cáncer y no saber dónde ir al hospital, con quién hablar, es muy difícil, muchas veces me encerraba yo solo. Me encerraba y ahí me quedaba. Hasta que ya me sentía mejor, ya me salía. Tenía una hermana que vivía enseguida de mí, pero también ella tiene su vida. Y se movieron. Yo me quedé ahí. En realidad yo he hecho mi vida muy solitaria aquí. Muy triste en veces, muy triste. Porque no puedes platicar. Si quieres platicar con tus quereres, con tus hijos, con tu hermana, con tu hija, con tu mamá, ¡no se puede! Están muy lejos y en realidad no tienes las finanzas para estar en los teléfonos o tenerlos aquí cerca de ti, que es lo que quisiera. Pero no han venido a visitarme, ya tienen un año. Y es que también tienen su vida allá, hay cosas que pasan allá, pero, por eso, no lo pienso yo mucho, porque es triste. Yo sé que la vida es difícil allá en los Estados Unidos y tienen cosas que hacer. Pero ellos me mandan para pagar donde estoy viviendo. Eso es otra cosa.

El dueño del departamento donde estaba viviendo, tuvimos una discusión y de un de repente, teniendo casa, teniendo departamento, ahora no tengo. Que no tenga casa, que no tenga donde vivir, no sé. Me tiraron todas las cosas a la basura, retratos, ropa, todo lo que tenía, sólo me quedé con la ropa que traía. Aquí me están ayudando. Estoy durmiendo en una casa abandonada. Estamos un sobrino y yo, pero está abandonada. Ponemos dos camitas ahí, no tiene puertas, porque está abandonada. Dormimos ahí, en la mañana él se va a trabajar, yo sigo buscando la ayuda de médicos y de una manera u otra, yo tengo que buscar.

Ando queriendo buscar mi dignidad. Porque en México, si se tiene apoyo de allá, creen que es fácil, pero es muy difícil. Una persona que está enferma de cáncer, ya terminal —es terminal. Porque yo no me siento como antes. Ya nada más es de venir aquí y platicar con las hermanas, ir para la casa y acostarme a dormir. Pero sólo Dios sabe lo que va a pasar. Y sí les digo: "No es lo más agradable como me la he pasado y no sé cómo voy a [*pausa*] si voy a vivir dos meses, tres meses. Pero aquí ando en la pelea".

Yo me peleé con el dueño del departamento. Fue de palabras. Discutimos. Yo me fui y él sacó todas mis cosas al bote de la basura. Cuando regresé, la casa estaba limpia. Los policías se bajaron y sacaron las macanas. Y vi que ya no era plática, que era algo más. Bueno, pues yo viendo que me iban a atacar, yo brinqué un cerco y me fui corriendo. Corriendo pensé: bueno, ¿por qué corro? No cometí ningún delito. Paré. Ah, ¡ni hubiera parado! Eran seis policías. Comenzaron a pegarme con las macanas y ya no son las de madera. Eran de fierro.

Así fue, me subieron, me pisaron la cabeza y me dieron toques en los ojos. Querían que gritara. Llegó otro y ya dijo: "Déjalo". Subieron, me sacaron fotos, me llevaron a la comandancia. Me llevaron primero al hospital. Me habían fracturado el dedo. No me lo dejaron bien. Y es que la policía les dijo que no me pusieran mucha atención. Por eso me dejaron el dedo que no lo puedo estirar. El comandante me dijo: "¿Sabes qué? Vete pa' tu casa".

"¿Y qué, no me van a hacer cargos de nada, con ningún delito?" "No", dijo el comandante. "Entonces, ¿por qué me hicieron esto? ¿No ve que ando todo quebrado, no puedo caminar? ¿Qué hice tan malo para que me quebraran los dedos, me golpearan las piernas?" "No", dijo: "¿Sabes qué? Mejor vete pa' tu casa, así déjalo". Salí de la comandancia y me tiré ahí. Ya en la noche, despacito, mejor me fui a dormir a la calle. No sé qué idea tenían, por qué me habían dicho que sacara mis cosas.

Total, aquí ando en la calle. Sin casa, sin familia, sin atención médica, sin dónde dormir, ¡sin nada! Y en una fase terminal de mi enfermedad.

llllllllllllllll

I'm Ramón Islas.[16] I got to the US when I was two years old. I'm originally from Nogales, Sonora, from the Buenos Aires neighborhood. I was taken there [to the United States] to have a better life. Now I'm forty-nine. I grew up there. Us kids went to school there, got married there, have our family there. I have kids of my own and eight grandkids. And that's the most important, best thing in life. To be with your kids, enjoy life. But the way things are now—I was removed in 2015.

I was diagnosed with cancer in 2012, skin cancer. I thought, they'll cure it. I was still in the US at the time. But they told me that I had a malignant tumor, that it was really fierce. And they started doing operations. They cut my big toe off, and they took out a tumor in my leg, in the muscle. After that, things actually got worse, started moving faster. The tumor got worse. It climbed up to my chest. Then I got it in my brain. All of this happened in the US between 2012 and 2014, when I had my last appointment. They said, "We're going to give you radiation treatment." Because they were already giving me chemotherapy, every three weeks. But the chemo wasn't going to do anything in my brain, which is why they were going to do the radiation, to control the cancer and the spots in my brain.

That was November 2014. By that time I had spent a year out of jail, a one-year furlough they'd given me. BOP [Federal Bureau of Prisons] gave me a one-year furlough to be with my family and get cancer treatment. Everything was great. They were giving me chemotherapy every three weeks. They gave me the radiation treatment. And everything was going well, no problems. But now my time was running out. I thought, I'm going to go to Immigration ahead of time, the way they indicated I should do, and I'm going to talk to them and tell them my situation. I was hoping they would say no problem, I mean you're sick, you have cancer, we'll give you more time so you can be in the US to finish your treatment.

Well, so I went and it didn't go like that. Completely the opposite. The worst imaginable thing. I never expected to be here again, not as a cancer sufferer. I thought, well, my future is just about hoping to get better or whatever God wills, meaning, waiting to die. And now I'm here. They deported me. I went to the immigration appointment to get them to give me more time to deal with my cancer, the radiation treatments and chemotherapy, but—who knows what exactly happened there, but they put me in a truck just like that, just that easy, from one day to the next. In less than five hours I was here in Nogales. No saying goodbye to anyone, no chance to grab stuff, nothing. Well, so, here I am. I walked into Nogales on December twelfth, 2014. It's been almost three years now.

I laugh about it, because I believe in God and I live by prayer. People here have helped me a lot with their prayers, I mean, with no treatments, no radiation, no chemo—more than two years—there's clearly something there, clearly something miraculous. They had given me one year to live, no more, and now I'm heading toward my fourth. I've lived here for almost three years so far, with no chemotherapy, not even a single pill. But those things are nothing, because *prayer* is that which does battle. People say, "Well I mean, it doesn't do anything." I always talk to Him now and I just about don't get sad, I don't get like that. Because I'm alone all the time. Being alone in Nogales is a real struggle. If you ask me, it's an impossible life. Because it's way, way different from how *I* grew up, anyway.

I was renting an apartment here. I don't have my family here. I have a cousin, an uncle, and an aunt, but we're not very close. I truly don't let myself think about the reality of being so alone because if I do, it makes me sad. I know that here I have to fight to obtain the things I need. Or talk to people, because talking, I find it lifts my heart, I forget the sadness, it lifts my spirits. Just me—because I know I have to take care of myself, because prayer and the power of God are my only companions. I sincerely believe that God does do things. But let's go back to talking about my experiences.

It's been pretty hard to get a hold of things, things you need to live. I mean, having cancer and not knowing what hospital to go to, who to talk to, it's really hard. A lot of times I used to stay inside by myself. I'd shut the door and just stay there like that, until I felt better, then I'd leave. I had a sister who was living next door to me, but she has her own life. They moved away. I stayed there. The truth is I've had a very solitary life here. Very sad sometimes, very sad. Because you don't get to talk about things. If you want to talk to the people you love, to your sons, your sister, your daughter, your mom, it's impossible! They're really far away, and the truth is you don't have the finances to be on the phone all the time or to have them here close to you, which is what I would like. But they haven't come to visit me. It's been a year now. And that's because they have their life there too, there's things that happen there, that's why I don't think about it much, because it's sad. I know life is hard there in the US and they have things to do. They do send me money to pay the rent where I'm living. That's different.

The owner of the apartment where I *was* living, we had an argument and all of a sudden, from having a home, having an apartment, now I don't. The idea that I don't have a home, don't have a place to live—I don't know. They threw all of my stuff in the trash: portraits, clothes, everything I had. All I had left was the clothes I had on. They're helping me here. I'm sleeping in an abandoned house. My nephew and I are there, but it's abandoned. We put two beds there. It doesn't have doors, because it's abandoned. We sleep there. In the morning, he goes to work and I keep looking for medical help. One way or another, I have to look.

I find myself wanting to look for my dignity. See, in Mexico, if somebody has support from over there, people think it's easy, but it's really hard. A person who's ill with cancer, terminal cancer—it is terminal. Because I don't feel like I did before. At this point it's just come here [to the KBI *comedor*] to chat with the sisters, go back home, and lie down and sleep. But only God knows what's going to happen. And I do say to people, "It's not the most pleasant thing in the world, how things have been for me, and I don't know how I'm going to—if I'm going to live two months, three months, but I'm still here, still in the fight."

I had a fight with the owner of that apartment. It was a verbal fight. We argued. I left and he took all my stuff out and put it in the trash can. When I came back, the house was cleaned out. The police got out of their trucks and got their nightsticks out.[17] That's when I saw that it wasn't a chat anymore; it was a bit more. Well, so when I saw they were going to attack me, I jumped a fence and took off running. I was running and then I thought, well, why should I run? I haven't committed any crime. I stopped. Agh, I shouldn't have stopped at all! There were six of them. They started to hit me with their nightsticks, and they're not the wooden ones anymore. They were made of metal.

That's how it was. They put me in the back of the truck, stepped on my head, and gave me electric shocks on my eyes. They wanted me to scream. Another one came and said, "Leave him be." They got in the truck, took pictures of me, took me to the station. They took me to the hospital first. They had broken my finger. It didn't get fixed right. And that's because the police told them not to give me too much medical care. That's why my finger got left where I can't stretch it out. The chief told me, "You know what? Get out of here, go home." I said, "What, you're not going to charge me with anything, any crime?" "No," he said. "So then why did you guys do this to me, sir? Do you see how I'm all smashed up and can't walk? What did I do that was so bad that you guys had to break my fingers, beat me on the legs?"

"No," he said, "you know what? Just get out of here, just leave it." I walked out of the station and lay down right there. Then during the night, slow and careful, I went and slept in the street instead. I don't know what they thought was going on, or why they had told me to get my stuff out.

All in all, I'm in the street. No home, no medical care, no place to sleep, nothing! And in a terminal stage of my illness.

11

Dismantling Access to Asylum

Introduced by Joanna Williams

For millennia, individuals and families have fled situations of insecurity and violence to seek safety in other locations. Religious and moral traditions—including the teachings of Christianity, Judaism, and Islam—encourage or even mandate a response of welcome to those seeking protection. While at times in recent centuries countries around the world have followed these mandates and responded with incredible hospitality, at other moments states have rejected those seeking asylum out of an attitude of xenophobia, which has resulted in individuals remaining in or being deported to persecution and even death. The US government has lately pursued the latter approach, systematically dismantling access to asylum and leveraging the suffering of many in order to discourage and deter the arrival of people fleeing violence to the US-Mexico border. The hundreds of individuals stranded in Nogales, Sonora, who are seeking protection from persecution bear the daily cost of these policies.

Throughout history we have witnessed the consequences of such restrictive policies. One of the most damning examples of this systematic rejection was before and during World War II, when countries throughout the world, including the United States, denied entry to Jews and others fleeing the Holocaust. In part to reckon with the human cost of such immigration policies, the international community drafted and ratified the 1951 Refugee Convention and its 1967 Protocol. The convention and protocol establish a principle of *non-refoulement*, under which member states cannot return a person to a territory where they have a "a well-founded fear of persecution for reasons of race, religion, nationality, political opinion or membership in a particular social group."[1] These agreements also prohibit policies or practices that punish refugees for seeking safety and outline basic standards for the treatment of refugees. The United States is party to the 1967 Protocol and incorporated the principle of *non-refoulement* into domestic law in 1980.[2] The Department of Homeland Security and the Department of Justice are tasked with implementing this legal standard and evaluating who qualifies for asylum in the United States.

Even after these international and domestic legal standards were established, the US government has routinely failed to carry out the protections outlined in the law. Political interests and ideologies often supersede the legal and moral commitment to offering protection to those who flee persecution. For example, during the Central American civil wars, people from Guatemala and El Salvador fled to the United States because they faced persecution based on their race and political opinion. Yet the US government claimed that their migration was primarily motivated by poverty and generalized violence.[3] Moreover, the US government provided military aid to the regimes that were persecuting their own citizens because it viewed opposition to them through the Cold War lens of a communist threat. Because of the US government's alliance with the governments of El Salvador and Guatemala, it wasn't in its political interest to recognize that many Salvadoran and Guatemalan migrants fit the refugee definition. Faced with this government failure, grassroots communities throughout the United States acted in solidarity with asylum-seekers out of their religious and moral convictions. The Sanctuary Movement was born to provide the protection that the government was unwilling to afford to asylum-seekers.[4] Through the Sanctuary Movement, churches declared themselves as sanctuaries in order to protect Central Americans from deportation to persecution. In the sanctuary declaration, churches committed to providing material support to refugees and to refuse entrance to immigration authorities who intended to enter their space to detain Central Americans.

Three decades later, the United States is in the midst of another moment of legal and moral reckoning in its response to asylum-seekers. From 2015 to 2017, the number of asylum applications filed by Salvadorans in the United States increased by 150 percent, to 47,260 in 2017. In the same period, Guatemalan applications doubled, to 33,398 in 2017, while the number of Honduran applications increased by 84 percent, to 26,736 in 2017. The number of Mexican asylum-seekers has not increased as dramatically, but Mexicans did file 28,593 asylum applications in 2017, which makes up 11 percent of the total number of asylum applications.[5] Central Americans are fleeing conditions that trace back to the civil wars and the instability

Several Central Americans, firm in the faith that Jesus Christ is with them, travel northward through Mexico by train to request asylum in the United States. Wenceslao Hernández Hernández.

generated by the US government's involvement in the region. As is discussed in the testimonies in this chapter, individuals and families face widespread threats by gangs, and the governments in the region are too weak and corrupt to protect their citizens.

Just as the United States during World War II and during the 1980s reacted to asylum-seekers with policies and practices of rejection and xenophobia, so too the government response to modern-day asylum-seekers is one of intentionally generating widespread suffering in order to deter migration. Numerous policies and practices produce despair, including narrowing the legal definition of who qualifies for asylum protection, dramatically expanding immigration detention, forcing people into limbo in Mexico, and collaborating with other countries in the region to prevent individuals from arriving at the US-Mexico border.

Although domestic US law codifies the internationally recognized standard of who qualifies for asylum protections, the interpretation and application of that law depends on immigration courts. Immigration courts are not part of the judicial branch but are instead administrative courts of the executive branch. That structure means that the attorney general has full power to issue precedent-setting decisions regarding the interpretation of asylum law. In 2018, Attorney General Sessions reversed protections for survivors of domestic violence and in his decision included sweeping language to generally discredit gang-based asylum claims.[6] In 2019, Attorney General Barr further restricted access to asylum by deciding that individuals threatened because of family ties do not qualify as suffering persecution on account of belonging to a particular social group. The most dramatic legal change, however, was the Trump administration announcement in July 2019 that ended asylum for anyone who did not first seek protection in any country that they traveled through on their way to the United States. This rule change, facing ongoing legal challenges, led to immediate deportations of people seeking asylum at US ports of entry back to Central American countries and intense resistance from advocates who outline the dangers that Central Americans face if they seek and are granted asylum in Mexico.[7]

Incarcerating noncitizens is allegedly a mechanism to ensure that individuals attend their immigration court hearings but in reality is used to isolate individuals from community support and make it more difficult to win protection in the United States. The system of immigrant incarceration, or "detention," has expanded dramatically under both President Barack Obama and President Donald Trump. In January 2009, there were thirty-two thousand immigrants in detention every day.[8] By October 2016 that population had grown to over forty thousand people.[9] In September 2019, fifty-two thousand people languished in detention.[10] This expansion is motivated in part by the profit interests of private companies, who run almost three-quarters of detention beds nationally.[11] Other Trump administration policies maximize suffering; most notably, the systematic separation of asylum-seeking families in the summer of 2018 that used criminal prosecution and immigration detention as mechanisms to keep parents away from their children. Communities and religious leaders' strong condemnation of the conditions in immigration detention and the cruel separation of parents and their children and this community mobilization did force the administration to cease the systematic separations.

To avoid sparking such widespread opposition the Trump administration has removed asylum-seekers from public consciousness, through policies that force them into limbo in northern Mexico. Since May of 2018, the administration has enforced a policy of metering at the ports of entry along the US-Mexico border, under which they only process a limited number of asylum-seekers each day. As a result of this policy, in August 2019 there were at least twenty-six thousand asylum-seekers waiting in northern Mexico, and depending on the border city waits range from two to six months just for an individual to begin the asylum process in the United States.[12] Even once a person or family is able to officially request asylum in the United States, they are increasingly being returned to Mexico to wait for their US court dates under a policy misleadingly titled "Migrant Protection Protocols" but more colloquially known as Remain in Mexico. As of January 2020, at least fifty-nine thousand asylum-seekers were returned to Mexico under this policy and must wait many months just for the first of a long series of court dates to evaluate their asylum claim. Because of obstacles in access to attorneys, 99 percent of people subjected to the program appear in court without an attorney. Moreover, between the inception of the program and January 2020, there were at least 816 reported cases of individuals who have been attacked, kidnapped, or raped in northern Mexico after being returned.[13] Remain in Mexico is a policy designed not to work, and it aims to use economic and physical insecurity to force people to give up on their asylum claims.

Another dimension of government policy to deny access to asylum aims to prevent individuals from even arriving at the US-Mexico border. This approach dates back to the Obama administration, which collaborated with the Mexican government to implement the Southern Border Plan. This plan dramatically increased immigration enforcement in Mexico and resulted in both an increase in deportations from Mexico to Central America as well as an increase in reports of human rights abuses.[14] The Trump administration has built on these efforts by leveraging economic interests to convince the Mexican government to expand immigration enforcement via a newly created National Guard.[15] Moreover, it has forged agreements with El Salvador, Honduras, and Guatemala to force people to seek asylum in those countries instead of coming to the United States.

The testimonies in this chapter make clear the way that these policies have generated suffering and despair. As in the 1980s, they expose the failure of government and the need for alternative responses by civil society. Faced with a government policy of generating hopelessness, we are invited to be communities of hope through our actions of direct aid and accompaniment as well as advocacy.

GUADALUPE

Me llamo Guadalupe Reynoso, de Tlacoapa, Guerrero. Tengo dos hijos, una niña de diecisiete años y un niño de quince, y mi madre, que depende de mí. La situación por la que vengo a pedir asilo es porque, desde 2013, mi pueblo ha sido saqueado por hombres armados. Pero se había mantenido al margen, porque los hombres del pueblo, los ciudadanos, lo protegían con una policía ciudadana. Pero llegó el momento en que los hombres se debilitaron. Ya no había dinero, no había cómo sustentar, porque eran asaltos cada quince días, cada mes . . . que venían a saquear a nuestros pueblos.

La disputa es porque se va a abrir una mina ahí en nuestros pueblos, una mina de oro. Ya está abierta una, en Iyotla, por una empresa estadounidense que se llama Terra Nova. Está como a una hora quince minutos de nuestro pueblo y está otra como a quince minutos. El único acceso a esta mina es mi pueblo. Y estos hombres armados que vienen de otro municipio, de Los Bajos, quieren apoderarse de nuestras casas, nuestros terrenos . . . o más bien, ya están apoderados, porque ellos ya se metieron a nuestras casas, ya viven ahí. Una casa que yo había hecho de madera, como cabaña, ya también la destruyeron.

Nosotros éramos comerciantes de trastes. Vendíamos ollas, cazuelas, todo eso de peltre y plástico. Yo también trabajaba para el sector salud. Era archivista. Cerca de mi casa estaba un hospital y ahí trabajaba. Vivíamos bien con nuestro negocito y mi trabajo. Mi padre murió de insuficiencia renal, le dimos hemodiálisis por año y medio, quedamos económicamente vacíos, pero gracias a Dios salimos adelante.

El once de noviembre de 2018 fue la fecha en que ya nos salimos. Entraron estos grupos a nuestro pueblo. A mi hijo me lo querían quitar, para llevárselo al grupo armado, y a mi niña, ocuparla como mujer o querida de alguno de ellos. Decidimos salirnos de ahí definitivamente. Yo conforme recuperé a mis hijos, nos salimos en la noche caminando.

Caminamos como doce horas por el monte, para no exponer a mis hijos, hasta la cabecera municipal, que es Leonardo Bravo, Chichihualco. El riesgo era que en el camino me los pudieran quitar. A mi mamá no me la traje. Mi esposo hace catorce años que murió. Yo siempre he sido toda para mis hijos. Este año ya no habían estudiado, por la situación violenta que se vivía. Llegamos a Zumpango del Río y ahí nos dieron refugio a 170 familias, que fuimos desplazadas por los hombres armados. Allí estuvimos viviendo en un auditorio por más de siete meses. Todos juntos. Así como aquí que se cocina mucha comida, que se baña uno en un solo baño para toda la gente, dos baños, todos trabajábamos igual: hombres y mujeres.

Fuimos a ver al gobierno de México, López Obrador. No nos dio solución, sólo nos dio un dinero para sustentarnos en la estancia ahí en Chichihualco. Nos dio dos mil pesos a cada familia, para renta de una casa por seis meses. Fue lo único. Nos pasamos un mes quince días afuera del Palacio Nacional para conseguirlo. Dijeron que nos regresarían a nuestros pueblos en seis u ocho meses, cuando entrara la Guardia Nacional. Llegó la Guardia, pero llegó a la costa donde se genera dinero, donde el gobernador tiene negocios y genera dinero. Pero nuestros pueblos siguen igual o peor. Ya no hay dinero, no hay trabajo, no hay gente, porque ellos ya se apoderaron de todo. Nuestro pueblo está regido por un grupo armado. Se llama Policía Comunitaria de Los Bajos. Son sicarios, pero disfrazados de comunitarios para que el gobierno no les haga nada. Y disfracen todo lo que hagan.

Llegamos de regreso de México y estuvimos dos meses en Los Bajos igual, en el grupo comunitario. Luego nos dijo el Presidente Municipal que teníamos que buscar la forma de sobrevivir, de trabajar. Pero pagaban cien pesos diarios y a las mujeres ochenta. Sí íbamos a trabajar, porque yo ya había perdido el trabajo de base que tenía. Yo antes ya tenía ISSSTE, ya ganaba cuatro mil pesos quincenales, ya llevaba nueve años, trabajo de base, pero lo perdí. El día domingo, dos de junio, entraron los hombres armados que estaban en mi pueblo, a una localidad que se llama El Naranjo, a diez minutos de donde estábamos ahora todas las familias. Ya tenían controlado todo el corredor: Filo de Caballos, Campo de Aviación, Los Morros, La Laguna, La Media Luna, Mirabán, Espuros, Xochipala, Mezcala. Tomaron todos los pueblos y entraron a la cabecera municipal. ¿Qué nos espera? ¡Nada! ¡Ni regresar! Si nos encuentran aquí, nos van a matar. Porque ellos matan sin más ni más.

Yo tengo un tío que era el acaparador de la goma de opio, desde hace como diez años. Ese negocio ya no vale nada, pero se le quedó el nombramiento. Esa mercancía ya no vale. Pero también comerciaba otras plantas medicinales que transportaba a México, al Centro Botánico Azteca. Ellos querían tumbar a mi tío para quedarse con el pueblo. Por ser familia nos vinculaban. Y empezaron a matar a la familia. Mi mamá tiene ocho hermanos. Él era el único metido en ese negocio. Pero a otro tío ya lo mataron. A un primo y a sus dos peones los mataron. Tenía huertas grandes y tenía dos muchachos que lo ayudaban y los mataron. Mi familia se salió toda. Unos se fueron a Morelos, otros al Estado de México. Otros se quedan y nosotros nos salimos para acá. A mi primo que vive en Morelos, lavador de autos, hace quince días lo mataron y también a la mujer. Le perforaron el pulmón. Mi tía pregunta cómo vemos la situación acá. Pero ella no se quiere venir porque no quiere perder su casa, aunque le están matando a los hijos. Entonces, yo me voy al otro lado porque ellos nos van a buscar y nos van a matar. Nosotros no tenemos ni a dónde ir. Perdimos todo, por ser familia, lo perdimos todo.

Mis tíos no me entienden. Ellos me dicen que si no he hecho nada mal, ¿por qué huyo? Ellos no me entienden. Pero ellos me van a buscar y me van a matar. Hay mucha gente a la que mataron. Tengo videos fuertes donde ese día que entraron, a dos señores de ahí, se los llevaron y los colgaron. Algo triste.

Yo quiero que mis hijos ya no padezcan, que ellos estén bien. Que nos quitemos de tanta delincuencia, que durmamos a gusto. Aquí me duermo tranquila, no siento la noche. En mi pueblo ya llevábamos años sin dormir, sin vivir en paz. Con temor y angustia no se puede vivir. Aquí la situación está un poco difícil, pero, la verdad, aquí yo ya me pierdo tranquila, me pierdo en la noche.

Si no fuera por esta situación, yo no hubiera perdido mi trabajo. No es un gusto, no voy a Estados Unidos para hacerme rica. Voy por la seguridad de mis hijos. Quiero vivir y prosperar. Es sufrimiento para uno. Imagínese, yo en mi casa me levantaba, ponía lumbre, hacía mi cafecito. Bien con mis hijos. Quiero que mi hija siga estudiando y que mi hijo agarre una carrera, aunque sea una carrera corta. Que se valgan por sí mismos. Un día yo voy a faltar.

La estancia aquí, me decían, son tres meses. Yo pensaba: "Si ya aguanté ocho meses fuera de mi casa" [*pausa*]. Si a mi hija me la detienen, no importa. Aquí llegamos el seis de agosto. Es cansado.

Aquí hay mucha gente que viene de allá, que trabaja para los cárteles de allá. Hay gente de Sonora, gente de Sinaloa, que aquellos hombres les pagan para que estos hombres les hagan los servicios. Por eso, me urge entrar. No me siento totalmente segura.

Y estoy muy agradecida por los servicios que aquí nos han dado.

IIIIIIIIIIIIIIIII

My name is Guadalupe Reynoso. I was born in Tlacoapa in Guerrero, Mexico. I have two children, a girl who's seventeen and a boy who's fifteen—and my mother, who is dependent on my support. I'm here to request asylum because of a situation where since 2013, my town has been being looted by men with guns. At first we had managed to avoid getting caught up in it.[16] The men of the town, the citizens, kept the town protected with a citizen police force. But the moment came when the men weakened. There was no money left, no way to feed our families, because attacks happened every other week, every month, where they came to loot our towns.

The reason for the dispute is that they're going to dig a mine there, where our towns are, a gold mine.[17] One is already dug, in Iyotla, by a US company called Terra Nova. That one's about an hour and fifteen minutes from our town. And another one is about fifteen minutes away. The only route to this mine is through my town. And these men with guns, who are from another municipality, from Los Bajos, they want to take control of our houses, control of our land—or rather, they're already in control, because they've already entered our houses, they already live there.[18] And a house that I built, a wood house, sort of a cabin, they destroyed that too.

We were kitchenware dealers. We sold pots and pans, all that enamel-ware and plastic stuff. I also worked in health care. I was a file clerk. A hospital was near my house and I worked there. We had a good life with our little business and my job. My father died from kidney failure. We had him on dialysis for a year and a half. Financially we were emptied out, but praise God, we were able to carry on.

November the eleventh, 2018, that was the day we finally left. They came into our town, these groups.[19] My son they wanted to take away from me and have him join the armed group, and my daughter they wanted to put to work as a girlfriend or sweetheart for one of them. We all decided to leave there for good. I agreed, and I got my children back and we left on foot that night.

We walked about twelve hours through the backcountry to avoid exposing my children, all the way to the municipal capital, which is Chichihualco, Leonardo Bravo.[20] The danger was that someone might take them away from me on the road. I didn't bring my mom along with us. My husband has been dead for fourteen years. I've always been everything for my kids. They hadn't been at school that year because of the violence that we were living through. We got to Zumpango del Río and were given shelter there,[21] me and my kids and 169 other families who had been displaced by the men with guns. We were in that area for more than seven months, living in an auditorium. Everyone living together. Just like the way it is here: the cooking food in big quantities, the washing yourself in one shared bathroom, you know, two bathrooms for all those people. We all worked on an equal basis, men and women.

We went to see the Mexican government, López Obrador.[22] He didn't have a solution for us; he just gave us some money to live on during the wait there in Chichihualco. He gave 120 dollars to each family for rent for six months.[23] That was it. We spent a month and a half outside the *Palacio Nacional* to get it.[24] They said they were going to return us to our towns in six or eight months, when the National Guard started.[25] The Guard did come to Guerrero—but to the coast, where people make money, where the governor has businesses and makes money; but our towns are the same or worse.[26] There's no money left, there's no work, there's no people, because these men took control of everything. Our town is ruled by an armed group. It's called "Community Police of Los Bajos." They're hired killers disguised as community people to keep the government from doing anything about them. And to disguise everything they're doing.

We got back from Mexico City, and we spent two months in Los Bajos the same way, at the "community" group's headquarters. Then the mayor told us we had to look for a way to survive, to work. But they were paying six dollars a day, five for women.[27] We did start going to work. Personally, I had already lost the steady job I had. I had my ISSSTE.[28] I was making 240 bucks biweekly.[29] I had nine years seniority, permanent status, but I lost it. On Sunday, June second, the men with guns who now had my town came into a place called El Naranjo, which is ten minutes from where all of us families were now. Now they had the whole corridor under their control: Filo de Caballos, Campo de Aviación, Los Morros, La Laguna, La Media Luna, Mirabán, Espuros, Xochipala, Mezcala. They took over all of those towns and came into the municipal capital. What can we expect now? Nothing! Not going home, nothing! If they find us here, they will kill us. Because these people kill without a second thought.

I have an uncle. He had been the opium-paste amasser for about ten years. That business isn't worth anything anymore, but he still had the appointment.[30] That product has lost its value. But he also dealt in other medicinal plants, which he would ship to Mexico City, to the Centro Botánico Azteca.[31] Well, these people, they wanted to take down my uncle so they could have the town. Since we're family, they connected us. And they started to kill our family. My mom has eight brothers and sisters. He was the only one involved in that business. But they killed a different uncle. They killed my cousin along with his two apprentices. He had big orchards, and he had two guys who used to help him. They killed them. My family got out, all of us. Some went to Morelos, some went to Mexico State. Some are still back there, and we left for here. They killed my cousin who was living in Morelos as a car washer, that was fifteen days ago, along with his girlfriend. They punctured her lung. My aunt asks us how things look here. But she doesn't want to leave and come here because she doesn't want to lose her house. Even though they're killing her children. So I'm not going anywhere, because those people will look for us and they will kill us. We don't have anywhere to go. We lost everything, just for having family ties, we lost all of it.

My aunts and uncles don't understand. They say if I haven't done anything wrong, why run away. They don't understand. But those people will look for me and they will kill me. There's lots of people they've killed. I have graphic videos from the day they came in, of two gentlemen from there that they took away and hanged. Really sad.

What I want is for my kids not to suffer, to be well. For us to get away from all the crime, to be able to sleep nice and comfortable. Here, I sleep without worrying. I don't feel the night. In my town, we had spent years without sleeping, without living in peace. You can't really live when you've got fear and anxiety. Things here are a little difficult, but honestly, I can lose myself without worrying here, lose myself in the night.[32]

If it weren't for this situation, I wouldn't have lost my job. It's not by choice; I'm not going to the United States because I want to get rich. I'm going for my children's safety. I want to know what it's like to thrive. It's an ordeal for a person. Imagine it, in my house I used to get up, get the fire going, make myself a little coffee—with my kids. I want my daughter to continue school and my son to get himself a degree, even a quick one. For them to stand on their own two feet. One day I won't be here.

The wait here is three months, that's what I've been told.[33] My thought has been that if I already managed to hold out for eight months, away from home . . . If they decide to keep my daughter in detention, that's okay. We got here on August sixth. It's tiring.

There are a lot of people here who come from there, who work for the cartels there. And there are Sonorans, Sinaloans, that those men pay for the services of these men.[34] That's why I need to get in. I don't feel totally safe.

I'm really grateful for the services we've been given here.

MARÍA ÁNGELES

Soy María Ángeles. Tengo veintitrés años. Soy originaria de El Salvador. Fuimos cuatro hermanos. Cuando yo tenía doce años, ya ayudaba a trabajar a mi mamá vendiendo enchiladas y pupusas. Gracias a este trabajo mi mamá pudo darnos estudio.

Yo tenía un padrastro. Mi padrastro maltrataba a mi mamá. Cuando peleaban, yo era pequeña, pero recuerdo que me metía entre los dos para impedir los golpes.

A los trece años, pedí permiso para tener novio. Del 2012 al 2013 estuve de novia y en el 2014 me acompañé de él. El trece de agosto de 2014 nació mi primera niña.

Nunca cruzó por mi mente dejar a mi mamá y venirme, pero a ella la mataron los pandilleros. Ya se habían separado mis papás, así que me quedé con mi niña de año y medio y tres hermanitos: una hermana de dieciséis, otro de once y una niña de ocho años. La causa de su muerte fue que ya no les quiso dar pupusas gratis a los mareros. A los cuatro meses de que se las negó, la asesinaron. Nosotros dejamos la casa y anduvimos de un lado a otro, porque nos vigilaban. Por eso dejé varios trabajos. En 2019, vi que ya no podía vivir así. A mi hermanito lo querían matar, lo amenazaban. La vez que ya decidí venirme fue en San Rafael. Decidí poner venta de pupusas y me empezó a pasar lo mismo que a mi mamá. Salí el diecinueve de mayo de este año, 2019.

Me vine con mis dos hermanitos más pequeños y mi niña, con doscientos dólares en la bolsa y sola con los tres. Pagué coyote hasta Guatemala. Me cobró mil [pesos] por los cuatro. Me dijo: "En Guatemala, va a encontrar un río y ahí vea cómo le hace". Encontré a un señor que me pasó sin cobrarme, sacándole la vuelta a Migración. Ahí empecé a pedir raite. Lo que traía lo dejé para comida de mi hija y hermanitos.

En Tapachula, compré dos boletos. A mi niña pequeña yo la cargaba, otro boleto para mi hermana y el niño se lo trajo el chofer como ayudante sin pagarle. Fueron cuatro noches de viaje hasta Tijuana. En ningún lugar me pidieron papeles.

En Tijuana, le pregunté al taxista cómo hacerle. Me dijo: "Te voy a dejar en el muro y ahí te avientas". Así lo hice. Subí al muro al niño de 11 años. Estando arriba, yo ayudé a la niña de ocho años a trepar. Él la jaló de las manos hasta subirla. Estando arriba la niña, la colgó tomándola de las manos y la dejó ir hacia abajo al lado de Estados Unidos. Luego subí a mi hija de tres años y mi hermano se la tiró a la niña de ocho años, que ya estaba abajo. Me ayudó a subir a mí. Se tiró él y al fin me tiré yo.

Como a los quince metros nos encontró Migración. "¿De dónde vienen? ¿Por qué?", me preguntaron. Le expliqué mi situación pero no me creyó. Dijo que todos decíamos lo mismo. Nos subió a la perrera. Luego nos subieron a otra patrulla, que nos llevó a la hielera. Me separaron de mi hermanito de once años. A mi hermanita me la iban a quitar. Finalmente nos sacaron a mí y a mi hija. Ya no supe más de mis hermanos.

Me sacaron por Tijuana. Sin dinero, sin conocer a nadie, me puse a pedir en la calle. A un señor que vendía tacos, le pedí el teléfono prestado. Hablé con mi tía que está en los Estados Unidos. Le dije que me habían quitado a mis hermanos. No me aceptaron el acta que traía sobre la patria potestad de mis hermanos. Yo no sabía ni dónde se habían quedado. También le dije a mi tía que me habían dado cita con el juez para el tres de septiembre y me habían regresado a México.

Después que llamé a mi tía, me asaltó un hombre. Sólo traía el dinero que me habían dado a los que pedí. Había logrado juntar doscientos pesos. El hombre me dijo: "Me das lo que traes porque tú no eres de aquí". Yo, con el temor que me quitara a mi hija, le di el dinero que me habían dado sin resistirme. Le entregué los doscientos. Me puse a pedir dinero de nuevo y me fui a la central. Un chofer se compadeció y me compró el boleto para Nogales. Me dijo que Tijuana era una ciudad peligrosa y que no me convenía estar ahí.

Llegué a Nogales. Yo me sentía asustada, desesperada. . . . Pedí a un taxista que me llevara a un lugar donde pudiera entrar a los Estados Unidos. Me llevó a un lugar que no sé dónde fue, pero había muchos furgones. Ahí me entregué a Migración. Migración me trató muy mal. Me dijo que si iba para estar de mantenida, que decía lo mismo que decían todos y que eso ya los tenía hartos. También me dijo que le diera gracias a Dios porque no me quitó el derecho a corte. Me detuvieron siete días. Una oficial me hizo una larga entrevista y me dijo que no me iban a dar asilo.

También hubo una abogada que me dijo que cometieron un delito con tener a mis hermanos detenidos de ocho a diez días. A uno se lo llevaron a Tucson y a otro a Michigan. Mi tía se movió, investigó y los reunieron en un albergue.

Cuando me deportaron aquí a Nogales, a la calle, me encontré con un señor que iba con unos platos de comida. Le pregunté: "¿Dónde estoy?" Con mucho miedo abrazaba a mi niña con fuerza para que no me la fueran a robar. Me dijo: "¡Usted no es de aquí!" "No", le dije. "Me acaban de sacar de Migración". En ese momento, como un ángel, apareció la Madre Alicia que me trajo a este albergue, donde esperaré hasta el día tres de septiembre, para ir a Tijuana y entrar a ver al juez. De ahí dependerá mi futuro.

||||||||||||||||

I'm María Ángeles, twenty-three years old, originally from El Salvador. There were four of us kids. When I was twelve, I was already helping my mom with her work selling enchiladas and *pupusas*.[35] It was thanks to that work that my mom was able to put us through school.

I had a stepfather. My stepfather abused my mom. When they would start fighting, I was little, but I remember I'd get in between them, to block the punches.

When I was thirteen I asked for permission to have a boyfriend. From 2012 to 2013 I was engaged, and in 2014 I went with him. On August thirteenth, 2014, my first child was born, a daughter.

It never entered my mind to leave my mom and come here, but the gang, they killed her. My parents had separated, so it was just me with my one-and-a-half-year-old daughter and three brothers and sisters: a sister who's sixteen, a brother who's eleven, and a little girl, eight years old. The reason for my mom's death was that she didn't want to give *pupusas* for free to the members of the gang anymore. Four months after she told them no, they murdered her. We left our house, and we kept moving around, because they would start watching us. I quit a lot of jobs for that reason. In 2019 I realized I couldn't live like that anymore. They were after my little brother; they were threatening to kill him. The time I finally decided to come was in San Rafael. I decided to put out *pupusas* for sale, and the same thing started happening to me that happened to my mom.[36] I left on May the nineteenth of this year, 2019.

I left with my brother and youngest sister and my daughter, with two hundred US dollars in my pocket, by myself with the three of them.[37] I paid for a *coyote* as far as Guatemala. He charged me sixty bucks for the four of us.[38] He told me, "In Guatemala, ma'am, you'll come to a river and then you'll have to figure out how to go about it." I found a gentleman who got me through without charging me, by dodging Immigration. From there

I started to hitchhike. What I had left I kept for food for my daughter and brother and sister.

In Tapachula, I bought two bus tickets. My little girl rode on my lap. The other ticket was for my sister, and my little brother the driver took along as his unpaid assistant. It was a four-night trip to get to Tijuana. Nowhere did they ask me for papers.

In Tijuana I asked the taxi driver how to go about it. He told me, "I'm gonna drop you off at the wall and you just throw yourself." That's what I did. I got the boy up the wall, the eleven-year-old. While he was on top, I helped the girl climb up, the eight-year-old. He pulled her by the wrists until she was up. Once she was on top, he hung her over and held onto her wrists and let her slide down toward the ground on the United States side. Then I got my daughter up the wall, the three-year-old, and my brother threw her to my eight-year-old sister, who was on the ground. He helped me get myself up. He jumped down and finally I jumped down.

In about fifty feet, we ran into Immigration. I was asked, "Where are you coming from and why?" I explained my case to him but he didn't believe me. He said we all said the same thing. He put us in the patrol truck. Then we were put in another truck, which took us to the cooler.[39] Then they separated me from my little eleven-year-old brother. They were also going to take my little sister away from me. Finally, they expelled me and my daughter. I got no more information about my brother and sister.

They sent me out through Tijuana. I had no money, didn't know anyone, so I started begging in the street. There was a gentleman selling tacos I asked to lend me his phone. I talked to my aunt in the United States, told her they had taken my brother and sister away from me. They hadn't accepted the certificate I was carrying that dealt with parental authority over my brother and sister. I didn't even know where they'd ended up. I told my aunt too that they had given me an appointment with the judge on September third and returned me to Mexico.

After I called my aunt, a man mugged me. All I had was the money I'd been given by the people I'd begged from. I'd managed to put together twelve bucks.[40] The man said to me, "You're gonna give me what you got because you're not from here." I was terrified he would take my daughter away from me, so I gave him the money they'd given me, no resistance. I handed over the twelve dollars. I started begging for money again, went to the bus station. A driver felt sorry for me and bought me the ticket to Nogales. He told me Tijuana was a dangerous city and it wasn't a good place for me to be.

I got to Nogales. I felt scared, desperate. I asked a taxi driver to take me to a place where I could enter the United States. He took me to a place, I don't know where it was, but there were a lot of boxcars.[41] I turned myself in to

Immigration there. Immigration treated me really badly. Asked me if I was coming there to sponge off the government. Said what I was saying was the same thing everyone else said and they were sick of hearing it. They also told me to thank the Lord because they hadn't taken away my right to a court hearing. They held me for seven days. I had a long interview with an officer, and she told me they weren't going to give me asylum.

There was also a lawyer, who told me that they had violated the law by keeping my brother and sister in detention for eight or nine or ten days. One of them had been taken to Tucson and the other to Michigan. My aunt got moving, looked into it, and they put them back together at the same shelter.

When they deported me here, to Nogales, to the street, I met a gentleman who was carrying some plates of food. I asked him, "Where am I?" I was really fearfully hugging my little girl tight so no one could try to steal her from me. He said, "You are not from here, ma'am, are you?" "No," I said, "I just got expelled by Immigration." Just then, like an angel, Madre Alicia appeared.[42] She brought me to this shelter. This is where I'll wait until September third, to go to Tijuana and go in to see the judge. My future will depend on that.[43]

NICOLE

Soy Nicole Camila Pérez, venezolana, treinta y seis años de edad, con el título de Técnico Superior en Informática y Licenciatura en Contaduría Pública. Obtuve mi título profesional en el año 2014.

Mi madre me educó con principios y valores democráticos, ser fiel a mis ideales y políticas de vida, a mantener siempre el amor por la libertad, la paz y a la democracia.

He sido víctima de discriminación, amenaza de muerte, persecución y agresión física, todo por tener posición política en contra del actual gobierno dictatorial de Nicolás Maduro Moros y por pertenecer a un partido político de la oposición venezolana. Ahora soy una perseguida política y tengo gran temor de perder la vida si regreso al país.

Detallo los hechos que ocurrieron y me han motivado a solicitar resguardo y protección.

Desde joven, comencé a militar en el partido Voluntad Popular, ya que dentro del colegio, el Colegio Universitario de Administración y Mercadeo, había un fuerte movimiento estudiantil en apoyo a los partidos de oposición, principalmente Voluntad Popular y Primero Justicia.

En el año 2014, comienzan en Venezuela las protestas más duras. Pasan de ser protestas sectoriales para convertirse en protestas generales. El doce de febrero, el dirigente Leopoldo López llama a lo que se dice la toma de Venezuela. Ese día todo el país se paralizó. La población cerró las calles, todas las plazas, todo el país atendió el llamado hecho por Leopoldo López en Caracas. Una gigantesca marcha fue reprimida brutalmente por la Guardia Nacional Bolivariana y los colectivos, asesinando a muchos jóvenes, lo que hizo que se extendieran las protestas. A los días siguientes, las protestas fueron aumentando, se formaron por parte de los estudiantes y jóvenes universitarios, lo que se denominó la resistencia. Estos jóvenes, exponiendo sus vidas, tomaron todos los rincones de Venezuela; de igual forma la represión por parte del Gobierno se recrudeció: los colectivos por orden de Nicolás Maduro y Diosdado Cabello fueron armados, recibieron la orden de disparar y asesinar a los jóvenes y estudiantes que estaban en las protestas. Yo, como no era partidaria del gobierno y viendo como era mi gente atropellada, perseguida y asesinada en las calles de Caracas y de toda Venezuela, no podía ser ajena a esta situación.

Nunca pensé que los hombres de confianza de mi jefa mantuvieran una vigilancia extrema sobre mí. El día seis de mayo de 2014, al salir de mi trabajo, de camino, detuve mi auto y le entregué a los jóvenes y estudiantes que se encontraban en la protesta en la plaza Altamira algo de agua para que se hidrataran y comida, ya que esos jóvenes estaban luchando por la libertad de Venezuela y estaban arriesgando sus vidas por nosotros. Pensé que esto era un pequeño aporte, de mi parte, a la lucha de la resistencia. Al día siguiente, al llegar a mi trabajo, fui escoltada por miembros colectivos a la oficina de mi jefa, quien al verme recriminó mi actitud, me exigió en un tono amenazante que le explicara cómo es que yo, siendo empleada de Banco de Comercio Exterior y sabiendo que es una institución del estado, estuviese apoyando las protestas y en contra del Gobierno y que eso a ella no le parecía correcto. Yo le dije lo primero que se me ocurrió y por supuesto que no me creyó nada, pero me dejó tranquila, no sin antes amenazarme, diciéndome que no quería que se volviera a repetir esa situación. Sus hombres, los colectivos, me escoltaron hasta la oficina. Al llegar a mi puesto de trabajo, también me amenazaron, diciéndome que si ellos se daban cuenta de otra actividad como esa, me costaría mi puesto de trabajo y perjudicaría a mi familia. Después de ver todo lo ocurrido, tomé la decisión de bajar un poco la ayuda y ser más discreta en cuanto al apoyo que yo pudiera dar a los jóvenes de la resistencia. Todo para resguardar mi vida y mi empleo en la institución.

A mediados del año 2017, fue convocado el pueblo a otros actos de protesta por el diputado Freddy Guevara, otro joven venezolano perteneciente al partido de Voluntad Popular. De forma inmediata se activó toda la población, esperanzada de que esta vez sí saldríamos de esta dictadura, que nos estaba matando día a día a todos los venezolanos de hambre y de tristeza. Yo, particularmente, enseguida atendí el llamado realizado por mi compañero de partido Freddy Guevara y me activé, tratando de no involucrarme mucho en el trabajo. Pero sí con algunos compañeros del partido Voluntad Popular, al cual apoyo y soy militante, procedimos a apoyar en nuestro sector a los estudiantes y jóvenes de las protestas. Recolectábamos insumos entre los vecinos.

A medida que las protestas iban aumentando, más jóvenes se unían y la represión también aumentaba de una manera desproporcionada. El gobierno activó todo su aparato represivo, e inclusive el mismo Diosdado Cabello les dio órdenes a los colectivos de que atacaran a todas aquellas personas que se encontraban en las protestas, sin importar si esas personas eran ancianos, mujeres o niños. La violencia de estos colectivos era tal, que a diario producían muchos heridos en cada punto donde se encontraba una protesta de los venezolanos. Aumentó considerablemente el número de muertos de la oposición. Las detenciones ilegales y arbitrarias por parte de la Policía Nacional Bolivariana y la Guardia Nacional Bolivariana eran tantas, que todos los centros de detenciones se encontraban abarrotados en todo el territorio nacional.

En vista de todo lo que estaba sucediendo, fue necesario recolectar entre los vecinos y el partido Voluntad Popular más agua, alimentos y medicinas. Mi compañero Martín y yo, cada dos días, muy temprano en la mañana, les entregábamos a los muchachos de las protestas todo lo recolectado, entre lo cual había agua, alimentos y algunos medicamentos. Pero aconteció que el día doce de junio de 2017, como de costumbre, temprano en la mañana antes de ir a mi trabajo, me preparaba para ir con mi compañero Martín a entregar los insumos recolectados. Y al haber salido de mi casa y caminado escasos trescientos metros, fuimos interceptados repentinamente por unos motorizados, nominados colectivos armados, de la dictadura del gobierno de Nicolás Maduro Moro.

Al ver a estas personas y la situación, traté de dialogar con ellos, pero fue un grave error, ya que esta gente estaba llena de odio y resentimiento hacia nosotros, la oposición. Y sus mentes estaban envenenadas por el dictador Nicolás Maduro, Diosdado Cabello, los hermanos Rodríguez y Freddy Bernal, entre otros. Uno de ellos me gritó de una forma muy vulgar y grosera: "Nicole, lo mejor que puedes hacer es quedarte quieta. Ya sabemos quién eres tú y a lo que te dedicas. Hemos visto que te la pasas ayudando y dándoles comida a los *guarimberos*. Eres una perra escuálida". Yo, al ver esta situación y la actitud que tenían, retrocedí y traté de meterme a mi carro. Pero no me fue posible, ya que una mujer morena, alta, de contextura gruesa, me jaló del cabello y me gritó: "Mira maldita escuálida de mierda,

¡pa' donde crees que vas tú?" Enseguida me dio un golpe en el estómago, el cual hizo que me cayera. Mi compañero, Martín, estaba siendo sujetado por dos colectivos y lo tenían apuntándole con un arma de fuego. Yo entré en pánico y entre lágrimas y sollozos pude ver una figura conocida. Este señor se me acercó y de una manera sigilosa me dijo,

> Coño, Nicole, ¡estás metida en tremendo peo! ¡Vale! Y todo por estar ayudando a esos coños de su madre, escuálidos que quieren y creen que tumbarán nuestra revolución. A ti te están pasando estas cosas por traidora a la patria, pero te puede ir peor y perder la vida. Piensa en tu familia y el dolor que les puedes causar y recuerda que yo sé bien quién eres, dónde vives, con quién vives, dónde trabajas. . . .Yo sé todo de ti y no te escaparás. Lo mejor que puedes hacer es cuidarte y cuidar de ti y tu familia y quedarte quieta para que no te pasen cosas malas. Si no lo haces y sigues con tus ayuditas, te va a ir peor y los voy a matar a ti y a los tuyos. Si tú sigues metiéndote donde no debes, recuerda bien lo que te estoy diciendo y advirtiendo, para que cuando te pase algo más grave, no te sorprenda.

Después de sus amenazas, les dio la orden a sus colectivos que se fueran, no sin antes haberse robado todos los insumos que estaban en mi carro. De regreso a mi casa y estando más tranquila, consulté con mis compañeros del partido y miembros de mi familia los hechos ocurridos. Me aconsejaron que colocara la denuncia en contra de este señor, Raúl González, y sus colectivos, denuncia que formulé ese mismo día. Me comunicaron que este es un delito que no se persigue, ya que no hubo personas de heridas graves ni muertos.

Finalizado el 2017, tomé un pequeño descanso por sugerencia de mis familiares. Ya entrando el año 2018, decidí mantenerme bajo perfil en la parte política y social de mi vida; por sugerencia de familiares y amigos, asistí a unas terapias psicológicas.

En 2019, le tocaba tomar la presidencia de la Asamblea Nacional al partido al cual pertenezco desde el 2011, Voluntad Popular. En vista de que nuestro líder, Leopoldo López, permanecía detenido y la gran mayoría de los dirigentes nacionales se encontraban en el exilio o perseguidos en el país por el régimen de Maduro, surgió un líder político, un joven ingeniero, Juan Guaidó. Toma el cargo de presidente de la Asamblea Nacional el cinco de enero de 2019 y se convierte en el presidente más joven en la historia de la Asamblea Nacional. Este nombramiento nos llenó de alegría, primeramente a los miembros de nuestro partido y segundo a todo un pueblo lleno de esperanza de un cambio. El nuevo presidente de la Asamblea Nacional convoca a una gran marcha a nivel nacional el veintitrés de enero de 2019, donde toda Venezuela se volcó a las calles en respaldo a este llamado. Yo, en lo particular, asistí con mis compañeros del partido Voluntad Popular. Nos colocamos nuestras camisas del partido, nuestra bandera tricolor en mano; yo con mi gorra de Venezuela y el corazón lleno de esperanza, nos fuimos a la juramentación del presidente interino Juan Guaidó. Mis compañeros y yo nos regresamos caminando y, al llegar a la esquina de San José con Las Brisas, nos encontramos con un punto rojo del Partido Socialista Unido de Venezuela, liderado por un grupo de colectivos del sector Las Brisas. Dos individuos de este grupo de colectivos armados comenzaron a apuntarme con sus armas y me amenazaron diciéndome: "Nicole, dentro de poco vas a amanecer muerta, perra escuálida de mierda, traidora a la patria de Bolívar y de nuestro comandante Chávez. Lo que te mereces es morir. Ya estamos cansados de decirte que te dejes de hacer estupideces. La próxima vez no lo contarás". Me quitaron mis pertenencias y yo, con mucho miedo, corrí y me metí a mi edificio. Recibí ayuda de mis vecinos para controlarme y estabilizarme.

Transcurrida la juramentación el día veintitrés de enero, todo el país estaba muy entusiasmado y emocionado, porque por fin íbamos a salir de esta dictadura narco-comunista. Nuestro presidente Juan Guaidó convocó a toda la población en general a sumarse a la entrada de la ayuda humanitaria, el día veintitrés de febrero del mismo año. Yo ese día asistí a la plaza Altamira en Caracas, donde me encontré con mis compañeros del partido Voluntad Popular en apoyo. La presencia de grupos de colectivos se podría ver en los alrededores de la plaza. A eso de las cuatro o cinco de la tarde, la tensión era muy fuerte y tomé la decisión de retirarme e irme a mi casa. Al llegar a la esquina, me encuentro con un grupo de colectivos identificados como colectivos de Las Brisas y un grupo de Guardia Nacional Bolivariana de Venezuela. Ellos al percatarse y darse cuenta que yo venía de la actividad en apoyo a la entrada de la ayuda humanitaria, ya que yo me encontraba identificada con mi camisa y gorra del partido Voluntad Popular, comenzaron a agredirme, a lanzar bombas lacrimógenas. Yo, evitando de que me golpearan con ellas o me asfixiaran, salí corriendo a mi edificio y me encerré en mi casa. Los colectivos y Guardias Nacionales lanzaron piedras, botellas y bombas lacrimógenas al interior del edificio, logrando partir los espejos y reventando las rejas y haciéndole daño a las paredes.

Al mes siguiente, nosotros estábamos continuando con la lucha por la libertad definitiva de Venezuela y acompañando a nuestro presidente interino Juan Guaidó; Venezuela estaba entrando en una etapa de desabastecimiento general y falta de los servicios básicos, como la luz y el agua, en todo el país. El día treinta de marzo de 2019, un grupo de vecinos y miembros del partido Voluntad Popular nos encontrábamos protestando pacíficamente en la avenida Fuerzas Armadas, por tener casi un mes sin los servicios de luz y agua. Transcurridas las horas y ya cayendo la tarde, un grupo de colectivos pasaron por la zona donde yo me encontraba protestando con mis vecinos y compañeros del partido. Uno de ellos me identificó, llamándome por mi nombre, y se me fue encima, agrediéndome con empujones, hasta que me tiró al piso. Estando yo en el piso, comenzaron dos individuos a darme de patadas en distintas partes de mi cuerpo. Ya en medio de tantos golpes, patadas, gritos y amenazas de muerte, yo pude identificar a Raúl González, el cual ya me había realizado amenazas de quitarme la vida a mí y a mi familia en el 2017. Este señor continuaba golpeándome y con un arma apuntándome directamente me decía, gritando, que esta vez sí me iba a matar y que le echaría mis restos a los perros, que acabaría con todas las personas escuálidas y traidoras como yo, que no merecemos vivir y que lo mejor era matarme. En medio de la angustiante situación, estos individuos recibieron una llamada y se fueron, pero no sin antes acentuar su amenaza de que lo que en realidad querían era matarme. Cuando desperté, me encontraba en una clínica, donde recibí atención médica. El primero de abril de 2019, interpuse la denuncia ante el Ministerio Público en contra de Raúl González y los colectivos armados del sector Las Brisas, dirigidos por el narco-gobierno dictador de Nicolás Maduro.

Durante mucho tiempo me negué a la posibilidad de irme de mi hermoso país, Venezuela. Me prometí no abandonarla nunca y luchar hasta la muerte por mis ideales, como me lo inculcó mi madre desde mi adolescencia. Fueron tantas las amenazas que recibí de muerte, por diferentes vías, el asedio que me tenían y el temor a perder mi vida, que tomé la difícil, triste y dura decisión de dejarlo todo, salir corriendo y huir de mi país, Venezuela, queriendo evitar lo peor.

Salí del país el veintiséis de abril de 2019 para proteger mi vida, recuperar mi libertad y mis derechos en un país que me acogiera, me brindara protección y me diera la oportunidad de hacer una nueva vida, sentirme segura, estar libre de angustia y no tener miedo. Por lo antes expuesto y en aras de salvaguardar mi vida, voy a pedir asilo a Estados Unidos, país que ha demostrado tener libertad y democracia.

llllllllllllllll

I'm Nicole Camila Pérez, from Venezuela, thirty-six years old, with an advanced specialist's degree in information technology and a bachelor's in accounting.[44] I obtained my professional qualification in 2014.

My mother brought me up on democratic values and principles, taught me to stay faithful to my ideals and personal policies and to always keep alive my love for freedom, peace, and democracy.

I've suffered discrimination, death threats, persecution, and physical attacks, all for being politically opposed to the current tyrannical government of Nicolás Maduro and for belonging to a political party that is part of the Venezuelan opposition. Now I am a political exile and am very much afraid that I will lose my life if I return to my country.

I will detail the events that took place that are my motivation for appealing for protection and personal security.

I got involved as an activist with the People's Will Party while still young.[45] There was a strong student movement at my college, the Technical College of Management and Commerce, that supported the opposition parties, mainly People's Will and Justice First.

The year 2014 was when the most intense protests began in Venezuela. At that point they went beyond being local-level protests and became nationwide protests. On February the twelfth, our leader, Leopoldo López, called for the Taking of Venezuela, as it was called. That day the whole country came to a stop. The populace closed the streets, closed all the squares. The whole country responded to the call of Leopoldo López in Caracas. A gigantic march was brutally repressed by the Bolivarian National Guard and the collectives, who murdered many young people, which caused the protests to extend into the following days.[46] The protests kept growing. They were made up of students and university-educated young people, what was dubbed the resistance. These young people put their lives on the line and took over every corner of Venezuela. The repression by the government correspondingly worsened. The collectives, by order of Nicolás Maduro and Diosdado Cabello, were armed, and they received the order to open fire and murder the young people and students who were taking part in the protests.[47] Since I wasn't on the government's side, and as I saw my people being trampled, persecuted, and murdered in the streets of Caracas and throughout Venezuela, I couldn't be oblivious to this situation.

It never crossed my mind that my boss's lieutenants were keeping me under close surveillance. On May sixth, 2014, after I left work in my car, I stopped along the way to drop off a few things with the young people and students at the protest in Altamira Square, a little water to keep them hydrated and some food. Since those young people were fighting for the freedom of Venezuela and risking their lives for us, I thought this was a small contribution I could make to the resistance's fight. The next day when I got to work, I was escorted by collectivists to my boss's office. As soon as she saw me she reprimanded me for my attitude. In a threatening tone she demanded I explain how it was that I, an employee of the Foreign Trade Bank, knowing that it was a state institution, came to be supporting the protests and working against the government. To her that didn't seem to make sense. I said the first thing that occurred to me to say, and of course she didn't believe me, but she left me in peace, though not before threatening me by saying she didn't want the same situation to arise again. Her lieutenants, the collectivists, escorted me to my office. When we got to my work area, they too threatened me by telling me that if they found out about any other activity like that, it would cost me my job and harm my family. Considering everything that had happened, I made the decision to stop helping so much and be more discreet with regard to any support I might be able to give to the young people of the resistance. Just to protect my life and my employment at the bank.

In mid-2017, the people were called to new acts of protest by National Assembly member Freddy Guevara, another young Venezuelan belonging to the People's Will Party.[48] Immediately, the whole populace went into action, given hope that this time we *would* emerge from this dictatorship that was killing every Venezuelan day by day, through hunger and sorrow. Personally, I responded right away to the call issued by Freddy Guevara, my fellow party member, by going into action. I tried not to get too involved in the work, but along with some fellow members of the party of which I'm a supporter and activist, People's Will, I did proceed to generate support in our neighborhood for the students and young people in the protests. We would gather supplies from among the residents.

As the protests kept growing, more young people were joining in and the repression was also growing, disproportionately. The government sent its whole repressive apparatus into action. In fact, Diosdado Cabello himself gave orders to the collectives to attack everyone at the protests without regard to whether they were senior citizens, women, or children. The violence of these collectives was such that, on a daily basis, in every location where there was a protest by the Venezuelan people, many individuals were being injured. The number of opposition deaths grew significantly. The illegal and arbitrary arrests by the Bolivarian National Police and the Bolivarian National Guard were so numerous that all the detention centers were packed, all over Venezuelan soil.

In view of everything that was happening, we needed to gather more water, food, and medicine from among residents and People's Will members. Every other day, first thing in the morning, my partner Martín and I would take everything that had been collected, which included water, food, and a few medications, and deliver it to the kids at the protests. But on June twelfth, 2017, something happened. As usual, early in the morning before going to work, I was getting ready to go with my partner Martín and drop off the supplies that we had collected. We left and had traveled barely three hundred yards when we were cut off suddenly by armed motorcycle collectivists, acting as agents of the dictatorship, the Nicolás Maduro government.

When I saw these people and what the situation was, I got out and tried to talk to them. But that was a grave mistake, because these people were full of hate and resentment toward us, toward the opposition, and their minds were poisoned by the dictator Nicolás Maduro, Diosdado Cabello, the Rodríguezes, and Freddy Bernal, among others.[49] One of them yelled at me, saying some very rude and vulgar things: "Nicole, the best thing for you to do right now is sit your butt down. We know all about you. We know about your work. We've seen how you like to spend your time, helping the safety zoners, giving them food.[50] You're a dirty bitch." I saw what the situation was, the attitude they had, so I stepped back and tried to get in my car, but this was not possible, because a tall, heavyset woman with dark hair and skin dragged me by the hair and yelled in my face, "You goddamn dirty piece of shit, where you think you're going?" She immediately punched me in the stomach, which caused me to fall down. My partner Martín was being held down by two of the collective members, and they had a firearm pointed at him. I was panic-stricken. Through my tears, I made out the shape of someone I knew. This gentleman came up to me and in a lowkey way said,

> Fuck me, Nicole, you're in the middle of some serious shit, aren't you? Yep, and all because you assisted those dirty fucking cunts who think they're going to take down our revolution. This stuff is happening to you for being a traitor to your country, but it can get worse, you can lose your life. Think about your family and the pain you'd be causing them. And remember: I know exactly who you are, where you live, who you live with, where you work. I know everything about you. You won't get past me. The best thing for you to do is be careful, take care of yourself and your family, and keep your butt out of trouble so bad things don't happen to you. Because if you don't, if you keep up with your little assistance, it's going to get worse. I'm going to kill you and I'm going to kill your loved ones. If you keep getting involved in things you shouldn't, remember the words I'm saying now, my warning, so when something more serious happens to you, you're not surprised.

Having made his threats, he gave the order to his collective members to leave, though not before stealing all of the supplies that were in my car. After returning home and calming down, I consulted with fellow party members and relatives regarding what had occurred. They advised me to put in a complaint against this gentleman, Raúl González, and his collective members—a complaint that I filed the same day. I was informed that this was an offense that doesn't get prosecuted because there were no serious injuries or deaths.

With 2017 at an end, I took a brief vacation at my family's suggestion. At the beginning of 2018, I decided to keep a low profile in my political and social life. At the suggestion of family members and friends, I went to some psychotherapy sessions.

In 2019, it fell to the party that I have belonged to since 2011, People's Will, to assume the speakership of the National Assembly. In view of the fact that our leader, Leopoldo López, was still under arrest and the great majority of the national leadership was in exile or being persecuted within the country by the Maduro regime, a political leader arose, a young engineer, Mr. Juan Guaidó, who assumed the role of speaker of the National Assembly on January fifth, 2019, becoming the youngest speaker in the history of the National Assembly. This appointment filled us with joy, firstly the members of our party and secondly an entire people full of hope that things would change. The new speaker of the National Assembly called a grand national-level march on January twenty-third, 2019, in which all of Venezuela poured itself into the streets, backing this call. Personally, I and other People's Will members put on our party shirts, and with the tricolor flag of our nation in my hand, my Venezuela cap on, and my heart full of hope, we headed to the swearing in of Interim President Juan Guaidó.[51] My fellow party members and I returned on foot, and when we got to the corner of San José and Las Brisas, we passed one of the United Socialist Party of Venezuela's red spots that a group of collectivists from Las Brisas was in charge of.[52] Two individuals from this group of armed collectivists started pointing at me with their guns and threatened me, saying, "Nicole, it's not going to be long before you wake up dead, dirty bitch, piece of shit, traitor to the homeland of Bolívar and Commander Chávez. What you deserve is to die. We're tired of telling you to stop doing stupid things. Next time you won't be telling the story afterward." They took my belongings, and I was too afraid to do anything but run to my building and get inside. I got help from my neighbors to get myself under control and stable.

After the swearing in took place on January twenty-third, the whole country was fired up and excited, because we were finally going to reach the end of this narcocommunist dictatorship.[53] Our president, Juan Guaidó, called on the whole populace of the country to join in on February twenty-third in favor of the entry of humanitarian aid. On that day I went to Altamira Square in Caracas, joining fellow members of the People's Will Party in support. The presence of groups of collectivists could be seen all around the square. At about four or five in the afternoon, the tension was very high and I made the decision to depart and go home. When I got to the corner, I passed a group of collectivists identifiable as Las Brisas collectivists as well as a group of Bolivarian National Guard soldiers. When they noticed me and realized that I was coming from the event in support of the entry of humanitarian aid, since I was identifiable by my People's Will shirt and hat, they began to attack me by throwing tear-gas canisters at me. To prevent them from hitting me with the canisters or asphyxiating me with the gas, I ran away to my building and locked myself in my home. The collectivists and National Guard soldiers threw rocks, bottles, and tear-gas canisters inside the building, managing to crack the mirrors, knocking out the railings, and damaging the walls.

In March, we were still carrying on the fight for final liberation of Venezuela and standing shoulder to shoulder with our interim president, Juan Guaidó. Venezuela was entering a period of general scarcity and lack of basic services such as electricity and water, throughout the country. On March thirtieth, 2019, I was part of a group of residents and People's Will members peacefully protesting on Fuerzas Armadas Avenue over the fact that we had gone almost a month without electricity and water service. After the hours had passed, as dusk was falling, a group of collectivists passed through the area where I was protesting with my neighbors and fellow party members. One of them called me out by name and came at me, attacking me, shoving me until he knocked me to the ground. While I was down on the ground, two individuals began to kick me in different parts of my body. Through all the punching, kicking, shouting, and death threats I was able to identify Raúl González, the same person who in 2017 had made threats to take my life and that of my family. This gentleman carried on beating me, and pointing a gun directly at me he kept saying, shouting, that this time he really *was* going to kill me, that he would feed my remains to the dogs, that he would wipe out every dirty traitorous person like me, that we didn't deserve to live, that the best thing to do was kill me. In the midst of this very distressing experience, the individuals received a phone call and left, though not before emphasizing the threat they had made, that what they genuinely wanted to do was kill me. When I woke up, I was in a clinic; I received medical attention there. On April first, 2019, I lodged a complaint in the public-prosecutions office against Raúl González and the armed collectivists of Las Brisas Sector directed by the dictatorial narcogovernment of Nicolás Maduro.

For a long time I rejected the idea of ever leaving my beautiful country. I promised myself never to abandon her and to fight for my ideals until I died, as my mother instilled in me since my adolescence. But the death threats I received from various sources became so numerous, I was so besieged and fearful of losing my life, that I made the difficult, sad, and harsh decision to leave it all behind, to run away, to flee my beloved Venezuela, in order to prevent the worst from happening.

I left the country on April twenty-sixth, 2019, to defend my life and to recover my freedom and rights in a country that would welcome me, offer me protection, and give me the opportunity to build a new life, to feel safe, to be free of distress and not live in fear. For the reasons laid out above, and in the interest of safeguarding my life, I am going to the United States—a country that has demonstrated that it has freedom and democracy—to request asylum.

12

Spiritual Life

Introduced by Samuel Lozano de los Santos, SJ

Migrants are men and women in motion. Throughout their long journey they experience a true Calvary of afflictions: insecurity, distance, disease, inclement weather, hunger, thirst, extortion, kidnapping, and even death. Despite this, they keep moving forward. Be it on a bus, aboard a train, on foot—they carry on.

Migrating is not merely moving, traveling, or walking; it is banking on seeing one's deep yearning realized. According to Pope Francis, "In essence, migrating is an expression of each human being's intrinsic yearning for happiness, the happiness that we seek and pursue."[1] It is a pilgrimage, seeking a goal that we set for ourselves. It is taking chances. As such, deprived of everything else, the only thing migrants have left to draw strength from is hope and the memory of loved ones for whom they pray along the way.

What do migrants want? What motivates them to want to be "over there"? They may be seeking new and better options for meeting basic needs, having a better quality of life, or even keeping themselves alive. However, most important of all perhaps, the majority of these pilgrims also carry with them a profound spirituality. They believe in a powerful force that moves with them, whom many call God, which inspires movement. This force inhabits and sustains them when they feel they have lost everything. How does this force manifest itself? It is reflected in others. When migrants are with people who embrace them without suspicion, this confirms, regenerates, and renews the promise that through the people around them God protects, guides, and accompanies them on this journey.[2]

People pray before eating in the *comedor*. Avery Ellfeldt.

Through dangerous lands, surrounded by people who could do harm, migrants find in their pilgrimage individuals who, grounded in shared humanity, align themselves with migrants. They welcome migrants without recriminations, condemnation, or racist attitudes, but with hospitality and solicitude. A place to sleep, a meal, clothing, shoes, or a phone call to family. To migrants, these gestures—small, yet simultaneously momentous—become palpable signs of hope, of a blessing from God amidst calamity. They are a manifestation of God's love.

The features of migrants' religious spirituality are expressed in different ways. These features become evident when they knock at the doors of shelters or *comedores*, hoping to be greeted by a caring presence that might help them fill some of their vast needs. You can see it in expressions of gratitude for assistance received, when they pray fervently, bow their head, and make the sign of the cross upon seeing a religious image. When migrants say goodbye, they ask for a blessing, that things will go well when crossing, or returning home. These religious expressions show that their hearts carry in them an altar, brimming with belief, experiences of faith, and many offerings—and that they offer themselves up too.

Sheltering someone who is a migrant offers the possibility of encountering oneself, encountering the deepest aspects of lived experience. Migrants find open doors and renewed faith showing itself through acts of compassion. They offer the chance for us to humanize ourselves and know who we truly are. In those moments, they humanize themselves. When we interact with, spend time with, and allow migrants into our lives, we soon discover that—despite the mishaps, mistreatment, and accumulated pain—they are individuals who keep hope alive.

It can be said that lives of pilgrimage—migrant lives filled with hope and surrounded by suffering—are sacred. "We must respect them, accept them, take them in and help them carry on."[3] Despite the physical and human walls that bar the path to their dreams, or which separate them from loved ones, many keep trying to cross. Why? Because inside they keep hope alive, and the faith that God will help them. They trust. They have a certainty that tells them there is a shared humanity that cannot be divided by political borders. It is simply through trust and encounters with people and places that take them in—heal, feed, and shelter them; keep them from the cold and give them water and strength—that these pilgrims will continue to experience the closeness of God and that He will not abandon them.

Spirituality in the life of many migrants means trusting their lives to God the pilgrim, who travels with them, offers consolation and protection, and gives them strength. It is not a spirituality of adventure. Rather, it is the

People pray for protection and find solace in the earth, Indigenous heritage, Christ's protection, and one another. Wenceslao Hernández Hernández.

Rosary cross. Avery Ellfeldt.

spirituality of life lived in the Spirit. A spirituality that knows suffering and endures, carrying on with hope and dignity.

NOMBRE RESERVADO / NAME NOT PROVIDED

Desde lo más profundo de mi corazón, te doy gracias, Señor, por ser bueno conmigo y por darme otra oportunidad de vida. También, yo lo sé, todo lo que haces por mí es para mi bien. Tu amor es inmenso conmigo. Todas estas pruebas que tú me pones, pruebas fuertes, son para saber qué tan fuerte es mi fe para contigo. Hoy me humillo hacia ti y me arrepiento de todo lo malo que he sido contigo. Te pido me quites todo lo malo que existe en mí y no te separes de mí en ningún momento. Guíame por el camino del bien y cuida de mí y de todos mis seres queridos. Tú solo eres perfecto y bondadoso. Gracias por tu paciencia, tu calma y por escucharme. Gracias, Jesús.

IIIIIIIIIIIIIIIII

From the bottom of my heart, I give thanks to you, Lord, for being so good to me and for giving me another chance at life. Also, I know, everything you do for me is in my best interest. Your love for me is vast. All this evidence you put before me, strong evidence, is to find out how strong my faith toward you is. Today I humble myself toward you and repent for all the ways I've been bad to you. I pray for you to take away from me all the bad that exists in me and not separate yourself from me for one minute. Guide me down the road of good and look after me and all my loved ones. You alone are perfect and full of goodness. Thank you for your patience, for your calm, and for listening to me. Thank you, Jesus.

NOMBRE RESERVADO / NAME NOT PROVIDED

Gracias por las personas que he encontrado en este camino. Sé que tu poder es grande y maravilloso. Gracias por las personas que me han ayudado. Bendiciones sobre todos y cada uno de ellos. Gracias, Señor, porque sé que mi familia también encuentra bendiciones y tu poder es grande. Te pido, Señor, guardes y cuides a mi familia, especialmente a mi padre, a mi madre y a mis hermanos. Deseo, Señor, que les ilumines el bien.

IIIIIIIIIIIIIIIII

Thank you for the people I've met on this journey. I know your power is great and wondrous. Thank you for the people who have helped me. Blessings on all of them, on every one of them. Thank you, Lord, because I know that my family also receives blessings and that your power is great. I pray, Lord, that you'll watch over my family and keep them, especially my father, my mother, and my siblings. My wish, Lord, is for you to illuminate the good for them.

ROSAURA

Gracias, Dios, por haber estado a mi lado en todos estos momentos tan difíciles para mí. Y es que a pesar de no poder cumplir con mi objetivo, sé que fue por algo. Tus pensamientos no son los mismos que los míos. Tú eres perfecto. Sólo queda esperar y ver lo que tú tienes para mí. Gracias por hacer que me dé cuenta de lo más hermoso que me has dado, que son mis hijos. Su amor es todo lo que poseo. ¡Gracias, mi Dios! Sólo tú sabes por qué me trajiste aquí a conocer personas tan hermosas que nos ayudan. Gracias, mil gracias. Yo sé que esto pasará y tú me guiarás, porque eres fiel. Dios fiel, sólo tú sabes mi situación, mi vida y sabes qué necesito de ti. Te amo, mi Dios, amén.

llllllllllllllllll

Thank you, God, for being by my side in all these moments that have been so difficult for me. Because despite not being able to fulfill my goal, I know it was for a reason. Your thoughts are not the same as my thoughts. You are perfect. All that's left to do is wait and see what you have in store for me. Thank you for making me realize the most beautiful thing you've given me, my children. Their love is all I possess. Thank you, dear God! Only you know why you brought me here, to meet people who are so beautiful and who help us. Thank you, thank you so much. I know that this will pass and that you will guide me, because you are faithful. Faithful God, only you know what my situation is, what my life is, and what I need from you. I love you, dear God. Amen.

NOMBRE RESERVADO / NAME NOT PROVIDED

Diosito, ¡quiero pedirte que me des otra oportunidad de pasar a los Estados Unidos! Sólo para hacerles una casa a mis hijos. Sólo te pido que me des esa oportunidad. Yo te prometo que si tú me ayudas, yo le voy a echar ganas trabajando, para lograr mi objetivo que tengo. ¡Por favor, Diosito! Te lo suplico, con todo mi corazón, que me ayudes junto con mi madrecita de

Guadalupe. Te pido que me cuides a mis hijas, a mis padres, para que a mi regreso pueda reunirme con ellos y poder abrazarlos. Te lo pido, Diosito.

||||||||||||||||

Dearest God, I want to pray that you'll give me another chance to get through to the United States. Only so I can make a home for my kids. I only pray that you'll give me that chance. I promise you if you help me, I'm going to give it my best and work hard to achieve the goal I have. Please, dearest God! I beg you with all my heart to help me, you and my dear mother of Guadalupe. I pray that you'll take care of my daughters, my parents, so that when I come back I can be with them again and be able to hug them. This I pray, dearest God.

MARÍA LUISA

Señor, te doy gracias por estar siempre conmigo. A pesar de todo, nunca me abandonas. Gracias, Señor, por cuidarme y por cuidar a mi familia y a todos los que me rodean. Gracias porque en este mes, viví muy mal por estar lejos de mi familia, pero a pesar de todo, siempre están en mi mente y en mi corazón y he tomado la decisión de regresar con ellos. Por eso te pido que me ayudes a llegar con bien a mi pueblo.

Te pido, Señor, porque en estos días encontré a mucha gente que intentó cruzar y no lo logró, ¡pobre gente! Señor, me da un poco de tristeza, porque algunos me platican cómo iban a cruzar caminando. Lo más triste es que me contaron que por el desierto había calaveras, cuerpos de personas que no lograron llegar, que les hizo falta agua y comida. Te pido, Señor, por ellos que sufren mucho.

Gracias a ti, aquí en Nogales hay gente muy buena, que nos abrieron las puertas de su casa y de su corazón. Te pido por ellos, pues nos dieron comida, ropa, zapatos y muchas cosas más. Bendícelos, Señor. Nunca imaginé encontrarme con gente tan buena. Te pido por todas las personas que ayudan a los migrantes. Gracias por tener gente buena en nuestro camino.

Te pido, Señor, por mi familia, especialmente por mi niña hermosa, que la extraño mucho. En este mes que estuve aquí, me di cuenta de muchas cosas. Una de ellas es el valor de mi familia y te doy gracias por haberme ayudado, de arrepentirme y regresar por mi niña. ¡Ella me necesita! La verdad, no sé si come bien, si la cuidan bien, si va al catecismo. Por eso te pido, Señor, que me cuides en mi camino. También ilumina a toda la gente que te necesita, ilumina a mi esposo, espero que me comprenda al haberme regresado. Bueno, Señor, es todo lo que te puedo decir. Más que nada, ayúdame a llegar con bien a casa. Te amo, mi Señor.

|||||||||||||||||

Lord, I thank you for being with me all the time. In spite of everything, you never leave me. Thank you, Lord, for taking care of me and for taking care of my family and all those around me. Thank you, because this month, I've had a really bad time, from being a long way from my family, but in spite of everything, you are always there, in my mind and in my heart. And I've made the decision to go back to them. And so I pray that you'll help me reach my hometown safely.

I pray to you, Lord, because in the last few days I've met a lot of people who tried to cross and, unfortunately, didn't succeed. Lord, it makes me a little sad, because some of them have told me that they were going to go all the way on foot! The saddest part is when they told me that in the desert, there were skeletons, bodies of people who didn't succeed in getting where they were going, who didn't have enough water and food. I pray for them, Lord. They suffer a lot.

Thanks to you, here in Nogales there are some really good people, who opened the doors of their houses and of their hearts to us. I pray for them, for they gave us food, clothes, shoes, and many other things. Bless them, Lord. I never imagined I'd run into such good people. I pray for all those who help those who migrate. Thank you for the fact that we have good people in our path.

I pray for my family, Lord, especially for my beautiful little girl I miss so much. During this month that I've been here, I've realized a lot of things. One of them is how valuable my family is—I thank you for helping me with that—and the value of repenting and going back for my daughter. She needs me! To tell the truth, I don't know if she's eating well, if they're taking good care of her, if she's going to her catechism class. So I pray, Lord, that you'll take care of me on the way. Also shine your light on all the people who need you. Shine your light on my husband—I hope he's understanding when I get back. Okay, Lord, that's all I wanted to say. Above all, help me get home safely. I love you, my Lord.

13

Valuing Voices

Tobin Hansen

Miguel, introduced in the book's opening and who has lived and worked in Oaxaca, Mexico, and the Pacific Northwest region of the United States, felt disillusion and desperation at his stymied desert crossing. On that blackened desert night in 2017, he asked himself, "What am I doing here? What am I doing so far from home?" Days later, he gave his *testimonio* and I dropped him off at a bus station in Nogales, ticket in hand to return to Oaxaca. I have not talked to Miguel since. I hope that he and others who offered *testimonios* find fulfillment. I speculate about where he is, how he is doing, and how he reflects on that desert night. As I struggle to understand his experience, years later, I wonder what answers he may have found.

This book has sought to shed light on these questions and, in the process, permit understanding of the lives of Miguel and others. If they flourish, it will be in spite of the grim inequalities embedded in immigration enforcement regimes. Although I do not know how Miguel is today, his travails from 2017 are laid bare. This book has outlined the uncertainty, isolation, ache, confusion, numbness, and pain that Miguel and so many feel. It has revealed the persistent trauma of harrowing desert crossings, abuses by government authorities, misogynistic violence against women and gender nonconforming people, disorienting deportations, the longing for legal refuge only to be denied. The *testimonios* of those who live with separation, hardship, pain, hunger, and occasional joy represent human potential, strength, resilience, agony, and affliction. The emotional texture of the narratives reveal feelings for loved ones and the future as well as perceptions of the world and self-worth. For you

People stand outside KBI's *comedor*. April Wong.

reading the *testimonios*, each detail, large and small, represents an opportunity to understand life differently and to question the order of the world.

Testimonios are more than just vehicles for experiential and emotional information, however. They reflect interpersonal solidarity and constitute political acts. Giving testimony, the act of living and telling, is one form of witnessing. Another is listening, observing, and documenting, to ensure the retelling of *testimonios*. Both forms are a refusal to be silent, defiance of things as they are, and a clamor for solutions. Since 2009, the Kino Border Initiative (KBI) has asserted its support for people on the move. Workers and volunteers have served hundreds of thousands of meals, given first aid tens of thousands of times, and offered hundreds of legal and asylum orientations and educational presentations. And people served at Kino have responded with their own action. Over the years, thousands of *testimonios* have been given, formally and informally. And each person giving *testimonio* could fill volumes recounting details of moments lived. But the brief *testimonios* presented here reflect commitment. Time is precious in Nogales and time dedicated to giving a *testimonio*—thirty minutes or an hour or three, often in a corner of the bustling *comedor*—pays tribute to people's experiences. Moreover, the act of collecting *testimonios* is one of listening, acknowledging, and imagining, in hopes that the impact of the story will persist beyond the fleeting moments of sitting with someone, heart and ears open.

While *testimonios* stand alone as political acts and experiential representations, global dynamics impact and shape them. Historical trajectories have wrought political, economic, and social systems that distribute opportunity and constraints in particular ways. Legal restrictions on movement; persistent global wealth inequality; and approaches to border "security" that emphasize policing instead of ensuring access to education, health care, and meaningful work configure the experiences reflected in these *testimonios*. The *testimonios* crystalize individual experience. Reading, rereading, thinking, and feeling with and through *testimonios*, however, necessitates consideration of the forces that go far beyond a human decision in isolation. What appear to be individual choices are a set of entangled pathways, leading to unspecified destinations. The chapter introductions historicize and contextualize the narratives by pointing to political sentiments, policy priorities, and their outcomes, as they are borne out by reporting and scholarly work. They sketch the contours of family life, as families seek to be together, away from violence, in a place where they might prosper together. The chapter introductions provide a sense of proportion, heft, and historical orientation. They are the sturdy wrapping in which the *testimonios*—in their rich texture, their intimacy and soulfulness—are enveloped.

The chapter introductions also draw attention to the political and economic structures that shape and constrain the choices available to the most vulnerable and marginalized people in the Latin America of the twenty-first century. These shifting structures have come about through the New World's colonial beginnings in the fifteenth century and continued through economic and social changes, the nation-building and state consolidation projects of independence, and further reordering of wealth accumulation and inequality and distribution of political power. The present-day perpetuation of inequality is exacerbated by immigration restrictionism. The insistence of rich countries in hardening the barriers to entry and seeking to erect new ones entrenches global inequality by denying people access to labor opportunities in a globalized world that promotes shifting capital flows, production sites, and financial instruments.

The *testimonios* and introductions invite reorientation to the world. Their substance and poignancy encourage moral calculation of valuing community members, citizens and noncitizens alike and effectuating or standing silent on public policy. The *testimonios* and book itself are an invitation to action. Community action is a start, in support of nonprofits who serve migrants and others in need. Housing, work, sustainable food, civics, and cultural literacy are all areas where action and support are needed. There are opportunities for solidarity with noncitizens surrounding issues before city and county governments, local school boards, housing authorities, and health care services. On a broader scale, pressuring and advocating congressional representatives, executive branch officials, and others in state and national government is necessary for enacting more humane immigration policies and reaffirming commitments to driver licenses and identification cards, in-state tuition for local colleges, access to education and health care for all people living in US communities, the rollback of draconian deportation policies, and an expansion of visa and asylum programs.

Restrictionist immigration policies have come about through a lengthy and twisting history of white supremacy, as discussed in chapter 9. Restrictionism has taken various forms, from Chinese Exclusion in 1882, limits on non–Western European migration in 1924, artificially low quotas on Western Hemisphere countries in 1965, and expanded grounds for inadmissibility and removal in legislation promulgated in 1986, 1996, and 2001. Moreover, since being sworn into office in 2017, President Trump has focused executive authority on limiting immigration. Even a partial list becomes wearying: he has signed executive orders that curtail travel to the United States from particular countries and have more than doubled year-on-year border apprehensions in 2019 to 851,508.[1] His policies have resulted in the deportation of more than three-quarters of a million people and restricted certain avenues of legal immigration. In articulating immigration restrictionism, he has called immigrants rapists and animals—quite literally denying their humanity—and blamed noncitizens for widespread voter fraud, gang violence, and a rise in violent crime. Moreover, he appointed Attorney General Jefferson Sessions, who narrowed consideration of domestic violence as grounds for granting asylum and rescinded the Deferred Action for Childhood Arrivals program and named a secretary of the Department of Homeland Security (DHS), Kirstjen Nielsen, who implemented the administration's family separation policy.

The impulse to foreclose possibilities of movement comes from other quarters as well. In March 2020, in response to the COVID-19 pandemic, the US Department of Health and Human Services Centers for Disease Control and Prevention, under the Public Health Services Act, ordered that certain people apprehended by US Customs and Border Protection (CBP) coming from Canada or Mexico be sent back. This included thousands of

Nogales at dusk. Looking south from Arizona. Avery Ellfeldt.

asylum-seekers in northern Mexico from Central America and elsewhere. Given that people seeking asylum were already congregating on the Mexican side of the US-Mexico border because of the metering and Migrant Protection Protocols previously implemented, as discussed in chapter 11, the numbers of people stuck in Mexico have increased. People fearing for their lives—such as Honduran, Salvadoran, and Guatemalan citizens who had made the arduous trek to Nogales, Mexico—to request asylum as stipulated by the 1951 UNHCR Convention and, since 1980, in US federal statute, must now wait indefinitely. Nongovernmental organizations in northern Mexico seeking to provide food and shelter and meet other basic needs were maxed out and struggling *before* the order, and now the compounding effects of this denial of due process and violation of international law are exacerbating hardship, uncertainty, and suffering.

The future is undetermined. There are few reasons for optimism regarding the US government's refusal to recognize the historical reasons that people move and become immobile. Intrenched inequalities and violence in Latin America go unaddressed. Inertia looks unfavorable for migration justice. People stuck or on the move tap into reserves of strength. Structural change is necessary to enable human flourishing. Education is critical for steps to be taken in this direction. People need to better understand the situation of those migrating, being deported, or seeking asylum in order to envision a world in which all people enjoy greater opportunity. This book has been written to contribute to efforts that facilitate that understanding.

NOTES

FOREWORD

1. Francis, "Homily of His Holiness Pope Francis."

PREFACE

1. In a very few cases, some or all of a *testimonio* was given in English or translated by another collaborator.

CHAPTER 1

1. All names are pseudonyms, except where noted, and some identifying details have been changed to protect individuals' privacy. See the Note on Names.
2. Vogt, *Lives in Transit*.
3. Tula and Stephen, *Este es mi testimonio* [This is my testimonio], 241.
4. Stephen, *We Are the Face*.
5. Gastélum Ceballos, "*Protección de la Ciudad de Nogales* [Protection of the city of Nogales]."
6. Heyman, *Life and Labor*, 67.
7. Rochlin and Rochlin, "Heart of Ambos Nogales"; see also St. John, *Line in the Sand*, 36.
8. Lim, *Porous Borders*.
9. Arreola, *Postcards from the Sonora Border*, 109.
10. Arreola, 110–11.
11. Truett, *Fugitive Landscapes*, 180; Sheridan, *Arizona*, 221; see also Almada Bay, *Sonora: Historia breve* [Sonora: A brief history]; Heyman, *Life and Labor on the Border*.
12. Chinese people and their descendants underwent periods of welcome as well as of severe anti-Chinese racism on the US and Mexican sides of the border.
13. St. John, *Line in the Sand*, 97.
14. Arreola, *Postcards from the Sonora Border*, 132.
15. Hernández, *Migra!*; Ngai, *Impossible Subjects*.

16. Kang, *INS on the Line.*
17. Hernández, *Migra!*, 80; Ngai, *Impossible Subjects*, 72–73.
18. Stephen, *Transborder Lives*, 145.
19. Andreas, *Border Games.*
20. De León, *Land of Open Graves.*
21. Cornelius, "Deaths at the Border"; De León, *Land of Open Graves.*
22. Spener, *Clandestine Crossings.*
23. Slack and Campbell, "On Narco-coyotaje."
24. US Department of Homeland Security (DHS), *2018 Yearbook*, 95.
25. Macías-Rojas, *From Deportation to Prison.*
26. Gomberg-Muñoz, *Becoming Legal.*
27. Colibrí Center for Human Rights, "Facts."
28. Secretaría de Gobernación, *Boletín Mensual de Estadísticas Migratorias 2019* [Monthly report of immigration statistics 2019], 165.
29. Albicker and Velasco, *"Deportación y estigma"* [Deportation and stigma]; Boehm, *Returned*; Caldwell, *Deported Americans*; Coutin, *Exiled Home*; Golash-Boza, *Deported*; Heidbrink, *Migranthood*; Slack, *Deported to Death.*
30. Secretaría de Gobernación, *Boletín Mensual de Estadísticas Migratorias 2019*, 165.
31. USDHS, *2018 Yearbook*, 103.
32. WHO, "Refugee and Migrant Health"; UNHCR, "Figures at a Glance."
33. FitzGerald, *Refuge beyond Reach.*
34. Stephen, *We Are the Face of Oaxaca*, "Fleeing Rural Violence"; see also Lusk and Villalobos, "Testimonio of Eva"; Tula and Stephen, *Este es mi testimonio.*
35. Stephen, "Bearing Witness," 94.

CHAPTER 2

1. Chasteen, *History of Latin America.*
2. Monroe, "President's Annual Message," 14.
3. Chasteen, *History of Latin America*; Pastor, *Exiting the Whirlpool*; Smith, *Talons of the Eagle.*
4. Kilty and Segal, "Poverty and Inequality."
5. Haenn, "New Rural Poverty"; Luccisano, "Mexico's *Progresa* Program."
6. Harris, "Dependency, Underdevelopment, and Neoliberalism," 85–89.
7. Luccisano, "Mexico's *Progresa* Program," 36.
8. Stephen, "Fleeing Rural Violence," 234; see also Hale, "More than an Indian."
9. Stephen, 253.
10. United Nations, *Situación de personas afrodescendientes en América Latina*; Del Popolo, *Los pueblos indígenas en América.*
11. Gonzales-Berry and Mendoza, *Mexicanos in Oregon*; Sheridan, *Arizona*; Truett, *Fugitive Landscapes.*
12. Massey, Durand, and Malone, *Smoke and Mirrors*, 27–29; see also Gomberg-Muñoz, *Labor and Legality.*
13. Stephen, *Transborder Lives*, 72–73.
14. Golash-Boza, *Deported*; Hernández, *Migra!*; Kang, *INS on the Line.*
15. Guatemala is divided into twenty-two departments. This term for the first-level administrative division of a country is common in Central and South America.

16. Yésica expressed the amount here in quetzales, the currency of Guatemala: thirty thousand quetzales, which works out to 3,911 dollars.

17. That is, get me across the border. *Pasarme.*

18. In Spanish, the word *comedor* refers to lots of different kinds of "eating places," including the dining room in a home. KBI's *comedor* for migrants was established in 2009 and is well known locally. In English, no one calls it anything other than *comedor.*

19. Casa Nazaret, the temporary housing for women provided by the Kino Border Initiative.

20. Mexican municipalities (*municipios*) correspond to American counties, being the second-level administrative division after states; quite often, though, the name of the municipality is the same as the name of the main city/town in it.

21. Fifty Mexican pesos.

22. Teaching the Mexican national anthem to those of the *coyote*'s migrant customers who were from Central America, to help them pass as Mexican if questioned by Mexican authorities.

23. Across the border. *Brincarme.*

24. He is referring here to the deportation officer who was in charge of his case.

25. People's usual way of referring to the authorities that arrest people at the border on account of their immigration status is as *la Migra, la Migración,* or *Migración.* The latter two are more polite/formal than *la Migra.* Santiago uses *Migración* here. I translate all of them as "Immigration." These terms are used equally for US immigration authorities (USBP/CBP) and Mexican immigration authorities (*Instituto Nacional de Migración* or National Migration Department).

26. The KBI *comedor.*

27. Nieves does not speak Spanish and told her story through an interpreter. Thus, her *testimonio* is in the third person.

28. Three hundred Mexican pesos. The two other amounts given in this paragraph are seventy pesos ("four dollars") and 6.36 pesos ("thirty-eight cents").

29. The tortillas would be made with the corn just mentioned.

30. "Here" refers to the US-Mexico border.

31. Carrying drugs across the border. *Llevar la mochila.*

32. Apparently, the load is picked up right at the border, as opposed to deep inside Mexico. If so, Samuel seems to mean that you go to the pick-up spot and that's where you're paid the higher rate for the previous load. And what if someone is apprehended on their way south, do they get paid nothing? Samuel doesn't spell it out. Perhaps everyone is paid five hundred dollars at the same time, when they drop off the load, and then those who want the higher rate have to go back for the remainder. Samuel doesn't even get as far as receiving the five hundred, so maybe that's why he does not give details.

CHAPTER 3

1. Wolf, *Mano Dura.*

2. Christopher Woody, "The 50 Most Violent Cities in the World," *Business Insider,* April 8, 2017, https://amp.businessinsider.com/most-violent-cities-in-the-world -2017-4.

3. The reigning violence was such that members of groups that habitually pointed out human rights violations by the Salvadoran Army—such as members of the church—were murdered. Such was the case of Archbishop Romero, who was killed on March 24, 1980, as he was conducting Mass. In 1989 the Atlacatl squad also murdered Jesuits Ignacio Ellacuría, Segundo Montes, Ignacio Martín-Baró, Amando López, Juan Ramón Moreno, and Joaquín López y López, along with Elba and Celina Ramos, a woman who worked for them and her daughter.

4. The *cobro de guerra* (war tax) is a fee that businesses of all sizes are charged by the Maras if they want to be allowed to continue their commercial activities.

5. US Department of the Treasury, "Treasury Sanctions Latin America Criminal Organization."

6. A group of gangs that belong to a neighborhood and that sometimes establish connections with other organizations.

7. In Guatemala, there are six years of compulsory public education, called *primaria*.

8. This is explained further below. Unlike in the United States, kidnapping in Latin America and elsewhere is not strongly associated with disturbed individuals who have obscure psychological motives, even when children are the victims, but rather with organized crime and financial motives.

9. "Rent" refers to the *cobro de guerra*. See note 4 above. Four hundred dollars is the equivalent of three thousand quetzales.

10. A *colonia* near the southern edge of the Guatemala City metropolitan area.

11. In contrast to her oldest son's murder. The Spanish sentence conveys this contrast very economically by making the kidnapped son a contrastive topic: *A él me lo secuestraron*, "Him, they kidnapped on me." I have instead added extra words: "This time, what happened was . . ."

12. Thirty thousand quetzales.

13. The Eloy Detention Center, an immigration detention center owned and operated by CoreCivic.

14. Both originated in Los Angeles. Calle 18 is named for 18th Street in the Rampart District. The *Mara Salvatrucha* is also known as MS-13.

15. To make money to get away.

16. The term "Christian" (*cristiano*), in the traditionally Catholic countries of Latin America, is normally used to mean non-Catholic/Protestant.

17. GRP is *Grupo de Reacción Policial* (Police Response Group), an elite unit of El Salvador's national police.

18. Tattoos.

19. *Comisión Mexicana de Ayuda a Refugiados* (Mexican Refugee-Assistance Commission), which has an office in Tapachula.

CHAPTER 4

1. United Nations Office of the High Commissioner for Human Rights, *Convention on the Elimination of All Forms of Discrimination against Women*, 2.

2. Organization of American States, "Inter-American Convention on the Prevention, Punishment, and Eradication of Violence against Women."

3. Miguel Ángel Vargas V., "7 claves sobre la desigualdad entre hombres y mujeres en México. Las mexicanas enfrentan más obstáculos que los varones en el trabajo, la política, la educación y las relaciones de pareja [7 key facts about inequality between men and women in Mexico. Mexican women face more obstacles at work, in politics, education and romantic relationships]," *Expansión en Alianza con CNN*, March 7, 2014, http://expansion.mx/nacional/2014/03/07/7-datos-sobre-la-desigualdad-entre-hombres-y-mujeres-en-mexico.

4. Vargas.

5. Vargas.

6. Instituto Nacional de Estadísticas y Geografía [National Institute of Statistics and Geography], "National Survey of the Dynamics of Household Relationships (ENDIREH)," 2016 and 2011, https://en.www.inegi.org.mx/programas/endireh/2016/; https://en.www.inegi.org.mx/programas/endireh/2011/.

7. Vargas, "7 claves."

8. Vargas.

9. Vargas.

10. "The guy who had gotten me away" refers to when he took her to see the tattooed man. By "left me behind" she means that the *pollero* either left her behind during the crossing or left her in Mexico and she got across another way. Either way, he didn't get her to South Carolina.

11. A *molcajete* is an ancient and common household item in Mexico, used for grinding chiles and making guacamole and other salsas. It is a stone bowl similar to a mortar, with a matching pestle (*piedra* or *tejolote*) of the same stone that is held in the hand. So what the mother threw here was basically a rock.

12. *Acosar* is "stalk" here. Both are terms used for aggressive, unwanted attention and harassment of women by men. Both have literal meanings connected with hunting. The literal meaning of *acosar* is a little closer to "hound" than *stalk*, connoting relentlessness, not stealth. Another possible and common translation for *acosar* is "harass." Stalking is focused, sustained, obsessive harassment, but *acosar* can refer to other types as well.

13. Policing functions are often divided into the preventive (patrol/response) and the investigative, and in Mexico, these functions are generally the work of completely separate agencies. Investigative agencies are formally affiliated with the prosecutor's office, so they are often called ministerial police or judicial police. Investigative cops generally have more prestige and influence than patrol cops—in general, not just in Mexico. In the United States, this person would belong to the investigative division of a police department and might be identified as a "detective" or something along those lines.

14. The fact that he had a wife and children doesn't mean he lived with them, or only with them. It's possible that he and his wife were separated, temporarily or permanently. Divorce per se is less common in Mexico than in the United States.

15. Similar to calling her "frigid," but that's a slightly different word: *frígida*, as opposed to *fría*. With *fría* the emphasis is not only on her alleged sexual dysfunction but also on her alleged unkindness.

16. Evidently the name of her second child. At the time of this incident, she was still pregnant with her third child, since she doesn't mention giving birth before recounting the incident (beginning with "One day . . ."). The reason

she mentions grabbing the milk must be that César was still very small. César is presumably the little boy she mentions being carried by the *coyote* in the next paragraph, though it might have been her then-newborn third child.

17. The paved section of the Tijuana River where it crosses the border is informally known as *El Bordo*. (At least one tire shop and one rehab center in the vicinity are named after it.) It resembles a drainage canal more than a river. The word *bordo* means "levee" in Spanish, but perhaps the similarity of sound between *bordo* and *border* is not a coincidence.

CHAPTER 5

1. UNICEF, *Convención internacional sobre los derechos del niño y la niña* [International Convention on Children's Rights], 6.
2. UNICEF, 7, 10.
3. Francis, "Address of His Holiness Pope Francis."
4. Twenty Mexican pesos.
5. Fifty Mexican pesos.
6. "Thugs" is a translation of *cholos*.
7. Twenty thousand Mexican pesos.
8. Thirty-five thousand Mexican pesos.
9. Seventy-five hundred Mexican pesos.
10. "Florence" refers to the Central Arizona Florence Correctional Complex (in Florence, AZ), which houses US Marshals detainees both before and after sentencing on federal criminal charges. "Eloy" is the Eloy Detention Center (in Eloy, AZ), which houses immigration detainees under contract with Immigration and Customs Enforcement (ICE). Both are private jails owned by the same corporation, CoreCivic (formerly known as the Corrections Corporation of America).

    Every migrant who completes a federal sentence passes into ICE custody, usually to be deported immediately, but if they request asylum, they may spend a long time in immigration detention awaiting the outcome of their request.
11. Being given an immigration bond means that, if you can come up with a certain amount of money, you can get out of immigration detention and carry on with your life while your case continues.
12. In Mexico, it's customary for parents to come to the school at lunchtime with their kids' lunch, rather than packing a lunch for their kids to take to school in the morning.
13. *La Reforma Educativa* is a policy introduced in 2013 during the term of President Enrique Peña Nieto.
14. Since her husband's income covers their expenses in the United States. There may be a reference here to a lack of adequate social insurance for the elderly in Mexico.
15. Marisol actually uses the English word *warning* here, presumably because there is no comparable procedure in Mexico that she is familiar with.
16. That is, cross the border.
17. *Clave Única de Registro de Población* (Population Registry Code), an ID number issued by the Mexican government to all residents and a prerequisite for

many government services. More or less the equivalent of a Social Security number.

CHAPTER 6

1. This strict policy notwithstanding, overstaying a visitor visa is nevertheless the most common form of unauthorized immigration. See Warren, *U.S. Undocumented Population Continued to Fall.*
2. USBP, "Border Patrol Strategic Plan," lays out the basic strategy.
3. Between 1994 and 2011, the number of USBP agents quintupled, from 4,945 to 21,444. All but 2,938 of them were assigned to the southwest border. See USBP, *Fiscal Year Staffing Statistics.*
4. USBP, "Border Patrol Strategic Plan," explains the intent, which was not to increase death and suffering for its own sake. The government simply posited that the increased death and suffering that would result from the new measures would have a deterrent effect on irregular migration and enhance the government's ability to control it, if not end it. Increased death and suffering were and are neither the goal nor an accidental side effect but a means to an end.
5. Louis Sahagun, "Nogales Wall Takes Toll in Injuries—and Costs," *Los Angeles Times*, September 8, 1994, http://articles.latimes.com/1994-09-08/news/mn -36023_1_illegal-entrants.
6. J. B. Miller, "Higher Wall, Harder Falls," *Nogales International*, September 1, 2011, https://www.nogalesinternational.com/news/higher-wall-harder-falls/article _437237b0-1b3a-5d39-9f4e-2c44b04a1451.html.
7. Genesis Lara, "Woman Breaks Multiple Bones Jumping from Border Fence," *Nogales International*, August 23, 2018, https://www.nogalesinternational.com /news/woman-breaks-multiple-bones-jumping-from-border-fence/article _8233b67e-a733-11e8-a914-3b03e3d3fd11.html; Paulina Pineda, "Woman Dies after Apparent Fall from Border Fence," *Nogales International*, June 21, 2016, https://www.nogalesinternational.com/news/woman-dies-after-apparent-fall -from-border-fence/article_1d0d569e-37f8-11e6-aadc-339f19764309.html.
8. The tiny ranch town of Altar, about an hour south of the tiny border town of Sásabe, grew into a key marketplace and staging area for cross-border traffic.
9. It will not be surprising that all four accounts presented here are of unsuccessful crossings. The *testimonios* in this book were collected in Mexico, at an aid center for repatriated migrants, rather than in the United States. The perspectives of individuals who have (recently) crossed successfully are absent here.
10. "We" refers to her and her husband.
11. Roughly "The Hunchback" or "The Hump."
12. This was on the phone, presumably, before they met her in person, so that they would recognize her.
13. This store is a large grocery-store chain.
14. Oxxo is a large convenience-store chain.
15. Twenty-one thousand pesos was worth a bit more than a thousand dollars (the amount left to pay after the other two thousand were paid): it was worth about twelve hundred. La Chepa must have given Nayeli Lizette and her husband a bad exchange rate on their pesos, effectively charging them about two hundred dollars extra.

16. The Sonoran Desert is one hundred thousand square miles and straddles the US-Mexico border, covering western Sonora and southwestern Arizona.
17. He uses the word *reserva*, which could equally refer to a natural preserve such as the Buenos Aires National Wildlife Refuge or an Indian reservation such as the Tohono O'odham Nation. He seems to have the latter meaning in mind, based on how the paragraph ends.
18. This is an unnatural translation, in that "emigrant" isn't a term in common use in American English. But to translate *emigrados* as "immigrants" would misrepresent the point of view. Throughout these testimonios, *emigrar, emigración, emigrado* have been consistently translated as "emigrate," "emigration," "emigrant," but only "emigrant" has seemed jarring enough to me to warrant a note.
19. The higher wall that was installed in Nogales in 2011, the year before this *testimonio*, consists of steel posts or "bollards" and is thirty feet tall.
20. Mexicans being deported from the United States are taken to the border and handed over to Mexican immigration authorities, specifically the repatriation department.
21. The Little Sisters of Our Lady of Sorrows, a Catholic order.
22. A topical antiseptic commonly found in the medicine cabinet of Mexican families. The closest American equivalent is Mercurochrome.
23. At this point, the Honduran switches from addressing him with the polite *usted* form, as he did at first, and starts using the more intimate *tú* form. But after the first sentence, he switches back to the *usted* form.
24. To pay for living expenses while in prison.
25. "That's what I went to the US for" is probably not referring to this specific crossing attempt. It seems that he had lived and worked in the United States previously and been able to help his son get the education to acquire the profession he practices now.
26. Over and above crossing fees paid to the *coyote's* organization, there is a *cuota*, or "toll," that must be paid to the drug cartel that "owns" the territory. Hence "to pay for the mafia."
27. They probably crossed at Sásabe, directly north of Altar, approximately thirty-six miles west of Nogales.
28. The *Grupos Beta* are a Mexican government agency (a branch of the National Migration Department) tasked with providing humanitarian aid to migrants, including when they are in distress in the desert on the Mexican side.

CHAPTER 7

1. Meyer, "One Year after National Guard's Creation."
2. Southern Border Communities Coalition, "Deaths by Border Patrol."
3. Takei et al., *Fatal Neglect*.
4. Danielson, *Our Values on the Line*.
5. USBP, *U.S. Border Patrol Fiscal Year Staffing Statistics*.
6. A. C. Thompson, "Inside the Secret Border Patrol Facebook Group Where Agents Joke about Migrant Deaths and Post Sexist Memes," *ProPublica*, July 1, 2019, https://www.propublica.org/article/secret-border-patrol-facebook-group-agents-joke-about-migrant-deaths-post-sexist-memes.

7. CBP Integrity Advisory Panel, *Final Report*.
8. Suárez et al., *Access to Justice for Migrants in Mexico*.
9. Knippen, Boggs, and Meyer, *An Uncertain Path*.
10. Danielson, *Our Values on the Line*.
11. Cantor and Ewing, *Still No Action Taken*.
12. A. C. Thompson, "Over 200 Allegations of Abuse of Migrant Children; 1 Case of Homeland Security Disciplining Someone," *ProPublica*, May 31, 2019, https://www.propublica.org/article/over-200-allegations-of-abuse-of-migrant-children-1-case-of-homeland-security-disciplining-someone.
13. Same metaphor in English and Spanish. For someone on the wrong side of the law, a place is *caliente*, or hot, if it's saturated with law enforcement.
14. Immigration agents were probably parked and sitting in their trucks. One encounters this a lot on southern Arizona's backroads.
15. Agents of USBP wear green uniforms.
16. "They told us" probably refers to their smugglers guiding them by phone.
17. Probably a reference to a tactical unit of USBP—such as BORTAC (Border Patrol Tactical Unit)—more military-like in aspect than regular USBP agents, hence the name *armis* (exactly like that in the Spanish; I've just copied it).
18. The word he uses here for the vehicle isn't *jeep*, as before, but *perrera*, which literally means "dog catcher's van." It's the usual word for the standard USBP truck that has a container on the back for transporting people.
19. He appears to be describing the Operation Streamline court proceedings, in which a large number of people are charged with illegal entry and found guilty all in a single court hearing.
20. Normally, when Operation Streamline defendants have a prior deportation, the case against them is structured this way. The prosecutor charges them with both illegal reentry after deportation, a felony, and illegal entry, a misdemeanor, and then offers them a plea deal; they plead guilty to the misdemeanor charge, and in exchange the prosecutor drops the felony charge.
21. The facilities of the Corrections Corporation of America in Florence, Arizona. The US Marshals Service houses its detainees there. This private-prison corporation has since rebranded itself as CoreCivic.
22. More likely ATVs. They would sound the same at night, and it seems from the following sequence of events that he never got a good look at them.
23. It's an international norm that anyone jailed or charged with a crime in a foreign country should have access to help and support from their country's consulate in that country. The personnel directory of the Mexican consulate in Tucson lists eight staffers in the *departamento de protección* (plus one department head), of whom four are assigned to the role of *asuntos penales* or criminal matters.
24. The Spanish text actually says, "the young woman from Immigration." Probably a Freudian slip: one kind of government official versus another, even though one is officially on his side and the other isn't. I am grateful to Engracia for confirmation of the intended meaning.
25. Two hundred and fifty Mexican pesos.
26. "Chapel" probably refers to a common type of roadside religious structure that has a modest amount of interior space.
27. Eight thousand Mexican pesos.

28. Five hundred Mexican pesos.
29. The *Procuraduría General de la República* is the Attorney General's Office, which is the Mexican counterpart of the Department of Justice and the Federal Bureau of Investigation; that is, a federal law-enforcement agency.
30. Respectively, the right to free movement, the right to due process, and the right to be secure in one's person.
31. The word translated as "activist" here is *político*, which as an adjective means "political" and as a noun means "politician" or anyone involved in politics.
32. In Mexico, most people use a voter registration card—known colloquially by the Spanish acronym INE, because it's issued by the *Instituto Nacional Electoral*, or National Electoral Institute—as their basic form of photo ID. Driver's licenses are issued by states, as in the United States, but are not as commonly used as ID.

CHAPTER 8

1. FitzGerald, *Refugee beyond Reach*; Rosas, "The Border Thickens."
2. DHS, "Migrant Protection Protocols."
3. Based on *Unidad de Política Migratoria, Registro e Identidad de Personas* [Migratory Policy, Records and Identification Unit], http://www.politicamigratoria .gob.mx/es/PoliticaMigratoria/Boletines_Estadisticos.
4. According to migratory legislation, only INM agents are authorized to request documentation that shows that someone is in the country with authorization. In actuality, however, many members of other law enforcement agencies take advantage of migrants not knowing the law and carry out extortion or theft.
5. Massey, Durand, and Malone, *Beyond Smoke and Mirrors*, 106–109; De León, *Land of Open Graves*.
6. Vogt, *Lives in Transit*.
7. Suárez et al., *Access to Justice for Migrants*.
8. Kovic and Kelly, "Migrant Bodies as Targets of Security Policies," 1.
9. In addition to using the word cuota or "toll," Rigoberto momentarily uses renta or "rent," the same word Ana Carolina (chapter 3) uses to refer to the cobro de guerra charged by the Maras. As for the Zetas, they are a notoriously brutal Mexican cartel.
10. The reference to "all of us" is initially puzzling. It was just the two of them who fled from Mexican Immigration; where did these other people come from? But they are traveling the same migration routes used by thousands. They must have fallen in with another group, perhaps in the cornfield. The Zetas knew to come to this particular spot to collect the toll, so it must be a regularly used spot. I am grateful to Engracia for this observation.
11. One hundred and thirty Mexican pesos.
12. Why mention the name of the train? Ferromex is the rail company that took over the whole northwest portion of Mexico's national railroad system when it was privatized and split up in the 1990s. Irapuato is toward the southern end of this rail network, so, for someone traveling north by train, Irapuato is one of the first places one would encounter a Ferromex train, and it would be a milestone of sorts. In Irapuato, one Ferromex track heads north, terminating at the US border in Ciudad Juárez. Another track goes west to Guadalajara.

In Guadalajara there is another route north, with arrival in Nogales or places further west (the tracks split off at the last minute in Benjamín Hill). Iván's choice of the Guadalajara-bound train thus puts him on the road to Nogales, which is where he gave this *testimonio*.

13. Apparently, this incident took place at night, in the dark, and the officers who were checking the train were using a type of baton (*tolete*, translated here as "nightstick") with a built-in flashlight, which lit up different things as they did their inspection.

14. In 2011, the drug cartel the Zetas murdered a group of seventy-two migrants near the town of San Fernando, Tamaulipas, about eighty-five miles south of the Matamoros-Brownsville and Reynosa-McAllen border communities. Those of the seventy-two victims who were identified were from Honduras, El Salvador, Guatemala, Ecuador, and Brazil.

15. Cristóbal is in Agua Prieta when he recounts this story, as he indicates at the end.

16. The Nogales *Grupo Beta* building is a short walk from the *comedor*. A typical routine for those who find themselves temporarily in Nogales is to have breakfast at the *comedor* and then spend the day at the *Grupo Beta*, calling their family, watching TV, and hanging out at the basketball court next door.

17. All three items are welding equipment. Welders use both heat (the welding machine and the torch) and pressure (the press) to join pieces of metal.

18. Cristóbal doesn't say so explicitly, but like anyone hired for day labor in this manner, he seems to have ridden in the back of the truck, not in the cab.

19. Mesquite is a plant typical of the Sonoran Desert, where Nogales is. It can grow as a shrub or a tree. The most common species in this area are the honey mesquite (*Prosopis glandulosa*) and the velvet mesquite (*Prosopis velutina*).

20. The word Cristóbal uses is a little less specific than "SUV": he says *camioneta cerrada*, "enclosed truck," which could refer to any truck or van other than a pickup (with an open bed). The vehicle would need to be large enough to seat seven people: a Chevrolet Suburban, for instance.

21. The local variety of red oak (*Quercus emoryi*) is traditionally harvested for its fruit, a small, slender acorn. It isn't found at low elevations, so Cristóbal's mention of this tree suggests they had climbed.

22. US phone numbers. The idea is that loved ones in the United States have money or can get a hold of it, to ransom you with.

23. That is, the man told him where the train tracks that led to Nogales were, and which direction Nogales would be in: north rather than south. Apparently, the man also pointed him toward Cananea, another city, in case that was where he wanted to go. This information would also help Cristóbal get to Nogales, avoiding taking the railroad tracks in the wrong direction, provided he knew that Cananea is southeast of Nogales.

CHAPTER 9

1. Hester, *Deportation: Origins of Policy*, 1; Kanstroom, *Deportation Nation*, 21–90. Historian Adam Goodman suggests that between 1892 and 2020 the US government deported some eight million people and expelled six times as many, mostly Mexican nationals, through the administrative procedure mentioned in

chapter 1 known as "voluntary departure." Voluntary departures, also called "returns," are a form of coercive expulsion that does not require a formal order of removal from an immigration judge or deportation officer.

2. Kanstroom, *Deportation Nation*, 35.
3. Kanstroom, 35.
4. Goodman, *Deportation Machine*, 5; Kanstroom, *Deportation Nation*, 74–76.
5. Ngai, *Impossible Subjects*.
6. Gomberg-Muñoz, *Becoming Legal*, 25–26.
7. De Genova, "The Deportation Regime."
8. Chavez, *The Latino Threat*; Golash-Boza, *Deported: Immigration Policing*.
9. De Genova, *Working the Boundaries*.
10. De Genova and Peutz, *The Deportation Regime*; Dowling and Inda, *Governing Immigration through Crime*; Gerken, *Model Immigrants*; Rosenblum and Kandel, "Interior Immigration Enforcement."
11. Golash-Boza and Hondagneu-Sotelo, "Latino Immigrant Men."
12. Inda, "Subject to Deportation."
13. Kanstroom, *Aftermath*, 12.
14. Hester, *Deportation: Origins of Policy*, 177.
15. Hester, 180.
16. USDOJ, *Sourcebook of Criminal Justice Statistics, 1981*, 378; USDOJ, *Sourcebook of Criminal Justice Statistics, 1996*, 416; USDOJ, "Matter of A-B-, Respondent," 381.
17. USDHS, *US Immigration and Customs Enforcement Fiscal Year 2019*, 22.
18. USDHS, 21.
19. Driving Under the Influence; USDHS, *US Immigration and Customs Enforcement Fiscal Year 2019*, 14.
20. Ewing, Martínez, and Rumbaut, *Criminalization of Immigration*.
21. The illegal reentry statue stipulates up to twenty years of imprisonment, though judges usually do not hand down sentences for that length of time.
22. A neighborhood in Tucson.
23. Buckeye is the colloquial name for Arizona State Prison Complex–Lewis.
24. Chronic anxiety.
25. Gerry demonstrates the bodily effects of his state of mind. He strains, flexing his shoulder muscles, shaking.
26. Is shameful.
27. Hill.
28. This refers to thirty-six hours in jail—the standard punishment for city ordinance violations.
29. To purchase alcohol or marijuana.
30. A hundred-dollar bill (US dollars).
31. Charge me with a probation violation.
32. Residence designed to facilitate social integration.
33. Group.
34. As a result of institutional, racialized segregation of living and recreational spaces.
35. Methamphetamine.
36. UAs are urine analyses to determine drug use.
37. She would help to ensure that Mike would not lose his Legal Permanent Resident status.
38. Board of Immigration Appeals, to whom respondents in immigration courts can appeal some lower court decisions.

CHAPTER 10

1. Boehm and Terrio, *Illegal Encounters*.
2. Martínez, Slack, and Martínez-Schuldt, "Rise of Mass Deportation," 36.
3. Colegio de la Frontera Norte, "Informe Anual de Resultados 2018" [Annual Report 2018], 25.
4. Gonzalez-Barrera, *More Mexicans Leaving than Coming to the U.S.*, 15.
5. Gomberg-Muñoz, *Becoming Legal*.
6. Castañeda, *Borders of Belonging*, 94–118.
7. USDHS, *US Immigration and Customs Enforcement Fiscal Year 2019*, 5.
8. Hansen, "Social Citizens and Their Right to Belong."
9. Slack, *Deported to Death*.
10. Caldwell, *Deported Americans*.
11. Guadalajara is located in the state of Jalisco.
12. People who spend time in a detention center or prison before being deported often have the final balance of their commissary account, money they have earned while incarcerated or received from family, returned to them in the form of a check instead of cash.
13. "Here" refers to the KBI *comedor*, where a team of volunteers cashes checks for those deported from US prisons.
14. Under US immigration law, citizens and lawful permanent residents can petition for family members, beginning the process for them to obtain legal residence. It often takes several years, however. On another note, the Repatriation office at the downtown port of entry in Nogales processes people on arrival. Representatives from the Mexican consulate use that space as well to provide services to the same people. The Mexican consulate itself is on the other side of the border, in Nogales, Arizona.
15. This is not uncommon, given how the 1996 laws (mentioned in the previous chapter) have introduced fast-track deportations by deporting officers and limiting the circumstances in which a noncitizen would go before an immigration judge.
16. This is his real name, not a pseudonym, unlike the other names (see chapter 1, note 1). Ramón's story has been made public through broadcasts on various media.
17. Evidently the landlord had involved the police already. When Ramón comes back, he doesn't say that the police arrived but merely that they exited their vehicles.

CHAPTER 11

1. UNHCR, *Convention and Protocol Relating to the Status of Refugees*.
2. Refugee Act of 1980.
3. Coutin, "Excavating the History of Central American Asylum Seekers."
4. Chinchilla, Hamilton, and Loucky, "The Sanctuary Movement and Central American Activism."
5. USDHS, Note that numbers include both affirmative and defensive asylum applications. Although there are important differences between the two processes, such matters are beyond the scope of this introduction.
6. USDOJ, *Matter of A-B-, Respondent*.

7. Spencer S. Hsu, "Federal Judge Strikes Down Trump Asylum Rule Targeting Central Americans." *Washington Post*, July 1, 2020, https://www.washington post.com/local/legal-issues/us-judge-strikes-down-trump-asylum-rule -targeting-central-americans/2020/07/01/96e57616-bb4a-11ea-bdaf-a129f 921026f_story.html.

8. Kerwin and Yi-Ying Lin, *Immigration Detention*.

9. Devlin Barrett, "Record Immigration Numbers Force Homeland Security to Search for New Jail Space," *Wall Street Journal*, October 21, 2016, https://www .wsj.com/articles/record-immigrant-numbers-force-homeland-security-to -search-for-new-jail-space-1477042202.

10. USDHS, "Detention Management."

11. Luan, "Profiting from Enforcement."

12. Leutert, Arvey, and Ezzell, *Metering Update: February 2020*.

13. Human Rights First, *A Year of Horrors*.

14. Boggs, "Mexico's Southern Border Plan."

15. Meyer and Hinojosa, "Recent U.S.-Mexico Agreement."

16. "It" refers to the situation involving mines and territorial disputes and armed attacks, which had affected multiple towns in the area, as she proceeds to explain.

17. This area of Guerrero is known as the Guerrero Gold Belt and is in the process of being intensively mined.

18. Los Bajos is a village to the west of Leonardo Bravo, which, as she indicates below, is the municipality where her town is.

19. As an indication of scale, there were reports of an incursion by about three thousand armed men into eight different communities from which people fled as a result.

20. A *cabecera municipal* is the same as a county seat in the United States, the city or town in which the municipality's/county's government is headquartered.

21. About an hour east of Chichihualco, the capital of Eduardo Neri Municipality.

22. President Andrés Manuel López Obrador had taken office on December 1, 2018. They literally traveled to Mexico City to ask for help, a journey of some 170 miles.

23. Two thousand Mexican pesos.

24. The *Palacio Nacional* is the equivalent of the White House in the United States; it is located on the Zócalo, the famous square in the heart of Mexico City. The community camped out there in a state of permanent protest.

25. Mexico's newest federal military police body, the National Guard, a signature initiative of the new administration, was formally established in mid-2019. According to reports, three hundred residents of a rural community in Leonardo Bravo Municipality, including eighty-four children and four people over the age of ninety, marched to Mexico City, installed a camp outside the *Palacio Nacional*, and spent forty-five days there before reaching an agreement to return to their municipal capital. They were promised housing, rental assistance, and sufficient public safety to return to their communities of origin.

26. Acapulco, the state capital, is on the coast.

27. One hundred Mexican pesos and eighty Mexican pesos.

28. The health-coverage program for government employees in Mexico. The agency is called the *Instituto de Seguridad y Servicios Sociales de los Trabajadores del Estado* (Government Workers Social Security and Social Services Agency). The hospital she worked at was thus a public institution, not a private institution.

29. Four thousand Mexican pesos.

30. Opium poppies have long been the primary cash crop of this region of Guerrero. The role of the local middleman, or *acaparador*—a local term, literally meaning "amasser" or "hoarder" (perhaps to be understood both in the sense of storing up the opium itself and of having a monopoly on the trade)—is to buy all the raw opium produced by the local farmers and then, at least in the village described in the report, process it into pure heroin. This exclusive role is granted by the cartel that buys the heroin for export, hence "the appointment." Moreover, the rise of fentanyl, a synthetic opioid, has shattered the profitability of opium production, thus devastating places that depended on it.

31. An herbal-remedy company.

32. "Things here are a little difficult" is an understatement: as she's said, and as she reiterates below, on the streets of Nogales she is not safe from the people who want to kill her. It's just that she's no longer living under siege, under the constant threat of thousands of armed men pouring in and dragging people away; by comparison, her current risk is more emotionally manageable, and she's able to relax in ways she couldn't. Note the word "honestly" (*la verdad*), acknowledging an expectation about her as an asylum-seeker: that she must be in a state of maximum terror all the time.

33. The wait for an asylum interview.

34. "Those men" are the cartel men in Guerrero. "These men" are the people here who do jobs for them. The local cartel bosses in Nogales are Sonorans and Sinaloans; she's saying that when the bosses in Guerrero want someone in Nogales killed, they have to go through the bosses here.

35. The *pupusa* is the national dish of El Salvador, a thick corn tortilla stuffed with one kind of filling or another.

36. Members of the gang started asking her for free food, the beginning of the same cycle that ended in her mom's death.

37. She gives this amount in US dollars, not Mexican pesos.

38. One thousand Mexican pesos.

39. *Hielera*, which could also be translated as "icebox" or "fridge." This is the common way of referring to Border Patrol holding cells, which are notoriously cold.

40. Two hundred Mexican pesos.

41. Probably the downtown crossing, the Deconcini Port of Entry. There is a gate there through which cargo trains pass from one country to the other.

42. Sister Alicia Guevara, who at the time was in charge of the Kino Border Initiative's shelter for women, Casa Nazaret. In Mexico and other parts of Latin America, religious women are referred to and addressed as *madre* (mother) by ordinary people.

43. Additional information from Engracia: María Ángeles did return to Tijuana to attend her court hearing. She was denied asylum, and she appealed the decision. She was deported to Mexico. Mexico refused to receive her, so the US immigration authorities had to take her back. There she waits. Her brother and sister were successfully reclaimed by her aunt.

44. *Técnico superior universitario*, an undergraduate degree similar to an associate degree.

45. The name in Spanish is *Voluntad Popular*.

46. Under Hugo Chávez and Nicolás Maduro, many institutions in Venezuela have been given the name "Bolivarian." Chávez dubbed his politics "Bolivarianism"

and his political project "the Bolivarian Revolution." The name comes from Simón Bolívar, the famous eighteenth-century revolutionary.

In the context of Venezuelan politics, the term "collectives" refers to ostensibly grassroots activist groups that are allied with Maduro and that opposition members see as effectively agents of the government.

47. Diosdado Cabello is a high-ranking figure in the ruling party, along with Maduro. At the time, he was the speaker of the National Assembly.

48. Leopoldo López, the leader of the People's Will Party, had been arrested in connection with the 2014 protests and remained imprisoned until July 2017, when he was transferred to house arrest.

49. Delcy Rodríguez, her brother Jorge Rodríguez, and Freddy Bernal are all Maduro allies who have held various offices.

50. "Safety zoners" is an attempt to translate *guarimberos*, which is a piece of Venezuelan political slang specifically used to mock opposition protestors. The name is based on the children's game of tag. In Venezuela, *guarimba* is the name for home base in the game, the safe zone where one is safe from being tagged. *Guarimba* was adopted as a slang term for the barricades or shelters used by protestors in the streets. Presumably, the mockery involves attributing childishness to the protestors.

51. At the January 23 rally, Guaidó declared himself president of Venezuela. Maduro had been sworn in for a second term on January 10, after a reelection of disputed legitimacy in May 2018. The ground for Guaidó's claim was the fact that Venezuela's Constitution names the speaker of the National Assembly as the successor to the presidency.

52. The United Socialist Party of Venezuela is Maduro's party. The "red spots" (*puntos rojos*) were curbside voter-mobilization kiosks alleged to have a vote-buying/voter-coercion function during the 2018 election. They consisted of a red pop-up canopy.

53. Nicolás Maduro and other members of the Venezuelan government have been indicted on drug-trafficking charges in the United States.

CHAPTER 12

1. Álvaro De Juana, "*Papa Francisco propone 3 acciones concretas para ayudar a los inmigrantes* [Pope Francis Proposes Three Concrete Acciones for Aiding Migrants]," ACI Prensa, February 21, 2017, https://www.aciprensa.com/noticias/papa -francisco-propone-3-acciones-concretas-para-ayudar-a-los-inmigrantes-13118.

2. Ps. 146:9; Deut. 10:17–19.

3. Rosa Die Alcolea, "*Palabras del Papa a los migrantes en Bolonia—Texto Completo* [Pope's Words to Migrants in Bologna—Complete Text]," Zenit, October 3, 2017, https://es.zenit.org/2017/10/03/el-papa-a-los-migrantes-en-bolonia -vosotros-sois-luchadores-de-la-esperanza/.

CHAPTER 13

1. USDHS, *2019 Enforcement Operations*, 3.

BIBLIOGRAPHY

Albicker, Sandra Luz, and Laura Velasco. "Deportación y estigma en la frontera México Estados Unidos: Atrapados en Tijuana." [Deportation and Stigma on the U.S.-Mexico Border: Trapped in Tijuana]. *Norteamérica*, 11, no. 1 (2016): 99–129.

Almada Bay, Ignacio. *Sonora: Historia breve* [Sonora: A brief history]. México, DF: Fondo de Cultura Económica, 2012.

Andreas, Peter. *Border Games: Policing the U.S.-Mexico Divide*. Ithaca, NY: Cornell University Press, 2000.

Arreola, Daniel D. *Postcards from the Sonora Border: Visualizing Place through a Popular Lens, 1900s–1950s*. Tucson: University of Arizona Press, 2017.

Beauvoir, Simone de. *El segundo sexo* [The Second Sex]. Mexico, DF: Debolsillo, 1999 [1949].

Boehm, Deborah. *Returned: Going and Coming in an Age of Deportation*. Oakland: University of California Press, 2016.

Boehm, Deborah A., and Susan J. Terrio, eds. *Illegal Encounters: The Effect of Detention and Deportation on Young People*. New York: New York University Press, 2019.

Boggs, Clay. "Mexico's Southern Border Plan: More Deportations and Widespread Human Rights Violations," Washington Office on Latin America, March 19, 2015, https://www.wola.org/analysis/mexicos-southern-border-plan-more-deportations -and-widespread-human-rights-violations/.

Caldwell, Beth C. *Deported Americans: Life after Deportation to Mexico*. Durham, NC: Duke University Press, 2019.

Cantor, Guillermo, and Walter Ewing. *Still No Action Taken: Complaints against Border Patrol Go Unanswered*. Washington, DC: American Immigration Council, 2017.

Castañeda, Heide. *Borders of Belonging: Struggle and Solidarity in Mixed-Status Immigrant Families*. Stanford, CA: Stanford University Press, 2019.

Chasteen, John Charles. *Born in Blood and Fire: A Concise History of Latin America*. New York: W.W. Norton, 2001.

Chavez, Leo R. *The Latino Threat: Constructing Immigrants, Citizens, and the Nation*. Stanford, CA: Stanford University Press, 2008.

Chinchilla, Norma Stoltz, Nora Hamilton, and James Loucky. "The Sanctuary Movement and Central American Activism in Los Angeles." *Latin American Perspectives* 36, no. 6 (2009): 101–26.

Colegio de la Frontera Norte. "Informe Anual de Resultados 2018" [Annual Report 2018]. Tijuana: Encuesta Sobre Migración en la Frontera Norte, 2019. https://www.colef.mx/emif/datasets/informes/norte/2018/Emif%20Norte%20Informe%20Anual%202018.pdf.

Colibrí Center for Human Rights. "Facts." Accessed July 14, 2020. https://colibri center.org/.

Cornelius, Wayne A. "Deaths at the Border: Efficacy and Unwanted Consequences of U.S. Immigration Control Policy." *Population and Development Review* 27, no. 4 (2001): 661–85.

Coutin, Susan Bibler. *Exiled Home: Salvadoran Transnational Youth in the Aftermath of Violence.* Durham, NC: Duke University Press, 2016.

———. "Falling Outside: Excavating the History of Central American Asylum Seekers." *Law and Society* 36, no. 3 (2011): 569–96.

Customs and Border Protection (CBP) Integrity Advisory Panel. *Final Report of the CBP Integrity Advisory Panel.* Homeland Security Advisory Council. Washington, DC: US Department of Homeland Security, 2016.

Danielson, Michael S. *Our Values on the Line: Migrant Abuse and Family Separation at the Border.* Washington, DC: Jesuits Conference of Canada and the United States and Kino Border Initiative, 2015.

De Genova, Nicholas. "The Deportation Regime: Sovereignty, Space, and the Freedom of Movement." In *The Deportation Regime: Sovereignty, Space, and the Freedom of Movement*, edited by Nicolas De Genova and Nathalie Peutz, 33–65. Durham, NC: Duke University Press, 2010.

———. *Working the Boundaries: Race, Space, and "Illegality" in Mexican Chicago.* Durham, NC: Duke University Press.

De Genova, Nicholas, and Nathalie Peutz, eds. *The Deportation Regime: Sovereignty, Space, and the Freedom of Movement.* Durham, NC: Duke University Press, 2010.

De León, Jason. *The Land of Open Graves: Living and Dying on the Migrant Trail.* Oakland: University of California Press, 2015.

Del Popolo, Fabiana, ed. *Los pueblos indígenas en América (Abya Yala): Desafíos para la igualdad en la diversidad* [Indigenous peoples in the Americas (Abya Yala): Challenges for equality in diversity]. Santiago, Chile: Comisión Económica para América Latina y el Caribe, 2017.

Dowling, Julie A., and Jonathan Xavier Inda, eds. *Governing Immigration through Crime: A Reader.* Stanford, CA: Stanford University Press, 2013.

Ewing, Walter A., Daniel E. Martínez, and Rubén G. Rumbaut. *The Criminalization of Immigration in the United States.* Washington, DC: American Immigration Council, 2015.

FitzGerald, David Scott. *Refuge beyond Reach: How Rich Democracies Repel Asylum Seekers.* New York: Oxford University Press, 2019.

Francis, Pope. "Address of His Holiness Pope Francis, 'Víctor Manuel Reyna' Stadium, Tuxtla Gutiérrez," February 15, 2016. https://w2.vatican.va/content/francesco/en/speeches/2016/february/documents/papa-francesco_20160215_messico-famiglie.html.

———. "Homily of His Holiness Pope Francis, Ciudad Juárez Fair Grounds," February 17, 2016. http://w2.vatican.va/content/francesco/en/homilies/2016/documents/papa-francesco_20160217_omelia-messico-ciudad-jaurez.html.

Gastélum Ceballos, Francisco Octavio. "Protección de la Ciudad de Nogales: Sonora contra avenidas extraordinarias" [Protection of the city of Nogales, Sonora, against flash floods]. Tesis de Maestría de Ciencias en Ingeniería. Querétaro, Mexico: Universidad Autónoma de Querétaro, 2008.

Gerken, Christina. *Model Immigrants and Undesirable Aliens: The Cost of Immigration Reform in the 1990s.* Minneapolis: University of Minnesota Press, 2013.

Golash-Boza, Tanya Maria. *Deported: Immigrant Policing, Disposable Labor, and Global Capitalism.* New York: New York University Press, 2015.

Golash-Boza, Tanya Maria, and Pierrette Hondagneu-Sotelo. "Latino Immigrant Men and the Deportation Crisis: A Gendered Racial Removal Program." *Latino Studies* 11, no. 3 (2013): 271–92.

Gomberg-Muñoz, Ruth. *Becoming Legal: Immigration Law and Mixed Status Families.* Oxford: Oxford University Press, 2017.

———. *Labor and Legality: An Ethnography of a Mexican Immigrant Network.* Oxford: Oxford University Press, 2011.

Gonzalez-Barrera, Ana. *More Mexicans Leaving than Coming to the U.S.: Net Loss of 140,000 From 2009 to 2014; Family Reunification Top Reason for Return.* Washington, DC: Pew Hispanic Center, 2015. https://www.pewresearch.org/hispanic/2015/11/19/more-mexicans-leaving-than-coming-to-the-u-s/.

Gonzales-Berry, Erlinda V., and Marcela Mendoza. *Mexicanos in Oregon: Their Stories, Their Lives.* Corvallis: Oregon State University Press, 2010.

Goodman, Adam. *The Deportation Machine: America's Long History of Expelling Migrants.* Princeton, NJ: Princeton University Press, 2020.

Haenn, Nora. "New Rural: The Tangled Web of Environmental Protection and Economic Aid in Southern Mexico." *Journal of Poverty* 8, no. 4 (2004): 97–117.

Hale, Charles. *Más que un Indio (More than an Indian): Racial Ambivalence and the Paradox of Neoliberal Multiculturalism in Guatemala.* Santa Fe, NM: School for Advanced Research Press, 2006.

Hansen, Tobin. "Social Citizens and Their Right to Belong." In *Illegal Encounters: The Effect of Detention and Deportation on Young People,* edited by Deborah A. Boehm and Susan J. Terrio, 32–44. New York: New York University Press, 2019.

Harris, Richard L. "Dependency, Underdevelopment, and Neoliberalism." In *Capital, Power, and Inequality in Latin America and the Caribbean,* edited by Richard L. Harris and Jorge Nef, 49–95. Plymouth, UK: Rowman, 2008.

Heidbrink, Lauren. *Migranthood: Youth in an Era of Deportation.* Stanford, CA: Stanford University Press, 2020.

Hernández, Kelly Lytle. *Migra!: A History of the U.S. Border Patrol.* Berkeley: University of California Press, 2010.

Hester, Torrie. *Deportation: The Origins of U.S. Policy.* Philadelphia: University of Pennsylvania Press, 2017.

Heyman, Josiah McC. *Life and Labor on the Border: Working People of Northeastern Sonora, Mexico, 1886–1986.* Tucson: University of Arizona Press, 1991.

Human Rights First. *A Year of Horrors: The Trump Administration's Illegal Return of Asylum Seekers to Danger in Mexico.* New York: Human Rights First, 2020. https://www.humanrightsfirst.org/sites/default/files/MPP-aYearofHorrors-UPDATED.pdf.

Inda, Jonathan Xavier. "Subject to Deportation: IRCA, 'Criminal Aliens,' and the Policing of Immigration." *Migration Studies* 1, no. 3 (2013): 292–310.

Kang, S. Deborah. *The INS on the Line: Making Immigration Law on the U.S.-Mexico Border, 1917–1954*. New York: Oxford University Press, 2017.

Kanstroom, Daniel. *Aftermath: Deportation Law and the New American Diaspora*. New York: Oxford University Press, 2012.

———. *Deportation Nation: Outsiders in American History*. Cambridge, MA: Harvard University Press, 2007.

Kerwin, Donald, and Serena Yi-Yang Lin. *Immigration Detention: Can ICE Meet Its Legal Imperatives and Case Management Responsibilities?* Washington, DC: Migration Policy Institute, 2009. https://www.migrationpolicy.org/research/immigrant-detention -can-ice-meet-its-legal-imperatives-and-case-management-responsibilities.

Kilty, Keith, and Elizabeth Segal. "Poverty and Inequality in the Latin American–U.S. Borderlands: Implications of U.S. Interventions: Introduction." *Journal of Poverty* 8, no. 4 (2004): 1–5.

Knippen, José, Clay Boggs, and Maureen Meyer. *An Uncertain Path: Justice for Crimes and Human Rights Violations against Migrants and Refugees in Mexico*. Research Report, 2015. https://www.wola.org/sites/default/files/An%20Uncertain%20Path _Nov2015.pdf.

Kovic, Christine, and Patty Kelly. "Migrant Bodies as Targets of Security Policies: Central Americans Crossing Mexico's Vertical Border." *Dialectical Anthropology* 41, no. 1, (2017): 1–11.

Leutert, Stephanie, Savitri Arvey, and Ellie Ezzell. Metering Update: February 2020. Austin: University of Texas at Austin, Robert Strauss Center for International Security and Law, 2020. https://www.strausscenter.org/publications/metering-update/.

Lim, Julian. *Porous Borders: Multiracial Migrations and the Law in the U.S.-Mexico Borderlands*. Chapel Hill: University of North Carolina Press, 2017.

Luan, Livia. "Profiting from Enforcement: The Role of Private Prisons in U.S. Immigration Detention." Washington, DC: *Migration Information Source*, May 2, 2018. https://www.migrationpolicy.org/article/profiting-enforcement-role-private -prisons-us-immigration-detention.

Luccisano, Lucy. "Mexico's *Progresa* Program (1997–2000): An Example of Neo-liberal Poverty Alleviation Programs Concerned with Gender, Human Capital Development, Responsibility and Choice." *Journal of Poverty* 8, no. 4 (2004): 31–57.

Lusk, Mark, and Griselda Villalobos. "The *Testimonio* of Eva: A Mexican Refugee in El Paso." *Journal of Borderlands Studies* 27, no. 1 (2012): 17–25.

Macías-Rojas, Patrisia. *From Deportation to Prison: The Politics of Immigration Enforcement in Post–Civil Rights America*. New York: New York University Press, 2016.

Martínez, Daniel J., Jeremy Slack, and Ricardo Martínez-Schuldt. "The Rise of Mass Deportation in the United States." In *The Handbook of Race, Ethnicity, Crime, and Justice*, edited by Ramiro Martínez Jr., Meghan E. Hollis, and Jacob I. Stowell, 173–201. Hoboken, NJ: John Wiley and Sons, 2018.

Massey, Douglas S., Jorge Durand, and Nolan J. Malone. *Beyond Smoke and Mirrors: Mexican Immigration in an Era of Economic Integration*. New York: Russell Sage Foundation, 2002.

Meyer, Maureen. "One Year after National Guard's Creation, Mexico Is Far from Demilitarizing Public Security." Washington Office on Latin America, May 26, 2020. https://www.wola.org/analysis/one-year-national-guard-mexico/.

Meyer, Maureen, and Gina Hinojosa. "Explainer: The Recent U.S.-Mexico Agreement to Regional Migration Flows." Washington Office on Latin America, June 14, 2019. https://www.wola.org/analysis/u-s-mexico-agreement-migration/.

Monroe, James. "President's Annual Message." Washington, DC: Library of Congress, 1823. https://memory.loc.gov/cgi-bin/ampage?collId=llac&fileName=041/llac041.db&recNum=4.

Ngai, Mae M. *Impossible Subjects: Illegal Aliens and the Making of Modern America.* Princeton, NJ: Princeton University Press, 2004.

Organization of American States. "Inter-American Convention on the Prevention, Punishment, and Eradication of Violence against Women (Convention of Belém do Pará)." Presented June 9, 1994. https://www.oas.org/en/mesecvi/docs/BelemDo Para-ENGLISH.pdf.

Pastor, Robert A. *Exiting the Whirlpool: U.S. Foreign Policy toward Latin America and the Caribbean.* 2nd ed. New York: Routledge, 2018.

Refugee Act of 1980. Pub. L. No. 96-212, 94 Stat. 102 (1980).

Rochlin, Fred, and Harriet Rochlin. "The Heart of Ambos Nogales: Boundary Monument 122." *Journal of Arizona History* 17, no. 2 (1976): 161–80.

Rosas, Gilberto. "The Border Thickens: In-Securing Communities after IRCA." *International Migration* 54, no. 2 (2015): 119–30.

Rosenblum, Marc R., and William A. Kandel. "Interior Immigration Enforcement: Programs Targeting Criminal Aliens" (R42057). *U.S. Congressional Research Service.* Washington, DC: Library of Congress, 2012.

Secretaría de Gobernación. *Boletín Mensual de Estadísticas Migratorias 2019* [Monthly report of immigration statistics 2019]. México, D.F.: Unidad de Política Migratoria, 2020.

Sheridan, Thomas E. 2012. *Arizona: A History.* Tucson: University of Arizona Press.

Slack, Jeremy. *Deported to Death: How Drug Violence Is Changing Migration on the U.S.-Mexico Border.* Oakland: University of California Press, 2019.

Slack, Jeremy, and Howard Campbell. "On Narco-coyotaje: Illicit Regimes and Their Impacts on the U.S.-Mexico Border." *Antipode* 48 (2016): 1380–99.

Smith, Peter H. *Talons of the Eagle: Dynamics of U.S.–Latin American Relations.* 3rd ed. New York: Oxford University Press, 2007.

Southern Border Communities Coalition. "Deaths by Border Patrol Since 2010." July 2, 2020. http://www.southernborder.org/deaths_by_border_patrol.

Spener, David. *Clandestine Crossings: Migrants and Coyotes on the Texas-Mexico Border.* Ithaca, NY: Cornell University Press, 2009.

St. John, Rachel. *Line in the Sand: A History of the Western U.S.-Mexico Border.* Princeton, NJ: Princeton University Press, 2011.

Stephen, Lynn. "Bearing Witness: Testimony in Latin American Anthropology and Related Fields." *Journal of Latin American and Caribbean Anthropology* 22, no. 1 (2017): 85–109.

———. "Fleeing Rural Violence: Mam Women Seeking Gendered Justice in Guatemala and the U.S." *Journal of Peasant Studies* 46, no. 2 (2019): 229–57.

———. *Transborder Lives: Indigenous Oaxacans in Mexico, California, and Oregon.* Durham, NC: Duke University Press, 2007.

———. *We Are the Face of Oaxaca: Testimony and Social Movements.* Durham, NC: Duke University Press, 2013.

Suárez, Ximena, Andrés Díaz, José Knippen, and Maureen Meyer. *Access to Justice for Migrants in Mexico: A Right That Exists Only on the Books.* Washington, DC: Washington Office on Latin America, 2017.

Takei, Carl, Mary Small, Carol Wu, and Jennifer Chan. *Fatal Neglect: How ICE Ignores Deaths in Detention.* American Civil Liberties Union, Detention Watch Network,

and Heartland's Alliance's National Immigration Justice Center, 2016. https://
www.detentionwatchnetwork.org/sites/default/files/reports/Fatal%20Neglect
%20ACLU-DWN-NIJC.pdf.

Truett, Samuel. *Fugitive Landscapes: The Forgotten History of the U.S.-Mexico Borderlands.* New Haven, CT: Yale University Press, 2006.

Tula, María Teresa, and Lynn Stephen. *Este es mi testimonio: María Teresa Tula, lucha-
dora pro-derechos humanos de El Salvador* [This is my *testimonio*: María Teresa Tula,
human rights advocate of El Salvador]. Boston: South End Press, 1994.

United Nations. *Situación de las personas afrodescendientes en América Latina y desafíos
de políticas para la garantía de sus derechos* [Situation of Afro-descendant people
in Latin America and policy challenges for rights protection]. Santiago, Chile:
United Nations, 2017.

United Nations High Commissioner for Refugees (UNHCR). *Convention and Protocol
Relating to the Status of Refugees.* Geneva: UNHCR, 2010. https://www.unhcr.org
/en-us/3b66c2aa10.

United Nations International Children's Fund (UNICEF). *Convención internacional sobre los derechos del niño y la niña: Adoptada por la Asamblea General de las
Naciones Unidas el 20 de noviembre de 1989* [International Convention on Children's Rights: Adopted by the United Nations General Assembly on November
20, 1989]. Asunción: UNICEF in Paraguay, 2004. https://www.dequeni.org.py/es
/userfiles/files/py_convencion_espanol.pdf.

United Nations Office of the High Commissioner for Human Rights. "Article 1
of the Convention on the Elimination of All Forms of Discrimination Against
Women." Entered into force September 3, 1981. https://www.ohchr.org
/Documents/ProfessionalInterest/cedaw.pdf.

———. *Convention on the Elimination of All Forms of Discrimination against Women.*
United Nations. Entry into force September 3, 1981. https://www.ohchr.org
/Documents/ProfessionalInterest/cedaw.pdf.

———. "Figures at a Glance." Accessed July 14, 2020. https://www.unhcr.org/en-us
/figures-at-a-glance.html.

US Border Patrol (USBP). "Border Patrol Strategic Plan, 1994 and Beyond: National
Strategy." Washington, DC: US Border Patrol, 1994. http://cw.routledge.com
/textbooks/9780415996945/gov-docs/1994.pdf.

———. *U.S. Border Patrol Fiscal Year Staffing Statistics (FY 1992–FY 2019).* Washington, DC: US Border Patrol, 2019. https://www.cbp.gov/sites/default/files/assets
/documents/2020-Jan/U.S.%20Border%20Patrol%20Fiscal%20Year%20Staffing
%20Statistics%20%28FY%201992%20-%20FY%202019%29_0.pdf.

US Department of Homeland Security (USDHS). *Annual Flow Report: Refugees and
Asylees: 2017.* Washington, DC: Office of Immigration Statistics, 2019.

———. "Detention Management." Washington, DC: US Immigration and Customs
Enforcement, July 8, 2020. https://www.ice.gov/detention-management.

———. "Migrant Protection Protocols." Washington, DC: US Immigration and Customs Enforcement, 2019. Release date January 24, 2019. https://www.dhs.gov
/news/2019/01/24/migrant-protection-protocols.

———. *2018 Yearbook of Immigration Statistics.* Washington, DC: Office of Immigration Statistics, 2019.

———. *U.S. Immigration and Customs Enforcement Fiscal Year 2019 Enforcement and
Removal Operations Report.* Washington, DC: US Immigration and Customs
Enforcement, 2019.

US Department of Justice (USDOJ). "Matter of A-B-, Respondent." 27 I&N Dec. 316. A.G. 2018.

———. *Sourcebook of Criminal Justice Statistics, 1981.* Bureau of Justice Statistics. Washington, DC: US Government Printing Office, 1982.

———. *Sourcebook of Criminal Justice Statistics, 1996.* Bureau of Justice Statistics. Washington, DC: US Government Printing Office, 1997.

US Department of the Treasury. "Treasury Sanctions Latin American Criminal Organization." Washington, DC: US Department of the Treasury, October 11, 2012.

Vogt, Wendy. *Lives in Transit: Violence and Intimacy on the Migrant Journey.* Oakland: University of California Press, 2019.

Warren, Robert. *US Undocumented Population Continued to Fall from 2016 to 2017, and Visa Overstays Significantly Exceeded Illegal Crossings for the Seventh Consecutive Year.* New York: Center for Migration Studies, 2019. http://cmsny.org/publications/essay-2017-undocumented-and-overstays. Washington, D.C.: US Government Printing Office, 1997.

Wolf, Sonja. *Mano Dura: The Politics of Gang Control in El Salvador.* Austin: University of Texas Press, 2017.

World Health Organization (WHO). "Refugee and Migrant Health." Accessed July 14, 2020. http://www.who.int/migrants/en/.

CONTRIBUTORS

JORGE A. ANDRADE GALINDO has a doctoral degree in anthropological sciences from the Universidad Autónoma Metropolitana and has been researching immigration for 20 years. In the last ten years he has focused on human rights, in particular of migrants in transit through Mexico. He co-founded the San José migrant shelter in Huehuetoca, Estado de México, which he co-directed from 2012 to 2014. His publications have examined migrant holding centers and transit routes to the United States.

SEAN CARROLL, SJ, is a Jesuit priest who has been the executive director of the Kino Border Initiative (KBI) since 2009. Prior to his work at KBI, he worked in pastoral ministry at St. Patrick's Church in Oakland, California, from 2000 to 2004 and Dolores Mission Church in Los Angeles from 2004 to 2008. He also served as assistant for pastoral ministries of the California Province of the Society of Jesus from 2006 to 2008.

MARLA CONRAD has a master's degree in social justice and human rights from Arizona State University. She has worked with migrants and their families since 2003 and in 2011 joined KBI to work as an advocate. She has helped establish services and programs that help migrants and refugees with varied needs and promoted respect for human rights by taking action to address abuses.

CECILIA GUADALUPE ESPINOSA MARTÍNEZ is a feminist human rights defender born in Ciudad Juárez, Chihuahua, Mexico. She cofounded the Paso del Norte Human Rights Center in 2001 and since 2010 has worked at the National Network of Human Rights Defenders, where she is codirector.

TOBIN HANSEN is pro-tem instructor of cultural anthropology at the University of Oregon, where he received his PhD in 2019. His research examines migration and deportation, race, masculinities, prisons, and gangs. He is a volunteer at KBI.

DAVID HILL has been living in Nogales, Arizona, and helping provide essential services to migrants in Nogales, Sonora, since 2010. He has a master's degree in classics from the University of Texas at Austin and a master's degree in linguistics from the Massachusetts Institute of Technology.

SAMUEL LOZANO DE LOS SANTOS, SJ, is coordinator of the Catholic Church's social ministry in the Diocese of Nogales. His work expresses solidarity with deported people, migrants in transit, unhoused people, and others at the margins.

MARÍA ENGRACIA ROBLES ROBLES, ME, is originally from Jalisco, Mexico, and is a Missionary of the Eucharist. She has been a professor of early childhood education with a specialty in psychological education. Her bachelor's degree is in religious and biblical sciences. Engracia has most enjoyed her community-based popular education work.

SATHYA HONEY VICTORIA is a translator and photographer currently living and working in Guanajuato, Mexico. She is especially interested in matters relating to justice and to art.

JOANNA WILLIAMS is the director of education and advocacy at KBI. She obtained her bachelor of science in foreign service from the Georgetown University School of Foreign Service and her master's in public policy from Arizona State University.

INDEX